The Political Economy of the East Asian Crisis and its Aftermath

The Political Economy of the East Asian Crisis and its Aftermath

Tigers in Distress

Edited by

Arvid John Lukauskas and Francisco L. Rivera-Batiz

Columbia University

Edward Elgar

Cheltenham, UK • Northampton, MA, USA

Published by
Edward Elgar Publishing Limited
Glensanda House
Montpellier Parade
Cheltenham
Glos GL50 1UA
UK

Edward Elgar Publishing, Inc.
136 West Street
Suite 202
Northampton
Massachusetts 01060
USA

A catalog record for this book is available from the British Library

Library of Congress Cataloging in Publication Data
The political economy of the East Asian crisis and its aftermath : tigers in distress / edited by Arvid John Lukauskas and Francisco L. Rivera-Batiz.
p. cm.
Includes bibliographical references and index.
1. Financial crisis—East Asia. 2. East Asia—Economic conditions—1945–
I. Lukauskas, Arvid John. II. Rivera-Batiz, Francisco L.

HB3816.5 .P647 2001
332'.095—dc21

00–062290

ISBN 1 84064 400 1
Printed and bound in Great Britain by MPG Books Ltd, Bodmin, Cornwall

Contents

Figures

Tables

Boxes

Contributors

Pedro Alba is lead economist of the Poverty Reduction and Economic Management Department in the Europe and Central Asia Region at the World Bank. His research includes: 'Thailand's Corporate Financing and Corporate Structures,' World Bank Policy Research Working Paper, 1998 (with S. Claessens and S. Djankov); 'The Role of Macroeconomic and Financial Sector Linkages in East Asia's Financial Crisis,' Washington, DC: World Bank, 1998 (with A. Bhattacharya, S. Claessens, S. Gosh and L. Hernandez); and 'Contagion in a Financially Integrated World: Lessons from East Asia's Recent Experience,' World Bank Policy Research Working Paper, 1998 (with S. Claessens and S. Gosh).

Mario Blejer is Senior Advisor in the Monetary and Exchange Affairs Department of the International Monetary Fund. His publications include: *Inflation Targeting in Practice: Strategic and Operational Issues and Applications to Emerging Market Economies*, Washington, DC: International Monetary Fund, 2000; *Financial Sector Transformation: Lessons from Economics in Transition*, Cambridge: Cambridge University Press (co-editor with M. Skreb); and *Central Banking, Monetary Policies, and the Implications for Transition Economies*, Amsterdam: Kluwer Academic Publishers, 1999.

Michael David Bordo is a professor of economics and director of the Center for Monetary and Financial History at Rutgers University in New Brunswick. His publications include: *The Defining Moment: The Great Depression and the American Economy in the Twentieth Century*, Chicago: University of Chicago Press, 1998 (with C. Goldin and E. White); *A Retrospective on the Bretton Woods System*, Chicago: University of Chicago Press, 1993 (with B. Eichengreen); and *Money, History and International Finance*, Chicago: University of Chicago Press, 1989.

Graciana del Castillo is visiting professor in the department of economics at Columbia University. Her publications include: 'Déjà vu All Over Again? The Mexican Crisis and the Stabilization of Uruguay in the 1970s,' *World Development*, 1998 (with M. Blejer); 'Policy Fundamentals, Interest Rate Differentials and Expected Devaluation in the Presence of an Active Crawling Peg

System,' *Journal of International Money and Finance*, 1992; and 'Obstacles to Peace-Building,' *Foreign Policy*, 1994.

Albert Fishlow is the Paul A. Volcker Senior Fellow for International Economics and Director of Economic Studies at the Council on Foreign Relations. He is the author of: *Growing Apart: The Causes and Consequences of Global Wage Inequality*, New York: Council on Foreign Relations, 1999 (with K. Parker); *Contending with Capital Flows: What is Different About the 1990s*?, Ithaca, NY: Cornell University Press, 1998 (with B. Eichengreen); and 'Inequality, Poverty and Growth: Where do we Stand?,' *Annual Conference on Development Economics*, Washington, DC: World Bank, 1995.

Stephan Haggard is a professor and research director of international relations at the Institute on Global Conflict and Cooperation, Graduate School of International Relations and Pacific Studies, University of California at San Diego. His publications include: *The Developing Nations and the Politics of Global Integration*, Washington, DC: Brookings Institution, 1995; *The Political Economy of Democratic Transitions*, Princeton, NJ: Princeton University Press, 1995 (with R. Kaufman); and *Voting for Reform: Democracy. Political Liberalization, and Economic Adjustment*, New York: Oxford University Press, 1994 (co-editor with S.B. Webb).

Leonardo Hernandez is an economist at the Central Bank of Chile. Some of his recent papers include: 'Capital Controls in Chile: Effective? Efficient?,' Central Bank of Chile Working Paper, 1999 (with F. Gallego and K. Schmidt-Hebbel); 'Contagion in a Financially Integrated World: Lessons from East Asia's Recent Experience,' World Bank Policy Research Working Paper, 1998 (with P. Alba, S. Claessens and S. Gosh); and 'Sustainability of Private Capital Flows to Developing Countries: Is a Generalized Reversal Likely?,' *Cuadernos de Economia*, 1997 (with H. Rudoph).

Miles Kahler is the Rohr Professor of Pacific International Relations at the Graduate School of International Relations and Pacific Studies, University of California at San Diego. His publications include: *Capital Flows and Financial Crises*, Ithaca, NY: Cornell University Press, 1998 (ed.); *Liberalization and Foreign Policy*, New York: Columbia University Press, 1997 (ed.); and *International Institutions and the Political Economy of Integration*, Washington, DC: Brookings Institution, 1995.

Daniela Klingebiel is a senior financial economist in the Financial Economics Unit of the World Bank. Her recent publications include: 'Electronic Finance: Reshaping the Financial Landscape Around the World,' Washington, DC: World

Bank, 2000 (with S. Claessens and T. Glaessner); 'Stock Markets in Transition Economies,' Financial Sector Discussion Paper No. 4, Washington, DC: World Bank, 2000 (with S. Claessens and S. Djankov); 'Controlling the Cost of Banking Crises', Conference on Bank Structure and Competition, Chicago, Illinois: Federal Reserve Bank of Chicago, May 2000 (with P. Honohan).

Arvid John Lukauskas is an associate professor of political science and international and public affairs at Columbia University. His publications include: 'Explaining Styles of Financial Market Opening in Chile, Mexico, South Korea and Turkey,' *International Studies Quarterly*, 2000 (with S. Minushkin); 'Managing Mobile Capital,' *Review of International Political Economy*, 1999; *Regulating Finance: The Political Economy of Spanish Financial Policy from Franco to Democracy*, Michigan: University of Michigan Press, 1997; and 'The Political Economy of Financial Restriction,' *Comparative Politics*, 1994.

Andrew James MacIntyre is an associate professor and associate dean at the Graduate School of International Relations and Pacific Studies, University of California at San Diego. Among his publications are: *Business and Government in Industrializing Asia*, Ithaca, NY: Cornell University Press, 1994 (ed.); *The Dynamics of Policy Reform in South-East Asia and the South-West Pacific*, Singapore: Oxford University Press, 1992 (co-editor with K. Jayasuniya); and *Business and Politics in Indonesia*, Sydney: Allen & Unwin, 1991.

Maria-Angels Oliva is a postdoctoral fellow at the Sloan School of Management at the Massachusetts Institute of Technology. Her recent research includes: *Strategic Trade Analysis: Theory, Policy and Evidence*, New York: Oxford University Press, forthcoming, 2000 (with L.A. Rivera-Batiz); and 'M&As, Bargaining and Synergy Traps,' in C. Aliprantis, N. Yannelis and A. Alkhan (eds), *Economic Theory and Applications*, Springer Verlag, Amsterdam, 1999 (with L.A. Rivera-Batiz).

Paolo Pesenti is a senior economist in the International Research Function of the Federal Reserve Bank of New York. His research includes: 'The Asian Crisis: An Overview of the Empirical Evidence and Policy Debate,' in P.R. Agenor, M. Miller, D. Vines and A. Weber (eds), *The Asian Financial Crisis: Causes, Contagion and Consequences*, Cambridge: Cambridge University Press, 1999 (with G. Corsetti and N. Roubini); 'Paper Tigers? A Model of the Asian Crisis,' *European Economic Review*, 1999 (with G. Corsetti and N. Roubini); and *Financial Markets and European Monetary Cooperation: The Lessons of the 1992–93 Exchange Rate Mechanism Crisis*, Cambridge: Cambridge University Press, 1998 (with W.H. Buiter and G. Corsetti).

Francisco L. Rivera-Batiz is an associate professor of economics and director of the Program in Economic Policy Management in the School of International and Public Affairs at Columbia University; he is also an associate professor of economics and education in the department of international and transcultural studies at Teachers College, Columbia University. Among his publications are: 'The East Asian Financial Crisis: What Went Wrong?,' in L. Guijun and J. Jayachandran, (eds), *China in the Globalization of the World Economy*, Beijing: University of International Business and Economics Press, 1999; *Island Paradox: The Puerto Rican Economy in the 1990s*, New York: Russell Sage Foundation, 1996 (with C. Santiago); and *International Finance and Open Economy Macroeconomics*, Prentice-Hall, 1994 (with L. Rivera-Batiz).

Luis A. Rivera-Batiz is an associate professor at the Faculty of Management of McGill University in Montreal. He is the author of: *Strategic Trade Analysis: Theory, Policy and Evidence*, New York: Oxford University Press, forthcoming, 2001 (with M.A. Oliva); *International Finance and Open Economy Macroeconomics*, Englewood Cliffs, NJ: Prentice Hall, 1994 (with F. Rivera-Batiz); and 'Economic Integration and Economic Growth,' *Quarterly Journal of Economics*, 1991 (with P. Romer).

Robert Wade is a professor of political economy and development at the London School of Economics. His publications include: 'From "Miracle" to "Cronyism": Explaining the Great Asian Slump,' *Cambridge Journal of Economics*, 1998; 'The Asian Debt and Development Crisis of 1997–?: Causes and Consequences,' *World Development*, 1998; and *Governing the Market: Economic Theory and the Role of Government in East Asian Industrialization*, Princeton, NJ: Princeton University Press, 1992.

Preface

Most of the chapters contained in this volume were presented at a conference entitled 'The East Asian Crisis: Tigers in Distress,' held on 14–15 March 1999 at Columbia University. The purpose of the conference was to provide an assessment of the causes and consequences of the East Asian crisis of 1997–98 and to examine its aftermath. More specifically, as organizers, we sought to pull together scholars in the fields of economics and political science in order to stimulate discussion on the ways in which economic and political forces interacted in the evolution of the crisis.

The conference was sponsored by the Program in Economic Policy Management (PEPM) at Columbia. PEPM is a graduate program that imparts to professionals and policy makers the skills required for the effective design and implementation of economic policy in market economies, with a strong emphasis on the problems facing developing countries. The Program has operated as a partnership between the World Bank and Columbia University since 1991. At Columbia, the Program was established as a collaboration of the School of International and Public Affairs (SIPA), the Economics Department and the Graduate School of Business, with the administrative leadership of SIPA.

In addition to the editors and contributors of this volume, the conference was blessed with a superb group of participants and discussants, including Sam Cross (Columbia), Koichi Hamada (Yale), Robert Hodrick (Columbia), Robert Immerman (Columbia), Robert Kaufman (Rutgers), Diana Kunz (Columbia), John P. Mei (New York University), Helen Milner (Columbia), and Hugh Patrick (Columbia). Representing the World Bank at the conference was Abdul Monem Al-Mashat, of the World Bank Institute. Dean Lisa Anderson represented SIPA.

The authors are grateful to Maya Haddow, Yi-Ping Ong, Marisol D. Sanchez-Mercado, Pamela Terry-Shell, and Deborah Wilson for assistance at various stages of the project. Financial support from the Dean's Office at the School of International and Public Affairs at Columbia is also gratefully acknowledged.

Arvid John Lukauskas
Francisco L. Rivera-Batiz

May 2000

1. Introduction: The political economy of the East Asian crisis

Arvid John Lukauskas and Francisco L. Rivera-Batiz

On the morning of 2 July 1997, the Bank of Thailand announced that it was abandoning the pegged exchange rate system it had utilized for many years and would no longer intervene in setting the international value of its currency. After months of buying the baht in foreign exchange markets with the goal of preventing a depreciation of the currency, losing billions of dollars in the process, Thailand's central bank had decided to let the baht float. Immediately, the currency's value spiraled downwards, losing close to 15 per cent of its value that day. The following months witnessed additional currency crises in Malaysia, the Philippines, Indonesia and the Republic of Korea, and a collapse of the financial systems and economies of these countries. The East Asian financial crisis was born.

The rapidity and severity of the crisis caught both academics and policy-makers by surprise. The region had experienced phenomenal economic growth in preceding years, leading many scholars to proclaim that the twenty-first century would belong to Asia. Many observers admired the close state–business relations characteristic of these countries, claiming that they permitted the implementation of a coordinated investment program that helped spur rapid economic development and modernization. In the course of a few short months, the crisis shattered this glowing appraisal, leading to sharp indictments of crony capitalism in several countries and a dim view of East Asia's long-term economic prospects.

Three years after the East Asian financial crisis started, this book provides an assessment of the causes of the crisis, its consequences, and the policy lessons to be drawn from the episode. The volume presents the view that the crisis and its aftermath were not simply the reflection of purely economic and financial phenomena but also the product of fundamental political forces. The chapters look at the crisis in historical perspective, examine the comparative evidence on financial crises across various regions, discuss the impact of political institutions and regime type on economic policy, and analyse how major international actors, including the United States and international organizations such as the International Monetary Fund (IMF), influenced events before, during and after the crisis.

The volume is divided into four parts. Part I explores how the East Asian crisis compares with other financial and debt crises in emerging markets, discussing several historical episodes and providing background on the similarities and differences between the East Asian crisis and other recent crises. Part II analyses the domestic political economy of the crises in the various East Asian countries, examining the role played by various private and public actors, political institutions, financial liberalization, and the problem of moral hazard. Part III focuses on the international political economy of the crisis, discussing how external economic and political forces influenced the decisions that led to the crises (and the policy prescriptions afterwards), as well as its international repercussions, including contagion effects on Latin America and other emerging markets. Finally, Part IV offers a roundtable discussion of the policy lessons of the crisis by four leading experts on international political economy.

1. THE CRISIS IN HISTORICAL AND COMPARATIVE PERSPECTIVE

Financial crises are neither new phenomena nor are they rare, isolated creatures in market economies. In Chapter 3, Michael Bordo notes that capital flows to emerging markets have historically been subject to booms and busts. He concludes: 'the lesson we learn from history is that there has always been optimism followed by pessimism in a world with imperfect and asymmetric information. Lenders are not fully informed about internal conditions in emerging countries, and borrowers may not put funds made available to their best use.' In Latin America, he observes, there were four major boom–bust cycles before the Great Depression dried-out sources of capital to the region. The first wave occurred in the 1820s, when British capitalists ploughed funds into newly-independent Latin American nations to finance mining and infrastructure investments, only to experience panic, crash and defaults by all these states years later. The second Latin boom was in the 1850s and 1860s, to finance railroads, and it ended in 1873 with massive defaults. The third cycle was in the 1880s, to finance railroads and infrastructure in Argentina and Uruguay, and concluded with the crash of 1890 and the Barings crisis in London. The last Latin American boom–bust wave occurred in the 1920s, to finance municipal infrastructure projects, and ended in the Great Depression and another round of defaults.

The East Asian crisis reflects the historical boom–bust experience with capital flows to emerging markets, but Bordo argues that it differs in several respects from past crises. First, today's globalized capital market appears to be less stable and more prone to reversals than in the nineteenth century. Second, contemporary capital flows are subject to much greater moral hazard problems. He asserts: 'what is different in today's boom–bust episodes from earlier ones is the belief that domestic financial institutions are protected by an internal safety net and that foreign lenders will not suffer losses on their loans in hard currencies because funds to compensate them will be made available by the multiple international lending agencies and the monetary authorities of the advanced countries. In earlier times losses were actually sustained by lenders, and by borrowers who were then cut off from further loans.'

Financial crises have proliferated in recent years. Estimates are that between 1976 and 1996 as many as 59 developing countries had at least one major banking crisis. Furthermore, 87 countries had at least one major currency crisis between 1975 and 1995. A substantial literature has emerged seeking to explain these crises. Research on the sources of banking crises in developing countries has considered the part played by macroeconomic volatility, lack of corporate and bank transparency, incompetent management of the maturity and currency composition of bank assets and liabilities, inadequate regulatory and supervisory institutions, moral hazard, bank fragility and political interference in bank management, among other factors.[1] Models of balance of payments crises have examined the role of persistent budget deficits, chronic monetary expansion and inflation, postponed macroeconomic adjustment, self-fulfilling speculative bubbles and financial panic in such crises.[2]

In Chapter 2, Francisco L. Rivera-Batiz argues that the East Asian crisis reflects a broader phenomenon facing emerging markets in general, which he refers to as 'emerging market disease.' He notes that emerging market policymakers face a basic underlying dilemma. Their development strategy relies on raising investment rates while attracting foreign capital through domestic and international financial liberalization. The resulting capital inflows, and the wide array of projects that these funds allow to finance, produce a boom in the economy, providing an aura of long-lasting, if not ever-lasting, growth. But, Rivera-Batiz argues, ingrained in this investment and economic boom are the seeds of an eventual slowdown or bust, which reverses some, if not all, of the gains achieved by the country. The reason is that capital inflows generally lead to a domestic real currency appreciation. A persistent appreciation, in turn, slows export growth, raises imports and, thus, worsens the current account balance. This has three potentially devastating consequences. First, a sluggish export sector can undermine the confidence of investors in the future growth of the economy. Second, a widening current account balance deficit, even if initially financed enthusiastically by foreign capital, leads to an accumulation of external debt that, at some point, raises the specter of default. Third, a sustained real currency appreciation also means that devaluation expectations will gradually but surely develop. All of these will eventually precipitate capital flight and generate a domestic credit crunch, throwing the economy into a recession. If the domestic banking system is fragile, if the capital outflows are accompanied by financial panic, and if policymakers stubbornly refuse to devalue, the outcome is a full-fledged currency and financial crisis.

Rivera-Batiz shows in detail how the symptoms of emerging market disease developed in East Asia. There are, however, a variety of other cases, notably in Chile (1978–82) and Mexico (1994–95). In Chile, a process of financial liberalization began in 1975, two years after a military junta overthrew the government of Salvador Allende. Interest rate ceilings were eliminated, reserve requirements were reduced, and entry into the banking industry was relaxed. As a result, real interest rates soared over world interest rates. Combined with a stable, fixed exchange rate established in June 1979, the economy attracted a flood of foreign capital. In 1980 and 1981, Chile was booming and a climate of euphoria dominated both business and the government. During the same period, however, the real exchange rate appreciated sharply, reducing the rate of growth of exports and increasing imports. In 1981, the current account balance deficit grew to over 12 per cent of Gross Domestic Product (GDP). By mid-1982, devaluation expectations were running high, triggering massive capital flight. The main features of emerging market disease had shown their face. On 14 June 1982, the government was forced to let the peso float. A major financial crisis followed, throwing the economy into a sharp recession. The 1982–83 recession was the fourth largest in Chile this century, with aggregate output falling by 20 per cent and unemployment rising to a peak of 30 per cent of the labor force by late 1983.[3]

The symptoms of emerging market disease were also evident in the Mexican crisis of 1994–95. Financial liberalization began in 1988 and accelerated in the early 1990s, with the privatization of the banking system, the abandonment of interest rate controls, elimination of reserve requirements on peso-denominated bank deposits, and removal of most capital controls. The nominal exchange rate was narrowly controlled by monetary authorities, fluctuating for years around a value of slightly over 3 pesos per dollar. After years of exclusion, Mexico started to regain access to world capital markets. Indeed, financial liberalization, stable exchange rates and rising domestic investment led to a massive influx of foreign capital in the early 1990s. But the mechanisms behind emerging market disease were already operating to slow down the economy. A sustained, dramatic real appreciation of the peso contributed to an expanding current account balance deficit, which reached close to 8 per cent of GDP in 1994. Expectations of devaluation throughout 1994 resulted in a run on the peso, culminating in an explosive capital flight that caused the government to let the peso float in December 1994. A devastating economic and financial crisis followed in 1995.[4]

2. THE POLITICAL ECONOMY OF THE EAST ASIAN CRISIS: DOMESTIC FACTORS

The unfolding of the East Asian crisis has been characterized by major shifts in fundamental economic and political variables: a surge of capital inflows followed by massive capital flight; pegged exchange rates followed by their sudden abandonment; rapid growth replaced by deep recession; and, in some countries, long-lasting political regimes giving way to new governments. The chapters in Part II examine the domestic economic and political forces behind these drastic shifts. We start with the issue of capital flows.

The Consequences of Capital Account Liberalization

In September 1997, the International Monetary Fund, at its annual meeting held in Hong Kong, endorsed the idea of including, as part of its Articles of Agreement, the goal of capital account liberalization. This idea has met a silent death in the aftermath of the East Asian crisis. Nevertheless, the view that free mobility of capital, including portfolio flows, has enormous benefits for developing countries continues to be central to the ideology of not only the IMF, but also the World Bank and other international organizations. It is reflected in the following statement by Bradford De Long, former deputy assistant secretary for economic policy: 'the ability to borrow abroad has enabled successful emerging market economies to double or triple the speed at which their productivity levels and living standards converge to the industrial core' (De Long 1998).

Despite this consensus, a central theorem in the political economy of capital flows directly contradicts it. Back in the late 1970s, a group of political economists, including Carlos Diaz Alejandro, Jagdish N. Bhagwati, and Richard Brecher, established the theoretical underpinnings for studying the welfare effects of capital flows.[5] Their conclusion was that, when there are distortions in domestic markets, capital flows can have severe negative effects on countries that liberalize their capital account and may result in a contraction of GNP. The result is important because most developing economies are plagued by domestic distortions. They can be in the form of market imperfections or government-generated protectionism. They can be associated with imperfect or asymmetric information in financial markets, or with negative externalities in goods markets. They may be linked to corruption, cronysm, and rent-seeking activities, or due to labor market imperfections. Consider, as an example, the case of an economy that has weak, inefficient financial institutions that appear to be healthy and profitable because they enjoy government protection. In this situation, the opening of the capital account can have serious negative consequences since funds will flow precisely to the weak, but attractive-looking, institutions, which are more likely to move funds into unproductive domestic investments.

One of the main explanations of the East Asian crisis is that capital account liberalization in these countries took place in the presence of a weak and fragile domestic financial sector. Chapter 5, by Pedro Alba, Leonardo Hernandez and Daniela Klingebiel provides an extensive case study of Thailand. The authors show that the Thai crisis was associated with rapid and extensive capital account liberalization in the presence of a weak financial intermediation system that was not prepared to handle the massive changes in the economic environment from 1988 to 1997. Thai financial institutions did not have the managerial capacity for project evaluation, risk control and risk management to handle the massive funds available through capital inflows. This was coupled with an inadequate institutional and regulatory framework and weak market oversight due to poor disclosure and quality of financial information, as well as a concentrated ownership structure and cross-ownership links between financial and nonfinancial entities.

To make matters worse, Alba, Hernandez and Klingebiel suggest, the macroeconomic policy mix in Thailand contributed to the growing economic vulnerability in the 1990s. Monetary policy had kept interest rates high, encouraging further capital inflows and the accumulation of short-term liabilities. The authorities also did not permit the exchange rate to fluctuate, which could have ameliorated the flows of capital. Finally, although the fiscal policy stance remained conservative throughout 1987–96, it did become procyclical in 1993–96 and further expanded aggregate demand in an overheated economy. All these factors led to the rapid build-up of financial and corporate sector fragility that culminated in the crisis in 1997.

The authors conclude that opening the capital account and integrating with global financial markets should be contingent on adequate domestic institutional development. The benefits of openness have to be weighed against the risk of financial crisis, especially in countries with fragile financial systems, weak regulatory and supervisory frameworks and government guarantees on deposits. Moreover, the liberalization of the financial sector needs to be carefully managed since domestic market and policy distortions – such as the presence of close links between corporate and banking sectors, and (implicit) deposit insurance – can create incentives for excessive risk-taking in both financial institutions and the corporate sector.

Political Factors Behind the Crisis

The political dimensions of the Asian crisis have not received as much attention as the economic ones, although a few important works have appeared (one notable example is Pempel 1999). Yet, it is obvious that domestic (and international) political factors played a prominent role in the onset and subsequent evolution of the crisis. After all, economic policy is made in a political context. Both political scientists and economists have developed a body of writings on the political economy of financial crises, that can contribute greatly to our understanding of recent events in Asia.[6] This section looks at the political economy issues raised by the Asian crisis and reviews the key findings from the relevant political science literature. We begin by examining the domestic political factors that have contributed to the onset of the financial crisis.

Most observers agree that capital account opening, combined with weak prudential regulation of financial systems, was a primary factor in causing or aggravating the crisis. Alba, Hernandez and Klingebiel, for instance, demonstrate this in the case of Thailand. Why did governments open the capital account without implementing an appropriate regulatory regime? Here we examine how domestic politics affected this decision, leaving international explanations for later.

One prominent claim in the political economy literature is that financial globalization has empowered the holders of non-fixed assets *vis-à-vis* other domestic groups because they can credibly threaten to withdraw their capital from the country if their demands are not met (see, for example, Kurzer 1993). This 'exit option' enables these actors to influence government policy and advance their preference for greater financial openness. This argument may help explain the general trend toward opening worldwide, but the experiences of individual Asian countries differed greatly. Mobile capital holders were not always the most influential actors in these countries; even where they were, their preferences were not unambiguously in favor of opening. In Korea, for instance, support for capital account liberalization was weak. The chaebol, Korea's most powerful economic interests, feared increased foreign participation in bond and equity markets, although they pushed for the ability to tap Eurocurrency markets to gain access to low-cost capital (Lukauskas and Minushkin 2000). Specifically, they were concerned that their control over industrial groups and the financial sector might diminish if the government removed barriers to entry more broadly. For their part, many policymakers worried that completely open financial markets might increase macroeconomic and financial instability. Furthermore, virtually no social group and few government officials favored the entry of foreign financial institutions. In Indonesia and Thailand, on the other hand, private sector support for opening was considerable, particularly among large firms anxious to attract investment flows to finance huge infrastructure projects.

Why did authorities not implement appropriate prudential regulation as they undertook capital account opening? One answer is that these countries had underdeveloped financial systems and insufficient administrative resources, and it takes a very long time to design and implement sound prudential regulation. Supporting this interpretation is the observation that even industrialized countries with deep financial markets and highly developed bureaucracies, like the United States, have found it difficult to maintain appropriate financial regimes, as their high incidence of banking crises indicates. One might expect, therefore, that countries that are undergoing liberalization and financial deepening would particularly struggle to develop adequate regulatory systems quickly.

Nevertheless, political factors undoubtedly played a role in the lack of development of a stringent regulatory regime as well. Government leaders have good political reasons to eschew developing stringent regulatory regimes, at least in the short term (see, for example, Lukauskas 1997, ch. 2). Strict prudential regulation is not popular with key constituents. In fact, several social groups, notably, banks and corporations, typically oppose stringent prudential regulation. Tough regulation imposes opportunity costs on banks in the form of higher levels of reserves or provisions, and generally increases the cost of credit for firms (in the short run). In addition, building the administrative capacity to supervise financial markets is costly and demanding. Thus, establishing a sound regulatory regime is normally a low priority on the economic agenda of most governments. Indeed, experience tells us that reform in this area rarely occurs in the absence of a major banking or general financial crisis that results in high direct costs for the government or powerful private actors, like banks.

Another prominent contention in the literature is that government policy created moral hazard problems among banks, firms, and investors, both domestic and foreign. Implicit or, in some cases, explicit government guarantees encouraged firms to undertake risky projects in the belief that they would be bailed out if their projects were unsuccessful. For their part, these guarantees encouraged financial institutions to extend credit to firms without abiding by proper lending procedures in the belief that their losses would be covered if firms could not repay loans. The guarantees stemmed from a variety of sources, which varied across countries, including direct government stakes in banks or firms, industrial policies that targeted specific sectors or even individual firms, and generally intimate ties between business and state elites, sometimes based on familial relations.

The argument that political institutions in some East Asian countries established a climate that was conducive to the development of moral hazard problems has gained many adherents. Yet, the close ties between East Asian government officials and business interests, which Miles Kahler labels 'elite collusion' in this volume's concluding roundtable discussion, were, until recently, viewed in a highly favorable light by many writers. Admirers claimed that close state–business relations permitted policy makers to implement a coordinated investment program without falling victim to what is often termed 'government failure.' The success of East Asian financial and industrial policies, particularly in Korea, relative to those of other countries in the developing world, was considered to be strong proof of the effectiveness of this approach.

With the crisis, critics of East Asian policies began to charge that 'government failure' had existed all along, but that strong economic growth, due to the massive mobilization of inputs, not efficient investment, had hidden corruption and the negative effects of government intervention. The exact nature of the problem varied across East Asian states. In some countries, like Indonesia, the government designed policies to benefit particular groups, firms, or even individuals, often personally related to government leaders, leading critics to speak of 'cronyism.' This cronyism reflected the personalistic character of the authoritarian Suharto political regime. In Korea, the government established direct, intimate links with business, especially the chaebol, through a variety of formal and informal channels to aid in formulating and implementing industrial policy. Until recently, the government also owned the most important banks, making it easy to control their operations and carry out selective credit policies; even after banks were privatized, the government continued to exercise influence over their operations.[7] The close ties between the state, firms, and the banking system made the government directly responsible for the health of the banking system and created a government stake in the success of select firms and sectors, which ultimately created moral hazard problems. Firms believed that they would be bailed out if their investments did not fare well. Lenders, both domestic and foreign, calculated that lending to favored firms carried low risk because the government would be forced to cover losses in order to avoid the collapse of the payments system and a sharp drop in employment and output.

In Chapter 4, Stephan Haggard and Andrew MacIntyre assess the theories that suggest the East Asian financial crisis was the result of sins of omission, in the form of weak regulation, or that it was the result of commission, in the form of explicit or implicit guarantees against losses that generated moral hazard. The authors find both of these hypotheses wanting. The weak regulation hypothesis finds some support, in that financial policy was often poorly designed, but it cannot account for the behavior of banks, firms, and investors or the magnitude of the crisis. The moral hazard hypothesis is not entirely consistent with the evidence from the Indonesian, Korean, and Thai cases either. Governments in these countries had provided guarantees, but their nature was ambiguous and contested. In Indonesia, guarantees pertained only to a small set of firms and Suharto sent out mixed signals about the strength of the state guarantee starting in late 1997. In Korea, authorities allowed several large firms to fail before its crisis, signaling investors that government guarantees were no longer in effect. The Thai case offers greater support for the moral hazard hypothesis, but Haggard and McIntyre show that other political variables, such as the ability of politicians with a direct interest in regulated financial institutions to influence decision-making, were more fundamental in the onset of the crisis by weakening confidence in Thai markets.

Haggard and MacIntyre advance a third type of domestic explanation, centered on politically-generated uncertainty about how the government would handle financial weakness, contending that it better explains both the timing and intensity of the Asian financial crisis. This uncertainty stemmed from several sources. First, in all three countries, firms and banks questioned the credibility of the government's commitment to avoid bailouts and lobbied authorities to provide support. This lobbying led to a 'war of attrition' between the government and private actors that delayed reform and reduced investor confidence in the public sector's policy management. Second, the authors identify broader institutional and political arrangements that lessened the government's ability to respond effectively to economic events, such as the presence of divided governments (Korea), the fragmentation of party systems (Thailand), and fundamental uncertainty surrounding the viability of the government itself (Indonesia).

The Politics of the Aftermath of the East Asian Crisis

Chapter 6, by Luis Rivera-Batiz and Maria-Angels Oliva, examines in detail how conjunctural political elements and weak political systems affected the policy process in the aftermath of the East Asian crisis. They argue that the interaction of the economic shocks with political and institutional factors account for the severity of the crisis. In Thailand, the proliferation of political parties, parliamentary fragmentation, unstable party alliances, and the inability of parties to achieve an electoral majority, led to policy deadlocks that blocked the formulation of consistent policies and implementation of reforms after the crisis occurred. In Korea, the run up to the the hotly-contested December 1997 election paralysed policy actions despite the severity of the crisis in the region. The legislature failed to pass a major financial bill that represented the most significant policy initiative before the December election. Only after longtime dissident and reformer Kim Dae-Jung was elected president on 19 December 1997 did the National Assembly in Seoul pass the major financial reforms bills that were a condition for IMF disbursement of the $57 billion under the bailout package of 3 December. In addition, major disagreements on monetary policy and financial regulation and supervision between the Ministry of Finance and the Bank of Korea made a coordinated response difficult.

In Malaysia, the crisis led to a bitter clash between government technocrats in charge of economic policy and Prime Minister Mahathir Mohamad. Mahathir blamed the crisis on foreign speculators and favored the imposition of capital and exchange controls as the main policy reaction. He also resisted an IMF bailout as well as the austerity and credit-tightening measures favored by the organization. Ministry of Finance economists, on the other hand, advocated austerity measures and higher interest rates to deal with the country's rising external debt and keep capital from flowing abroad. Mahathir was able to impose his policy stance after the crisis erupted in July1997. However, in December, Finance Minister Datuk Seri Anwar Ibrahim introduced a set of 'home-grown' measures fashioned after IMF policies, including government spending cuts of 10 per cent and the delay of several of Mr. Mahathir's pet building projects. Intense pressure by Mahathir on the finance ministry led to a policy turn-around in July and September 1998 that reduced interest rates, restored public sector spending on infrastructure projects, and reimposed fixed exchange rates, with wide-ranging controls on currency trading and international financial transactions. Mr Anwar was dismissed on 2 September 1998 and accused of financial and sexual misconduct. He was later convicted and jailed.

As Rivera-Batiz and Oliva document, Indonesia was the country where political uncertainty reached its peak in the region. President Suharto's thirty-year government displayed inconsistent and, at times, chaotic policy behavior during and after the crisis erupted. Intra-governmental conflict between Suharto and central bank officials regarding the best policy course compounded the uncertainty. An IMF bailout was initially arranged in late October 1997, but the severity of the crisis and the government's incoherent policy reactions led to a revision of the agreement in early 1998. In February 1998, Suharto dismissed the central bank governor and considered replacing the central bank with a currency board, a move which was radically opposed by the IMF, the World Bank and most Indonesian economists handling the crisis. The currency board proposal was later abandoned. Throughout this period, uncertainly regarding the vitality of Suharto's regime itself was substantial, as the aging leader faced a deepening social and economic debacle. Critics perceived the government to be stalling key policy measures in order to protect the wealthy business dealings of Suharto's family and associates.

After an extended period of social and political unrest, Suharto stepped down in May 1998, giving way to B.J. Habibie, who was vice-president. President Habibie's administration, which operated under the influence of Suharto and his political party Golkar, did not reduce uncertainty significantly. The economic crisis raged on in the second half of 1998, with an acute food shortage and fears of widespread starvation. Moreover, a sensitive situation regarding East Timor independence from Indonesia dominated the headlines throughout 1999. When the country's military occupied the island in 1999 and the government refused to allow United Nations peacekeeping troops access, both the World Bank and the IMF suspended discussions regarding an expansion of loans over those provided under the 1997–98 bailout. Political scandals continued throughout 1999, with accusations that funds intended to salvage Indonesian banks were being diverted to government officials and political parties. In June 1999, democratic parliamentary elections were held and, in November, the parliament elected a new president, Abdurrahman Wahid.

The chapter by Rivera-Batiz and Oliva focuses on how political forces influenced the development of the crisis and its aftermath. Political scientists have also analyzed the reverse causal relationship: how an economic crisis may affect a country's political institutions. One traditional line of inquiry has asked whether crises lead to regime change, from authoritarian to democratic regimes, or vice versa. Initial research, focused on Latin America, examined how poor economic conditions might provoke authoritarian responses in democratic states. A good example of such a response occurred in Chile, where Pinochet seized power from the Allende government in 1973 after rapid, severe deterioration of that country's economic situation. More recently, scholars have considered whether poor economic performance can spur democratization. Stephan Haggard and Robert Kaufman (1995, ch. 2) have found that a sustained economic crisis often precedes democratic transitions. Crises cause the 'authoritarian bargain' with the private sector to break down and contribute to the strength of the opposition by mobilizing broader social movements. Examples of this phenomenon are Argentina, Bolivia, and the Philippines, where crises precipitated or hastened the demise of authoritarian regimes.

A related line of inquiry is whether crises lead to institutional experimentation, specifically, of economic policy-making structures, within the context of a given political regime. One argument is that crises increase the odds of major institutional change because actors are more willing to consider dramatic initiatives to deal with difficult circumstances, especially if perceptions are that the economic environment has changed irrevocably.[8] Stated another way, crises may provide the stimulus to break a country's path dependency. Historical examples of this dynamic are the institutional innovations associated with the New Deal in the USA, in response to the Great Depression, and the movement toward more technocratic economic policy-making structures in the countries affected by the 1980s debt crisis, such as Mexico.

The crisis had varied domestic political repercussions, sparking major political change in Indonesia and Korea, some changes in Thailand and the Philippines, but none in Malaysia. In Indonesia, the severe economic downturn following the collapse of the financial system, and the perception that the government was incapable of fashioning a coherent economic program in response, was a primary factor in the overthrow of the Suharto regime, as already noted. Certainly, opposition to Suharto was long-standing and had been increasing in recent years, but economic problems clearly made the difference, both by emboldening the opposition and adding to its ranks. In Korea, unhappiness over the economy enabled an opposition political party to win the presidency for the first time since the country's democratization in 1987. While this does not constitute a change in regimes, it does signal democratic consolidation in the country. Institutional change, for example, granting the central bank greater independence, is also taking place in Korea, but some of this was in the works before the crisis hit.

In the Philippines, President Fidel Ramos hastily abandoned attempts to seek a constitutional amendment to allow him to run for re-election for a third consecutive term in September 1997. Instead, in May 1998, Joseph Estrada, a populist candidate and former movie star, was elected president. Estrada, who was vice-president under the previous administration, based his campaign on reforms intended to deal with the social and economic effects of the crisis, promising the redistribution of wealth and to put 'food on the table' of the poor. In Thailand, the fractious, six-party ruling coalition broke down and Prime Minister Chavalit Yongchaiyudh had to resign on 4 November 1997. In Malaysia, on the other hand, Prime Minister Mahathir astutely deflected criticism over his government's role in the country's financial turmoil by blaming international speculators for economic problems. If anything, the crisis solidified Mahathir's hold on power, as he took advantage of events to force out politicians with views at odds with his own. His ruling National Front party amply won Malaysia's national election in November 1999, giving him a new five-year term after 18 years as prime minister.

Financial crises can spark major political responses but they can also lead to substantial policy reforms. Crises, for example, may affect the potential for long-delayed structural and regulatory reform. A common argument is that a crisis generates pressure in favor of structural adjustment by strengthening the hand of reformers, who can claim that their preferred set of policies are superior. In particular, if a country requires outside funding or advice to overcome the crisis, reformers may have the opportunity to enlist powerful external actors in their reform efforts (though this may not always be an advantage) or use conditionality demands to push through policy changes (Maxfield 1990; Öncü and Gökce 1991). In addition, leaders may become more receptive to new economic ideas or ideologies as old beliefs become discredited. Given the crisis environment, many may feel that very little can be lost by adopting a new strategy. A crisis also tends to weaken social opposition to structural adjustment. Dani Rodrik suggests that crises requiring tough stabilization programs make trade reform easier if governments package the two together, by reducing the politically difficult distributional effects of trade reform to second-order proportions (Rodrik 1994). It is not difficult to develop a parallel argument about financial reform.

Research, however, finds that although crises have sometimes pushed governments to liberalize financial markets further, in other cases, governments have reimposed or deepened financial controls.[9] A number of domestic factors determine the direction of financial policy in the wake of a crisis, including the political calculations of leaders, the interests of influential private sector groups, and the degree of political competition within the country. In the East Asian case, Korea, Indonesia, and Thailand deepened liberalization of their financial systems (and, more generally, their economies) in response to the crisis, albeit with some delay, while Malaysia did not. Malaysian policymakers actually deepened state intervention, for instance, implementing new capital controls on outflows (though they were only temporary measures). This divergence in policy direction was partly due to the need of Korea, Indonesia and Thailand to seek outside funding to carry them through the crisis. Most of this funding came from the IMF, which imposed financial reform as a condition of lending. In contrast, Malaysia never asked for IMF assistance. But domestic politics also played a role. In the Korean case, for instance, reformers seized upon the crisis to advance a relatively unpopular agenda. Simply put, the government would not have opened as quickly and as broadly as it did in the absence of the crisis and the subsequent international pressure by the IMF and the United States (Lukauskas and Minushkin 2000). In Malaysia, a relatively healthy economy, combined with Prime Minister Mahathir's dominant role in domestic politics, permitted the government to maintain its desired level of control over the economy, even allowing it to implement a new set of capital controls, which were roundly criticized by external and some internal actors.

3. THE INTERNATIONAL POLITICAL ECONOMY OF THE CRISIS

Previous sections examined how *domestic* economic and political factors in each East Asian country were linked to the eruption of the crisis and its severity afterwards. This section examines the external factors involved in causing the crisis as well as the consequences of the East Asian debacle for the rest of the world.

International Political Explanations of the Crisis

Many scholars view premature financial opening as a primary cause of the East Asian crisis. We have already considered some of the domestic explanations for this policy choice. To what extent did international factors also play a role in premature opening? It is possible to identify both indirect 'structural' as well as direct international pressures on countries to open their financial markets, pressures which need not be mutually exclusive.

The structural argument claims that heightened capital mobility has become an exogenous constraint on policymaking, forcing states to engage in competitive financial deregulation to attract and retain international capital flows. Specifically, governments may need to eliminate restrictions on international financial transactions in order to attract or retain investment capital; if not, capital will simply go elsewhere (see, for example, Cerny 1993; Cable 1995). The increased ability of capital to move rapidly across national borders has also decreased the effectiveness of capital controls and augmented their cost.[10] In this view, East Asian countries, like many other developing countries, opened their capital account in response to these new incentives.

Direct external pressure might also have pushed East Asian (and other developing) countries to liberalize their financial markets before they were ready or willing to do so. Indeed, the pressure on middle-income developing countries to open their capital account increased noticeably in the early part of the 1990s. In particular, the USA and several international organizations, notably, the IMF and the Organization for Economic Cooperation and Development (OECD), stepped up their demands on countries to liberalize markets (Wade and Veneroso 1998). The economic turmoil in many regions of the world gave some of these international actors greater leverage over countries through their control over emergency lines of credit. The IMF, in particular, expanded its conditionality to incorporate a demand for financial reforms, including capital account liberalization and greater access for foreign intermediaries to domestic financial markets.

Robert Wade, in chapter 7, concentrates on the argument that direct pressures by the USA and a variety of international organizations on East Asian countries greatly contributed to their decision to open the capital account. Wade's primary thesis is that the crisis and the policy responses to it can only be understood by examining the role played by the USA as the world's leading international financial actor. The influence of the USA on the crisis began long before the US government took a leading role in managing the fallout. The East Asian crisis, Wade writes, was largely due to the sudden bursting of an investment bubble which the USA (along with Europe and Japan) helped create by channeling massive capital flows into selected Asian countries. Wade identifies several mechanisms by which this took place, showing how US policies throughout the 1980s and 1990s pumped huge amounts of liquidity into the international financial system. In East Asia, this liquidity helped to fuel excess investment in industry, which created surplus capacity in many sectors, and dramatic, unsustainable increases in asset and real estate values.

Wade also contends that the US government, pushed by Wall Street firms, pressed for rapid liberalization of financial markets throughout Asia in the 1990s. Most broadly, the USA stimulated the opening of financial systems by spreading policy-relevant knowledge favorable to open markets under its intellectual and moral leadership. But it also applied direct pressure on East Asian governments to open up, bilaterally and multilaterally, through organizations such as the World Bank, IMF, OECD, and World Trade Organization (WTO). Bilateral pressure was the greatest in the case of the Republic of Korea, where the US had insistently pushed for capital account opening and greater access to Korean markets for US intermediaries since the early 1980s (Woo-Cumings 1997). The IMF and World Bank also advanced this agenda, not only because of US pressure, but also because these organizations subscribed to a neoliberal economic ideology that favored few controls on financial flows.

Wade argues that US officials mostly ignored other dimensions of financial regulation, namely, the need for adequate prudential regulation, in their push to open up East Asian markets. He writes: 'attention to building "strong" regulatory arrangements and linking capital opening to the strength of those arrangements on the ground was deliberately discouraged lest it provide countries with excuses to delay – contrary to US objectives.' According to Wade, the capital account opening demanded by the United States was wholly unwarranted because these countries enjoyed ample domestic savings and had no need to open themselves up to volatile capital flows; moreover, these flows threatened to undo the beneficial relationships that had evolved between firms, banks, and government policymakers.

Another international-level explanation for the East Asian crisis focuses on the moral hazard problems created by IMF interventions in past financial crises, notably, the 1994–95 Mexican peso crisis. Critics argue that these IMF actions were largely motivated by political goals, specifically, the desire to aid geo-strategically important governments, and were not designed according to sound economic criteria. They have contended that the interventions bailed-out private international investors, leading them to believe that they would also be insured against major losses in the future. This discouraged financiers from exercising proper caution in their lending to developing countries and, consequently, they accepted too much risk. As a result, much of the flood of money into the East Asian countries went to undeserving borrowers, establishing an unstable, speculative economy that could easily be rattled if conditions went slightly awry or if investors lost confidence in the government.

The moral hazard argument (and the attendant claims about the IMF), though quite plausible, has relied more upon assertion than evidence. While foreign investors made poor lending decisions in East Asia, it is not obvious that they made them based on the presumption that they would be protected against losses. A number of factors might explain inappropriate lending, such as over-optimistic predictions about the growth rates of specific firms or the Asian economies generally, or over-confidence on the ability of governments to maintain fixed exchange rates.[11] Certainly, foreign investors had no explicit guarantee that they would be bailed out. The IMF has recently taken several steps to make private borrowers accept even more of the costs of debt restructuring, in a policy called 'burden sharing.'[12]

The International Economic Consequences of the Crisis: Contagion

The East Asian crisis presents classic examples of how economic events in one country are transmitted to others. This transmission has many mechanisms, ranging from the *spillover* effects of a crisis in one country to its trading or financial partners to the *contagion* effects of an economic crisis in one country to others with very little, if any, trade and financial linkages with the originating country. The mechanisms involved in the transmission of business cycles and economic disturbances among countries that are closely linked by trade and capital account transactions have been studied extensively over the years.[13] What has not been studied as carefully until recently, however, are the contagion effects of an economic crisis in one country to other economies with very little, if any, trade and financial linkages with the originating country.

Mario Blejer and Graciana del Castillo, in chapter 8, analyse the spread of the East Asian financial crisis across the globe, as waves of economic aftershocks were felt in a variety of other countries. The first signs of contagion in emerging markets appeared in October 1997. In Latin America, the impact was particularly significant in Brazil, Argentina and Mexico, whose currency and stock markets came under speculative attack. In these countries, the policy reactions in response to the contagion were swift, with tightening of monetary and fiscal policies that significantly raised interest rates. These initial impacts of the crisis were followed by: (1) trade effects linked to the increased competition from East Asian products cheapened by the devaluations in those countries; and (2) plummeting commodity prices, which worsened the terms of trade of copper producers (Chile and Peru) and oil producers (Mexico, Venezuela, Ecuador and Colombia). These developments contributed to deteriorating current account balance deficits and a slowdown of economic activity, both of which suggested the higher risks involved in emerging markets in the aftermath of the crisis. Still, by mid-1998 the policy responses in Latin America had been able to contain the short-run effects of the shock.

The East Asian saga took a turn for the worst in August 1998 when the Russian economy deteriorated, with a sharp devaluation of the ruble, a government default on domestic debt and a moratorium on payments by Russian commercial banks to foreign creditors. According to Blejer and del Castillo, the Russian crisis and that country's policy responses 'changed the character of the world financial crisis and led to a swift and rash reassessment by investors of their lending and investment strategies and a reevaluation of their financial instruments.' As a result of the increased risk-aversion, private sector financing for emerging markets dried up, spreads widened considerably, the price of securities in the secondary markets fell, and local interest rates rose. This worsened the situation in East Asia, Latin America and emerging markets in general. The frustration felt by some policy makers in emerging markets as financial events in faraway Russia spread to their own economies is seen in this statement made by Mexico's Secretary of the Treasury, Jose Angel Gurria, at the time of the crisis: 'Ninety per cent of Mexicans have never heard of the Duma, and yet the exchange rate and interest rates that they live with every day were being driven by people like Kiriyenko and Chernomydrin and Primakov' (as quoted in Edwards 2000, p. 1).

Blejer and del Castillo provide a detailed analysis of the impact of the Russian-led August 1998 debacle on the economy of Brazil. The difficulties in obtaining foreign financing, in the face of growing current account balance and budget deficits, threw that country into crisis. In November 1998, Brazil reached an agreement with the IMF that included a $41.5 billion international assistance package. This did not end the crisis. Domestic political opposition to the IMF-led adjustment program and a sustained policy of fixing the value of the real led to massive capital flight, which forced the central bank to let the currency float on 15 January 1999.

The extensive sequence of financial stress in emerging markets in the late 1990s, from East Asia to Russia to Latin America, has left many countries with substantially diminished growth. Blejer and del Castillo suggest that this slowdown is raising the danger of protectionism at the beginning of the new century. This is evident not only in the now frequent public protests against globalization and the WTO, but also in the escalation of trade conflicts and protectionist threats between various countries or groups of countries, including the USA, the European Community, Mercosur and the Andean Group. They recommend that 'rather than letting the crisis undermine their process of trade liberalization and integration, countries should pursue this goal even more determinedly.'

The Politics of the Crisis Aftermath

The international consequences of the East Asian crisis are not circumscribed to the economic arena. The politics underpinning the international community's response to the East Asian crisis has been the object of considerable controversy among scholars and policymakers, echoing the debate that surrounded the 1980s debt crisis. The most benign view is that advanced industrial states, using the IMF as their primary vehicle, aggressively moved to protect the integrity of the international financial system by providing needed temporary assistance, under strict conditionality, to countries unable to meet their external obligations. The prompt response helped to safeguard the international financial system as a whole, and IMF conditionality, including the imposition of structural adjustment programs, targeted problems that needed to be corrected if crisis countries were to enjoy sustained growth and modernization. In this view, the IMF acted as an honest broker, making a good faith effort to consider the interests of both the developing world and advanced industrial states, and to protect the stability of the international financial system.

Robert Wade's chapter and other recent papers offer a more sinister view, suggesting that the international community's response to the East Asian financial turmoil, centered on the IMF, was largely driven by US interests at the expense of crisis countries (Wade 1998; Wade and Veneroso 1998). The United States pressed for far-reaching economic and political conditionality on IMF emergency lending to further its agenda of getting developing countries to liberalize financial markets and, more generally, to adopt more open, Western-style market economies. His analysis reiterates a claim often made with respect to IMF intervention in the 1980s debt crisis: the IMF acted as a proxy for advanced industrial states, implementing measures that were inimical to the interests of developing countries (Pastor 1989).

IMF conditionality undisputedly has broadened throughout the 1990s to include demands for fundamental changes in economic and political organization, beginning with Russia in 1992. Many are troubled by this expansion of scope beyond the original mandate of the organization, which was to require only what was necessary to enable a country to regain access to international capital markets (Feldstein 1998). But not everyone shares Wade's belief that this shift has been due to the USA's ability to use the IMF to advance its agenda. After all, until recently, US officials could often be heard loudly complaining that they lacked the capacity to influence IMF operations. An alternative explanation is that IMF officials themselves have sought to extend the reach of their programs, either out of a genuine conviction that this was necessary to alleviate structural economic problems, or a desire to create a new mandate after the demise of the Bretton Woods monetary regime in the early 1970s.

Wade finds the scope of IMF conditionality especially objectionable in the Korean case, given the country's recent economic success, which easily surpassed that of most advanced industrial member states (Wade 1998). Among other conditions, the IMF demanded that the government take steps to dismantle the chaebol, the huge industrial groups that had dominated the Korean economy during the post-war era, as well as to end efforts to direct bank lending to priority sectors through official and unofficial means. Wade contends that such structures were associated with a large part of East Asia's economic success and should not be dismantled, especially due to external pressure.

Numerous authors have also contended that the Fund's crisis management failed to stem contagion from one country or region to another and, in several instances, actually deepened the economic decline of affected countries (see Calomiris 1998; Feldstein 1998; Stiglitz 2000). The IMF itself has admitted to making errors of judgment that worsened the crisis (Sanger 1998). The counter-argument is that although the IMF policy prescriptions did contribute to an immediate deterioration of the economic situation in these countries, they laid the groundwork for better performance in the future (Mussa and Savastano 1999 and Dornbusch 2000 share this view). IMF officials contend that structural reform is an essential element of achieving economic recovery; stabilization measures will be ineffective in the long-run if the root structural problems of the crisis economies are not tackled. Economic growth, in fact, surged in the East Asian countries that followed IMF prescriptions starting in 1999, leading IMF officials to claim victory for their approach. Notwithstanding the casual evidence, it is probably too soon to make any definitive judgment about the success of the IMF's policies.

4. THE POLICY IMPLICATIONS OF THE CRISIS

The final chapter of the volume presents a roundtable discussion on the policy implications of the East Asian crisis. The round table included Graciana del Castillo, Albert Fishlow, Miles Kahler and Paolo Pesenti. Three major issues were the focus of this discussion: how capital account liberalization should be conducted by policymakers, what type of exchange rate regime emerging markets should adopt and what should be the response of the international policy community to the multitude of emerging market crises in the 1990s.

Paolo Pesenti encourages policymakers to consider two basic postulates when approaching capital account liberalization: (1) domestic financial markets should be strong and adequately regulated and supervised *before* proceeding with the liberalization of international financial transactions; and (2) a high priority should be given to measures preventing the growth of large stocks of foreign-currency denominated debt as well as controlling the magnitude of the maturity mismatches of assets and liabilities of corporate and financial firms. Pesenti argues that governments should not interfere with capital outflows but rather implement regulations that change the term and currency composition of capital inflows, including high reserve requirements on foreign-currency deposits, limits on inter-bank loans in foreign currencies, and the use of high-risk weighting in setting capital standards for foreign currency loans. He also indicates that greater transparency in financial transactions and increased foreign ownership of domestic financial institutions could serve an important role in reducing systemic risk in the banking system.

Albert Fishlow argues that the East Asian crisis clearly displays the problems affecting fixed but adjustable exchange rate regimes. Sustaining a pegged exchange rate in the face of the massive capital flows observed in the world today requires a huge volume of international reserves, which countries cannot afford. Given this situation, he states that 'there are only two real possibilities for an effective exchange rate regime. One is to have a currency board, such as Argentina has. The other alternative is a floating rate.'

Currency boards received a lot of attention when Indonesia considered replacing its central bank with one in early 1998. Proponents of currency boards point to the increased credibility it provides to anti-inflationary policies by tying the hands of inept domestic monetary authorities. They also argue that a currency board prevents the speculative runs that fixed, but adjustable, rates are prone to, as evidenced by the East Asian crisis.[14] On the other hand, proponents of flexible exchange rates argue that currency boards are still subject to speculative attacks.[15] They also point out that eliminating exchange rate adjustments as a policy mechanism sharply curtails the ability of policy makers to smooth business cycles (see Perry 1997; Roubini 1998).

A final policy issue, posed by Miles Kahler, is how the leading international organizations will deal with the international monetary system in the aftermath of the East Asian crisis. Will they be content merely to manage the current crisis or will they seek major reform in an effort to prevent such crises in the future? The variety and scope of proposals to reform the international financial architecture in the wake of the Asian crisis is nothing short of remarkable. A consensus has emerged among many that muddling through with the current system is not wise; broader reform is urgently needed. As Kahler notes, however, such agreement may not be sufficient to achieve reform, since states must still resolve complex collective action problems that have often plagued efforts to cooperate on international monetary affairs.[16]

The literature on cooperation among nation-states in international financial and monetary affairs is vast, but yields few hard and fast rules about when cooperation is likely to emerge (see Rogoff 1985, 1999; Eichengreen 1999). Several studies have provided excellent accounts of why cooperation succeeded or failed in particular instances, but these analyses have come after the fact with the benefit of hindsight and do not help us predict when reform is most and least likely (see Eichengreen 1996). Nevertheless, scholars agree that systemic reform is only possible when major international powers favor it and when an effective mechanism for overcoming traditional collective action problems among states is available. Major states seem most willing to engage in reform when existing structures are incapable of preventing problems severe enough to disrupt the functioning of the international financial system itself. Many believe that the current period of globalization has ushered in an era that meets that description. However, the 1980s debt crisis clearly posed the threat of a systemic disruption, but no serious attempt to reshape basic institutions was forthcoming; instead, a piecemeal approach to reform ensued, one that did not alter any of the basic features of the monetary regime. Similarly, the financial meltdown of the 1930s yielded a major reform of the international architecture only a decade later (in the form of Bretton Woods). More recently, the 1994–95 Mexican peso crisis, which affected several Latin American countries through the tequila effect, failed to yield tangible architectural reforms.

What may be different this time around is a perception that the degree of financial interdependence is greater than ever before. Historians tell us that the current degree of financial integration is only matched by the late nineteenth and early twentieth centuries, and in many ways the mobility of capital is greater today. For example, the incredible speed at which transactions can occur increases the odds of rapid, destabilizing financial events. Thus, to a greater extent than before, advanced industrial countries may interpret major financial crises as an indication that the current set of institutional arrangements are inadequate to deal with the new degree of financial integration. In addition, several features of the current international environment may help to mitigate collective action problems among key states. First, an institutional framework to facilitate state cooperation is in place. The major industrial powers have cooperated for several decades, albeit imperfectly, through the G-7 framework, and a number of international agencies, like the Bank for International Settlements, exist and can build on ongoing efforts to develop international standards and regulations. Second, the current era is marked by the absence of major political divides among the leading powers, unlike the 1920s and 1930s, or even the 1980s.

The greater volatility induced by the globalization of financial markets, and the severe costs imposed by economic crises, has induced some states to cooperate in a variety of areas, including exchange rate management. As Barry Eichengreen notes: 'The spread of capital mobility and political democratization will make it prohibitively difficult to peg exchange rates unilaterally. Pegging will require international cooperation, and effective cooperation will require measures akin to monetary unification' (Eichengreen 1997, p. 3). On the other hand, proposals for East Asian joint exchange rate or monetary policy may be premature as the region lacks the strong, longstanding political and economic institutions required to establish a currency union, making such a prospect unlikely in the near future.

Still, one of the striking features of the aftermath of the East Asian crisis has been the emergence of a global debate on the international financial architecture, with concrete steps proposed not only in exchange rate management but also in areas such as strengthening domestic banking systems, 'bailing in' the private sector, improving the transparency of financial markets, reforming the Bretton Woods institutions, setting standards for financial reporting by countries and establishing international banking standards.[17] This debate is itself a contribution to the understanding of financial crises and their prevention.

NOTES

1. For example, Diamond and Dybvig 1983; Edwards and Vegh 1997; Kane 1998; Caprio and Honohan 1999; Chang and Velasco 1999 and Detragiache 1999.

2. See Krugman 1979, Obstfeld 1986, Edwards and Montiel 1989, Dornbusch et al. 1995, Chang and Velasco 1998, and the surveys by Flood and Marion 1998, and Krugman 1999.
3. For details of the Chilean economic crisis, see Velasco 1991 and Edwards 1996.
4. See Dornbusch and Werner 1994, Edwards 1996, Calvo and Mendoza 1996 and Sachs et al. 1996.
5. The original contributions in this literature were: Brecher and Diaz-Alejandro 1977 and Bhagwati and Brecher 1980. See also Barbone and Rivera-Batiz 1987. Bhagwati 1998 discusses the dangers of opening the capital account in developing countries.
6. This includes work of Haggard and Kaufman 1992 on the politics of stabilization and the pioneering research of Kahler 1986 on the political economy of the 1980s debt crisis. Among economists, the growing literature on political economy has been surveyed by Drazen 2000, and Persson and Tabellini 2000.
7. Selective credit programs covered between 50 and 70 per cent of available credit. The primary mechanisms were direct, subsidized loans, called 'policy loans,' to beneficiaries through deposit money banks; preferential rediscounting for lending to priority sectors at the central bank; credit floors and credit ceilings (Cole and Park 1983).
8. Social scientists sometimes refer to short bursts of rapid institutional change that alter long-standing, static arrangements as 'punctuated equilibria' (see Krasner 1984).
9. Lukauskas and Minushkin 2000 examine under which conditions countries might choose to open or close their capital account in the wake of a financial crisis.
10. See Goodman and Pauly 1993 on the effectiveness and cost of capital controls.
11. Herring 1998 and Rivera-Batiz 1999 have made this point forecefully.
12. See 'An Uneasy Share of the Debt Burden,' *Financial Times*, 15 March 2000, p. 13.
13. For a survey of this literature, see Rivera-Batiz and Rivera-Batiz (1994). In the East Asian case, there is now substantial evidence that the initial financial and currency crisis in Thailand led to substantial spillover effects on other countries in the region, inducing capital flight in Indonesia, Korea, Malaysia and the Philippines. See, among others, Glick and Rose (1998), Cerra and Saxena (2000), and Nagayasu (2000).
14. The economist Steven Hanke was the key advisor who encouraged Suharto to introduce a currency board. His views are presented in Hanke 1998. An analysis of the situations where a currency board may or may not work is presented by Rivera-Batiz and Sy 1999.
15. Speculative attacks have been observed in several countries with currency boards. As the Mexican peso crisis erupted in 1994, Argentina was subject to severe capital flight – referred to later as the tequila effect – that had all the appearances of a currency speculative attack. From December 1994 to April 1995, $8 billion in bank deposits left Argentina, which represented 16 per cent of the banking deposits in that country. Hong Kong, which also has a currency board, was subject to speculative attacks during the East Asian crisis. And Argentina was subject to another bout with capital outflows when the Russian crisis erupted in August 1998. Both Argentina and Hong Kong have had political factors that have created credibility problems for their currency boards. The Argentinean system is very young and statements by major Argentinean politicians hinting that the constitutional provision establishing the currency board needs to be reviewed do not help. In Hong Kong, the transfer of the island from British to Chinese control has generated serious questions about the currency board, despite the People's Republic assertions of two systems, one country.
16. Eichengreen 1996 presents a comprehensive historical overview of the mixed success of efforts at cooperation in international monetary affairs.
17. In the United States, Congress convened a panel of experts chaired by Allan Meltzer to study the reform of the IMF and World Bank; a brief summary of the recommendations of the panel is presented by Meltzer and Sachs 2000. Goldstein 1997 examines international banking standards. Those standards are likely to be controversial, as disputes will rage not only over their specific content but also over the governance of the institution setting them.

REFERENCES

Barbone, Luca and Francisco L. Rivera-Batiz (1987), 'Foreign Capital and the Contractionary Impact of Currency Devaluation, with an Application to Jamaica,' *Journal of Development Economics*, **26**: 1–15.

Bhagwati, Jagdish N. (1998), 'The Capital Myth: The Difference Between Trade in Widgets and Dollars,' *Foreign Affairs*, **77**: 7–12.

Bhagwati, Jagdish N. and Richard A. Brecher (1980), 'National Welfare in an Open Economy in the Presence of Foreign-Owned Factors of Production,' *Journal of Political Economy*, **10**: 103–115.

Brecher, Richard A. and Carlos F. Diaz-Alejandro (1977), 'Tariffs, Foreign Capital and Immiserizing Growth,' *Journal of International Economics*, **7**: 317–22.

Cable, Charles (1995), 'The Diminished Nation-state: a Study in the Loss of Economic Power', *Daedalus*, **124**: 25–53.

Calomiris, Charles (1998), 'The IMF's Imprudent Role as Lender of Last Resort,' *Cato Journal*, **17**: 275–94.

Calvo, Guillermo A. and Enrique G. Mendoza (1996), 'Mexico's Balance of Payments Crisis: A Chronicle of a Death Foretold,' Working Paper No. 20, Center for International Economics, Department of Economics, University of Maryland at College Park, March.

Caprio, Gerard and Patrick Honohan (1999), 'Restoring Banking Stability: Beyond Supervised Capital Requirements,' *Journal of Economic Perspectives*, **13**: 43–64.

Cerny, Philip (1993), 'The Deregulation and Re-regulation of Financial Markets in a More Open World,' in Philip Cerney (ed.), *Finance and World Politics: Markets, Regimes and States in the Post-hegemonic Era*, Aldershot: Edward Elgar, pp. 51–85.

Cerra, Valerie and Sweta Chaman Saxena (2000), 'Contagion, Monsoons, and Domestic Turmoil in Indonesia: A Case Study in the Asian Currency Crisis,' IMF Working Paper WP/00/60, European I Department, International Monetary Fund, March.

Chang, Roberto and Andres Velasco (1998), 'Financial Crises in Emerging Markets: A Canonical Model,' National Bureau of Economic Research, Working Paper No. 6606, June.

Chang, Roberto and Andres Velasco (1999), 'Liquidity Crises in Emerging Markets: Theory and Policy,' in Ben S. Bernanke and Julio J. Rotemberg (eds), *NBER Macroeconomics Annual 1999*, Cambridge, MA: MIT Press, pp. 11–57.

Cole, David and Yung Chul Park (1983), *Financial Development in Korea, 1945–1978*, Cambridge, MA: Harvard University Press.

Detragiache, Enrica (1999), 'Bank Fragility and International Capital Mobility,' paper presented at the conference on Is Globalization of Capital Markets a Boom or Bust to Development?,' Program in Economic Policy Management, Columbia University, New York, April.

DeLong, J. Bradford (1998), 'What's Wrong With Our Bloody Economies?,' *Los Angeles Times*, January 28.

Diamond, Douglas W. and P.H. Dybvig (1983), 'Bank Runs, Deposit Insurance and Liquidity,' *Journal of Political Economy*, **91**: 401–19.

Dornbusch, Rudiger (2000), 'Stiglitz versus the IMF: Another View,' mimeo, Department of Economics, Massachusetts Institute of Technology.

Dornbusch, Rudiger and Alejandro Werner (1994), 'Mexico: Stabilization, Reform and No Growth,' *Brookings Papers on Economic Activity*, No. 1, 253–315.

Dornbusch, Rudiger, Ilan Goldfajn and Rodrigo Valdes (1995), 'Currency Crises and Collapses,' *Brookings Papers on Economic Activity*, **2**, 219–95.

Drazen, Allan (2000), *Political Economy in Macroeconomics*, Princeton, NJ: Princeton University Press.
Edwards, Sebastian (1996), 'A Tale of Two Crises: Chile and Mexico,' National Bureau of Economic Research Working Paper No. 5794, October.
Edwards, Sebastian (2000), 'Contagion,' mimeo, Department of Economics, University of California at Los Angeles, March.
Edwards, Sebastian and Peter Montiel (1989), 'Devaluation Crises and Macroeconomic Consequences of Postponed Adjustment in Developing Countries,' *IMF Staff Papers*, **36**, 4.
Edwards, Sebastian and Carlos Vegh (1997), 'Banks and Macroeconomic Disturbances Under Predetermined Exchange Rates,' National Bureau of Economic Research, Working Paper No. 5977, March.
Eichengreen, Barry (1996), *Globalizing Capital: A History of the International Monetary System*, Princeton, NJ: Princeton University Press.
Eichengreen, Barry (1997), 'International Monetary Arrangements: Is There a Monetary Union in Asia's Future?,' mimeo, Department of Economics, University of California at Berkeley.
Eichengreen, Barry (1999), *Toward a New International Financial Architecture: A Practical Post-Asia Agenda*, Washington, DC: Institute for International Economics.
Feldstein, Martin (1998), 'Refocusing the IMF,' *Foreign Affairs*, **77**: 20–33.
Flood, Robert and Nancy Marion (1998), 'Perspectives on the Recent Currency Crisis Literature,' National Bureau of Economic Research, Working Paper No. 6380, January.
Glick, Reuven and Andrew K. Rose (1998), 'Contagion and Trade: Why Are Currency Crises Regional?,' mimeo, Department of Economics, University of California at Berkeley, August.
Goldstein, Morris (1997), *The Case for an International Banking Standard*, Washington, DC: Institute for International Economics.
Goodman, John and Louis Pauly (1993), 'The Obsolescence of Capital Controls? Economic Management in an Age of Global Markets,' *World Politics* **46**: 50–92.
Haggard, Stephan and Robert Kaufman (eds) (1992), *The Politics of Economic Adjustment*, Princeton, NJ: Princeton University Press.
Haggard, Stephan and Robert Kaufman (1995), *The Political Economy of Democratic Transitions*, Princeton, NJ: Princeton University Press.
Hanke, Steven H. (1998), 'How to Establish Monetary Stability in Asia,' *Cato Journal*, **17**: 295–301.
Herring, Richard J. (1998), 'Banking Disasters: Causes and Preventative Measures,' in Gerard Caprio, William Hunter, George Kaufman and Danny Leipziger (eds), *Preventing Bank Crises: Lessons from Recent Global Bank Failures*, Washington, DC: World Bank, pp. 209–36.
Kahler, Miles, (ed.) (1986), *The Politics of International Debt*, Ithaca, NY: Cornell University Press.
Kane, Edward J. (1998), 'Understanding and Preventing Bank Crises,' in Gerard Caprio, William C. Hunter, George G. Kaufman and Danny M. Leipziger (eds), *Preventing Bank Crises: Lessons from Recent Global Bank Failures*, Washington, DC: World Bank, pp. 269–77.
Krasner, Stephen (1984), 'Approaches to the State: Alternative Conceptions and Historical Dynamics,' *Comparative Politics*, **16**: 223–46.
Krugman, Paul (1979), 'A Model of Balance of Payments Crises', *Journal of Money, Credit and Banking*, **11**, 311–25.

Krugman, Paul (1999), 'Currency Crises,' in Martin Feldstein (ed.), *International Capital Flows*, Chicago: University of Chicago Press, pp. 421–40.

Kurzer, Paulette (1993), *Business and Banking: Political Change and Economic Integration in Western Europe*, Ithaca, NY: Cornell University Press.

Lukauskas, Arvid (1997), *Regulating Finance: the Political Economy of Spanish Financial Policy From Franco to Democracy*, Ann Arbor: University of Michigan Press.

Lukauskas, Arvid and Susan Minushkin (2000), 'Explaining Financial Market Opening in Chile, Mexico, South Korea, and Turkey,' *International Studies Quarterly* **44**: 695–723.

Maxfield, Sylvia (1990), *Governing Capital: International Finance and Mexican Politics*, Ithaca, NY: Cornell University Press.

Meltzer, Allan and Jeffrey D. Sachs (2000), 'A Blueprint for IMF Reform,' *Wall Street Journal*, 8 March.

Mussa, Michael and Miguel Savastano (1999), 'The IMF Approach to Economic Stabilization,' in Ben Bernanke and Julio J. Rotemberg (eds), *NBER Macroeconomics Annual 1999*, Cambridge, MA: MIT Press, pp. 79–121.

Nagayasu, Jun (2000), 'Currency Crisis and Contagion: Evidence from Exchange Rates and Sectoral Stock Indices of the Philippines and Thailand,' IMF Working Paper WP/00/39, Monetary and Exchange Affairs Department, International Monetary Fund, March.

Obstfeld, Maurice (1986), 'Rational and Self-fulfilling Balance-of-Payments Crises,' *American Economic Review*, **76**: 72–81.

Öncü, Aye and Dennis Gökce (1991), 'Macropolitics of Deregulation and Micropolitics of Banks,' in Metin Heper (ed.), *Strong State and Economic Interest Groups: the Post-1980 Experience*, Berlin: Walter de Gruyter & Co., pp. 99–118

Pastor, Manuel (1989), 'Latin America, the Debt Crisis, and the International Monetary Fund,' *Latin American Perspectives*, **16**: 790–810.

Pempel, T.J., (ed.) (1999), *The Politics of the Asian Economic Crisis*, Ithaca, NY: Cornell University Press.

Perry, Guillermo (ed.) (1997), *Currency Boards and External Shocks: How Much Pain, How Much Gain?*, Washington, DC: World Bank.

Persson, Torsten and Guido Tabellini (2000), *Political Economics: Explaining Economic Policy*, Cambridge, Mass.: MIT Press.

Rivera-Batiz, Francisco L. (1999), 'The East Asian Economic Crisis: What Went Wrong?,' in Lin Guijun and C. Jayachandran (eds), *China in the Globalization of the World Economy*, Beijing: University of International Business and Economics Press, pp. 20–32.

Rivera-Batiz, Francisco L. and Luis A. Rivera-Batiz (1994), *International Finance and Open Economy Macroeconomics*, Englewood Cliffs, NJ: Prentice-Hall.

Rivera-Batiz, Luis A. and Amadou Sy (1999), 'Currency Boards, Credibility and Macroeconomic Behavior,' paper presented at the conference on Is Globalization of Capital Markets a Boom or Bust to Development?, Program in Economic Policy Management, Columbia University, New York, April.

Rodrik, Dani (1994), 'The Rush to Free Trade in the Developing World: Why so Late? Why Now? Will it Last?,' in S. Haggard and S. Webb (eds), *Voting for Reform: Democracy, Political Liberalization, and Economic Adjustment*, New York: Oxford University Press, pp. 61–88.

Rogoff, Kenneth (1985), 'Can International Monetary Cooperation be Counterproductive?,' *Journal of International Economics*, **15**: 199–217.

Rogoff, Kenneth (1999), 'International Institutions for Reducing Global Financial Instability,' *Journal of Economic Perspectives*, **13**: 21–42.
Roubini, Nouriel (1998), 'The Case Against Currency Boards: Debunking Ten Myths about the Benefits of Currency Boards,' mimeo, Department of Economics, New York University.
Sachs, Jeffrey, Aaron Tornell and Andres Velasco (1996), 'The Collapse of the Mexican Peso: What Have we Learned?,' *Economic Policy*, **22**, April, pp. 13–63.
Sanger, David (1998), 'I.M.F. Now Admits Tactics in Indonesia Deepened the Crisis,' *New York Times*, 14 November, pp. A1, D11.
Stiglitz, Joseph (2000), 'The Insider: What I Learned at the World Economic Crisis,' *New Republic*, 6 April, pp. 13–23.
Velasco, Andres (1991), 'Liberalization, Crisis and Intervention: The Chilean Financial System, 1975–1985,' in V. Sundararajan and T. Balino (eds), *Banking Crises: Cases and Issues*, Washington, DC: International Monetary Fund, pp. 113–174.
Wade, Robert (1998), 'The Asian Debt-and-Development Crisis of 1997 – ?: Causes and Consequences,' *World Development*, **26**: 1535–53.
Wade, Robert and Frank Veneroso (1998), 'The Gathering World Slump and the Battle over Capital Controls,' *New Left Review* **231**: 13–42.
Woo-Cumings, Meredith (1997), 'Slouching Toward the Market: the Politics of Financial Liberalization in South Korea,' in Michael Loriaux, Meredith Woo-Cumings, Kent Calder, Sylvia Maxfield, and Sofía Pérez (eds), *Capital Ungoverned: Liberalizing Finance in Interventionist States*, Ithaca, NY: Cornell University Press, pp. 57–99.

PART I

The Crisis in Comparative and Historical Perspective

2. The East Asian crisis and the anatomy of emerging market disease

Francisco L. Rivera-Batiz

1. INTRODUCTION

In 1997, after what had been a decade of remarkable growth, the economies of Thailand, the Philippines, Malaysia, Indonesia and Korea all came to a sudden and grinding halt, suffering a severe crisis from which it has taken them years to recover. What became known as the East Asian crisis was not foreseen by most observers. On the contrary, these countries had been characterized in previous years as 'miracle economies' and their economic policies as exemplary. In 1993, for example, the World Bank gave the region glowing marks, noting that, in these countries, 'fundamentally sound development policy was a major ingredient in achieving rapid growth. Macroeconomic management was unusually good and macroeconomic performance unusually stable, providing the essential framework for private investment' (World Bank 1993, p. 5).

What went wrong in East Asia? What turned-around the situation of countries that, just a few months earlier, had been hailed as examples of economic stability and as showcases of the way economic policies should be handled? It is the purpose of this chapter to discuss the background behind the crisis, its unfolding in 1997 and 1998, and its consequences.

The East Asian crisis emerged in the form of a sequence of severe currency crises. First was Thailand, on 2 July 1997, when its central bank abandoned frantic efforts to keep the baht from depreciating in value and decided to let the exchange rate float. This was followed by the Philippine peso on 11 July 1997, when the central bank of the Philippines also decided to let the peso float after losing close to $1 billion in foreign currency reserves a day in the previous week as a result of capital flight. Then, on Monday, 14 July 1997, Malaysia's central bank stopped intervening in foreign exchange markets, letting the ringgit float after a loss of over $10 billion in reserves in just two weeks. In Indonesia, the central bank first widened, on 11 July 1997, the trading band around which it was permitting exchange rate changes, from 8 per cent to 12 per cent. However, by 13 August 1997, Bank Indonesia – facing massive capital flight

– could not prevent the rupiah from reaching its new band limit. The following day, the central bank decided to let the currency float.

Although the Thai baht, the Philippine peso, the Malaysian ringgit and the Indonesian rupiah fell sharply in value during July, August and September, the Korean won had remained relatively stable. The Korean central bank actively intervened to prevent the currency from depreciating, By October and November, the pressures from capital outflows were unsustainable and the Bank of Korea, facing dwindling foreign exchange reserves and a breakdown of its external payments system, allowed the won to depreciate against the dollar.

The tide of capital outflows encountered by the five East Asian economies was the proximate cause of their currency crises. It was a sharp turnaround compared to the situation in the previous ten years. During the early and mid 1990s, financial analysts all over the world encouraged investors to plunge into 'emerging markets,' the most dynamic of which were found indeed in East Asia. An example of this, one of a multitude of voices in a self-propelling chorus of encouragement, is the following statement published in a 1994 article in the *Columbia Journal of World Business*: 'The Asian stock markets have been hot and there are no signs of cooling off. Attracted by solid economies, credible reform and a trend of liberalization, global investors continue investing on a grand scale in these countries ... the rates of economic growth in East Asia will continue at the highest levels in the world during the next decade' (Clemente 1994, p. 92).

The experts at international organizations did not fare much better in predicting at all what was happening in East Asia. In its annual *World Economic Outlook* in May 1996, the International Monetary Fund forcefully stated: 'it is likely that the emerging Asian economies will continue to boom during the next 12 months, although growth could slow down in some of them ... In the Philippines, economic recovery is expected to continue on a firm basis during the next 12 months' (International Monetary Fund 1996, p. 10). And the World Bank, in its annual outlook, was still stating in September of 1997 that: 'even though growth [in East Asia] is likely to slow down, a severe crisis like that of Mexico is unlikely' (World Bank 1997).

What caused the East Asian crisis? Previous research has considered the role of a wide array of forces, including currency overvaluation, moral hazard and excessive risk-taking among financial institutions, the growth of short-term foreign-currency debt, domestic bank fragility, speculative lending bubbles, financial panic, herd effects and contagion.[1] Although these forces are important, this chapter argues that a focus on them has missed the fundamental, underlying economic phenomenon behind the crisis. We suggest that the crisis is a reflection of a more basic problem facing emerging markets in general, not just East Asia. The fact is that the investment and economic boom in these countries, which puts them in the category of emerging markets, also plants the seeds of an eventual slowdown, or a bust, that reverses some, if not all, of the economic progress. In some countries, such as Mexico, this process of boom and bust has continued for decades.

We refer to this economic phenomenon as 'emerging market disease.' The term disease, rather than virus or flu (which has been used by some experts in the case of the East Asian crisis) is utilized because the forces involved are not short-term in nature but are rather long-term and endemic to the development strategy followed in the countries involved. In essence, emerging markets seek to achieve high rates of economic growth through the rapid and substantial expansion of domestic investment accompanied by macroeconomic stabilization and a major liberalization of international financial transactions. The flood of capital inflows associated with this strategy allow the economies to boom, providing an aura of everlasting prosperity. However, the seeds of a future slowdown or bust are being planted at the same time, through the impact of the capital influx on the exchange rate. Capital inflows exert upward pressure on the value of the domestic currency. A persistent real currency appreciation eventually slows down export growth, increases imports and worsens the current account balance. This has serious consequences. A sluggish export sector will reduce output growth and undermine the confidence of investors on the future of the economy. Furthermore, a widening current account balance deficit, even if initially financed enthusiastically by foreign capital, leads to an accumulation of external debt that, at some point, raises the risk of default, whether in the public or private sector. The sustained real appreciation of the currency also means that expectations of devaluation will inevitably materialize, sooner or later. All of these developments eventually precipitate a withdrawal of funds from the country and a credit crunch that plunges the economy into recession. If the domestic banking system is fragile, and if the capital flight is aggravated by policymakers who tenaciously refuse to devalue, the result is a crisis.

The economic forces behind emerging market disease have been known for a long time. In Latin America, the 'capital inflows problem' has been studied for decades (Diaz-Alejandro 1985; Dornbusch 1986). The best-known cases of the disease in this region have been in Chile (1978–82) and Mexico (1980–84 and 1990–95), but there are other examples in Argentina, Brazil and Uruguay.[2] Some of the symptoms of emerging market disease are akin to what has been called 'Dutch disease.'[3] The latter describes the case of countries where a boom based on the exploitation of natural resources leads to a disastrous de-industrialization in the rest of the economy. Dutch disease erupts as a repercussion of the massive capital that flows into an economy stimulated by the discovery and exploitation of natural resources. These inflows increase the value of domestic currency, hurting the international competitiveness of local exports and shrinking the industrial base of the economy. Countries that were expected to grow rapidly due to their natural wealth end up instead with a sluggish expansion. In emerging market disease, the influx of capital is not necessarily linked to the exploitation of natural resources but is instead associated with rising domestic investment rates, financial liberalization and an opening of the capital account.

This chapter shows how the five East Asian crisis countries: Indonesia, the Republic of Korea, Malaysia, the Philippines, and Thailand, have displayed the main symptoms of emerging market disease. The next section begins with a discussion of the key long-run growth trends in East Asia. Later sections document the period before the crisis, its unfolding and its consequences. The last section outlines the policy implications of the analysis.

2. PATTERNS OF LONG-RUN GROWTH IN EAST ASIA

A glance at some fundamental indicators of economic development shows why the East Asian economies involved in the crisis were generally considered 'miracle economies' in the years preceding the debacle. Table 2.1 displays the changes in real per-capita Gross Domestic Product (GDP) in these countries as well as in the United States between 1960 and 1995. The country with the highest growth rate was the Republic of Korea, which grew at an average rate of 6.5 per cent per year, making it one of the fastest-growing countries in the world during this time period. In 1960, Korea had per-capita income below that of Angola, Madagascar, Mozambique, Senegal, the Dominican Republic, Bolivia, Ecuador and Honduras, among many other developing nations. Yet, by 1996, Korea was catalogued as a high-income country by the World Bank (this rank was lost after the 1997–98 crisis). Thailand, Malaysia and Indonesia also exhibited a rapid expansion of per-capita income, each growing an average of over 4 per cent per year. This earned them the rating of 'high-performing economies' by the World Bank in 1993. The country with the slowest growth was the Philippines, whose GDP per-capita increased at an average rate of 1.3 per cent per year. But even the Philippines was showing a rising growth rate in the 1990s, leading Michael Taylor, an economist with Morgan Stanley, to describe the situation of that economy in 1995 as 'a truly unexpected Asian economic miracle' (as quoted in the *New York Times*, 7 May 1995, p. A6.

Table 2.1 shows that, except for the Philippines, the East Asian economies surpassed the US average rate of growth of per-capita income between 1960 and 1995. They also outperformed the industrialized world in general, diverging from the experience of most other developing countries, which grew slower than the industrialized economies in the period of 1960 to 1995 (see Barro and Sala-i-Martin 1995).

Associated with this economic growth was a substantial expansion of these countries' human and physical capital. Consider first the human component by looking at demographics. Table 2.2 shows the population levels in the East Asian countries in 1998 as well as the total fertility rates in 1960 and 1990. Indonesia is the most populous of the East Asian countries, with a population of 204 million in 1998. It is followed, in order of decreasing population, by the Philippines, Thailand, Korea and Malaysia. All five countries showed sharp drops in total fertility rates between 1960 and 1990. In Korea, there was a 120 per cent drop in the fertility rate between 1960 and 1990 while for Thailand the reduction was 112 per cent, in Indonesia and Malaysia it was 66 per cent, and in the Philippines 58 per cent.

Table 2.1 Growth of real GDP per capita in East Asia, 1960–95

	Per-capita GDP, 1960 (in 1995 $)	Per-capita GDP, 1995 (in 1995 $)	Rate of growth, 1960–95 (%)
Indonesia	621	2 602	4.1
Rep. of Korea	883	8 505	6.5
Malaysia	1 381	6 613	4.5
The Philippines	1 112	1 756	1.3
Thailand	923	5 034	4.8
United States	9 774	19 621	2.0

Sources: Barro and Lee 1994 and World Bank 1998. The data are expressed in constant 1995 dollars and have been adjusted for differences in purchasing power among the various countries.

Table 2.2 Demographic transition in East Asia, 1960–90

	Population 1998 (millions)	Total fertility rate*	
		1960	1990
Indonesia	204	5.43	2.80
Rep. of Korea	46	5.64	1.70
Malaysia	22	6.81	3.50
Philippines	75	6.97	3.90
Thailand	61	6.44	2.10

* The total fertility rate is defined as the number of children that would be born to a woman if she were to live to the end of her child-bearing years and bear children at each age according to the prevailing age-specific birth rates in the country.

Source: World Bank 1995, 2000c.

The demographic transition in East-Asian lowered both birth and death rates. However, death rates dropped before birth rates did. The result was a temporary 'bulge' in the age structure that, over time, made its way into an increased working-age population relative to the non-working, or 'dependent' population. As a recent Asian Development Bank publication has emphasized: 'part of East Asia's rapid growth in income per person between 1965 and 1990 is due to the rising share of the working-age population relative to the total population. During these years, the working-age population grew almost 1 percentage point faster than the total population in East Asia' (Asian Development Bank, 1997b, p. 76). This increased working-age population allowed a greater flow of resources into savings and investment, spurring the growth of GDP per capita (Bloom and Williamson, 1997).

Although the labor force grew rapidly, not all the educational and occupational categories increased at the same pace. The labor force growth in the East Asian economies was accompanied by an unprecedented increase in educational attainment. This means that, although the labor force was rising, the unskilled labor force, that is, the number of workers with no educational attainment, was actually *declining*. Table 2.3 presents the sharp drop in the adult population with no schooling at all. In Indonesia, the proportion of the population 25 years of age or older with no schooling was equal to 75.5 per cent in 1960. By 1990, only 32 per cent of the Indonesian population had no formal education. In the Republic of Korea, the corresponding drop was from close to 57 per cent to just 11 per cent over the thirty-year period. Similar patterns are exhibited by Malaysia, the Philippines and Thailand.

Table 2.3 Rising schooling in East Asia, 1960–90

	Proportion of the population over 25 years of age with no schooling 1960 (%)	1990 (%)
Indonesia	75.5	32.0
Rep. of Korea	56.9	11.0
Malaysia	58.5	25.6
The Philippines	33.5	9.1
Thailand	48.1	22.0

Source: Barro and Lee 1994.

The expansion of schooling is reflected in a sharp decline of adult illiteracy rates. While in developing countries overall, the adult illiteracy rate was 25 per cent in 1998, in Korea it was 2 per cent, in Thailand and the Philippines it was 5 per cent, in Indonesia 10 per cent, and in Malaysia 13 per cent.

The comparative success of East Asian countries in raising the human capital of their labor force has been linked to a specific set of policies. First, the resources allocated by the government to education were generally greater than those in other developing economies. In 1960, developing countries allocated an average of 1.3 per cent of their GNP to public educational expenditures; in Malaysia, however, the corresponding proportion was 2.9 per cent, in Indonesia it was 2.5 per cent, in Thailand it was 2.3 per cent, and in Korea 2.0 per cent. Second, the proportion of public spending dedicated to primary and secondary education was much higher than in other developing economies in Africa and Latin America. This allowed both the quantity and quality of public primary and secondary education to increase quickly. Indeed, the high-growth East Asian countries all have performed at the highest levels in international assessments of educational progress in secondary schools, exceeding the scores in most countries, including high-income economies (Hanushek and Kim 1995). Third, public spending was complemented with substantial private investment in education, especially at the secondary and higher education levels. Fourth, the expansion in the supply of skilled labor was accompanied by a sharp increase of the demand for such labor, associated in turn with colossal capital accumulation, as is discussed next. This allowed the human capital to gain employment in a growing economy, instead of becoming unemployed or underemployed. As a result, human capital accumulation explains a substantial portion of the income growth in the region. In Korea, as much as 43 per cent of the growth in per-capita GDP between 1960 and 1990 can be accounted for by the expansion of the skilled labor force (Rivera-Batiz 1999b).

The high-growth East Asian economies have displayed rapid rates of physical capital accumulation. Table 2.4 shows gross investment spending as a fraction of GDP. With the exception of the Philippines, investment rates more than doubled from the 1960s to the 1990s. This expansion was gradual but it was sustained all the way up to the period before the crisis. In Indonesia, investment spending rose from an average of about 10 per cent of GDP in the 1960s to about 35 per cent in the 1990s. For the Republic of Korea, the increase was from 18.4 per cent to 36.9 per cent; for Malaysia it was from 19.2 per cent to 39.8 per cent, and for Thailand from 20.5 per cent to 42.1 per cent. These investment rates sharply exceed global investment rates, which have averaged between 20 and 25 per cent over the last twenty years. Only the Philippines has had lower investment rates, but even these have been around the worldwide average.

One of the most popular explanations for East Asian growth has focused on the export sector. It is argued that, by focusing on production for export markets, developing economies can in principle generate substantial short-term gains in efficiency, forced upon them by the pressures of international competition.[4] It is also pointed out that long-term gains in economic growth are often the result of the introduction of new technologies and products, obtained through greater international trade, as fostered by an externally-oriented development strategy (see Romer 1990; Rivera-Batiz and Romer 1991).

Table 2.4 Investment rates in East Asia, 1960–96

	Investment as a percentage of Gross Domestic Product			
	1960–69 (%)	1970–79 (%)	1980–89 (%)	1990–96 (%)
Indonesia	9.8	21.8	29.1	34.8
Rep. of Korea	18.4	27.3	30.0	36.9
Malaysia	19.2	25.5	30.3	39.8
The Philippines	19.6	25.6	22.1	22.5
Thailand	20.5	25.8	27.6	42.1

Source: World Bank 1995, Asian Development Bank 1997a.

There is no question that exports have boomed in East Asia. Table 2.5 displays the increase in exports as a fraction of GDP between 1960 and 1998. In Korea, for instance, the ratio of exports to GDP rose from 9 per cent in 1960 to 41 per cent in 1998. In Thailand, the ratio of exports to GDP expanded from 5.6 per cent in 1960 to 47.4 per cent in 1998. This positive and significant correlation of increased exports with output growth has led many to conclude that export promotion was the key to economic expansion in the high-growth East Asian countries, suggesting that these policies would produce similar results in the rest of the developing world. As the World Bank concludes: 'The export-push strategy appears to hold great promise for other developing countries. Creating a free trade environment for exporters, providing finance and support services for small and medium-sized exporters, improving trade-related aspects of the civil service, aggressively courting export-oriented direct foreign investment, and focusing infrastructure on areas that encourage exports are all attainable goals' (World Bank, 1993, p. 25).

The view that export promotion has been the key force behind the accelerated growth in high-performing East Asian countries has been questioned in recent years. Some experts have reversed the direction of causality between export growth and output growth, indicating that export growth may have been caused by other forces which simultaneously stimulated output growth. As Dani Rodrik puts it, in his analysis of Korea and Taiwan:

> the standard story is incomplete and quite misleading on the importance it attaches to the role of export orientation in growth performance. ... The increase in the relative profitability of exports around the mid-1960s was modest in both countries, and can account fully neither for the initial jump in the export–GDP ratio at that time nor for the subsequent steady increase in the ratio. (Rodrik 1995, p. 56)

Instead of export promotion, Rodrik finds that it was the expansion of investment that led to sharp growth, at least in Taiwan and South Korea. He argues that, by removing impediments to investment and establishing a sound investment climate, the Korean and Taiwanese governments were able to engineer a sharp rise in private investment, which then led to the growth of both output and exports. The policy implication, as Rodrik puts it, is that 'the South Korean and Taiwanese "miracles" can best be understood by taking seriously what the two governments thought and said they were doing: namely, coordinating and encouraging private (and public) investments with a high degree of linkages with the modern sector' (Rodrik 1995, p. 97).

Table 2.5 Export growth in East Asia, 1960–98

	Exports/GDP (%)	
	1960	1998
Indonesia	3.0	53.4
Rep. of Korea	9.0	41.3
Malaysia	22.9	99.3
The Philippines	7.0	45.3
Thailand	5.6	47.4

Source: Barro and Lee 1994 and World Bank 2000d.

This section has presented some of the major indicators of long-run economic performance in East Asia since 1960. There appears to be little doubt that, except for the Philippines, the East Asian countries under consideration displayed remarkable long-run growth of physical and human capital and substantial increases in income per-capita between 1960 and 1995. No clues to the crisis could be found in this area. Ironically, on 21 May 1997, a few weeks before the crisis began to develop, the World Economic Forum, a business-financed research organization in Geneva, released its ranking of the most competitive economies and those with the biggest growth potential. Malaysia was ranked as the ninth most competitive economy in the world; Indonesia was ranked as the fifth in terms of biggest growth potential and Thailand was ranked tenth, out of the 53 countries, which included industrialized nations as well as many emerging markets and economies in transition.

One of the few voices of caution regarding the future of East Asia's economic growth in the mid 1990s was that of Paul Krugman, who argued that East Asia was due for a slowdown. Based on studies that found East Asia's growth to be due mostly to accumulation of human and physical capital, instead of technological change, he suggested that diminishing returns inevitably implied a slowdown of growth. Krugman, however, did not predict the growth collapse in the late 1990s, concluding that 'growth in East Asia would continue to outpace growth in the West' (Krugman 1994, p. 78).

3. BEFORE THE TYPHOON: A LOOK AT SOME KEY MACROECONOMIC FUNDAMENTALS

A look at some of the key macroeconomic indicators in East Asia during the period leading up to the crisis does not easily uncover any compelling signs of distress or potential trouble.

Overall, economic growth in the five economies was still going strong and did not appear to be threatened by any major forces. Table 2.6 shows that, for the five East Asian economies, the average rate of growth of real GDP in 1996 was 7.1 per cent, slightly higher than the average growth rate in the period of 1990 to 1995, which was 6.9 per cent, and significantly greater than growth in the 1980s, which averaged 5.6 per cent per year. In Malaysia and Indonesia, real GDP had been growing at 8 per cent or higher per year since 1990. In South Korea, growth had hovered over 7 per cent since 1980. For the Philippines, growth was rising sharply, from less than 2 per cent per year in the 1980s, to 2.3 per cent in 1995 and 5.7 per cent in 1996. And although growth in Thailand had slowed-down in 1996, it was still a respectable 5.5 per cent, higher than for most other countries in the world. Indeed, the 7.1 per cent average real GDP growth rate characterizing the East Asian economies in 1996 exceeded the 6.6 per cent achieved by developing countries in general and the 2.5 per cent growth rate in industrialized nations.

The growth spurt displayed by the East Asian countries from the early 1990s to mid-1997 led most observers to predict strong growth for these economies in the future. For instance, the Asian Development Bank in its annual economic outlook completed in mid-1997 predicted that the growth of real GDP in Indonesia would be a strong 8.0 and 7.9 per cent in 1997 and 1998, respectively. For Korea, the estimate was that real GDP would rise between 6.3 and 6.9 per cent a year. The forecast for Malaysia was for 8.5 per cent growth in 1997 and 1998. For the Philippines, the outlook stated that 'growth prospects over the next two years are bright: GDP is expected to grow at an annual rate of 6-6.5 per cent' (Asian Development Bank 1997a, p. 96). Real GDP growth for Thailand was expected to be 6.3 per cent in each year, 1997 and 1998. These figures suggest that, on the eve of the crisis, most experts saw no dark clouds in the sustained expansion of East Asia in the 1990s.

Table 2.6 Growth of real GDP before the crisis: East Asia vs. the world, 1980–96

	Average annual rate of growth of real GDP (%)		
	1980–89	1990–95	1996
East Asia*	5.6	6.9	7.1
Indonesia	5.3	8.0	8.0
Rep. of Korea	7.8	7.8	7.1
Malaysia	5.8	8.8	8.6
The Philippines	1.9	2.3	5.7
Thailand	9.0	7.3	5.5
Industrialized countries	2.7	1.8	2.5
Developing countries	4.3	5.8	6.6
Latin America	1.0	2.9	3.5

* The average for East Asia is a weighted average of the growth rates of the five East Asian countries considered.

Source: International Monetary Fund 1998.

Price instability was not a major concern either. Inflation rates were high by the standards of industrialized countries, but they were significantly lower than in most other developing countries and they were declining. Table 2.7 shows that, in the 1980s, the average inflation rate in East Asia was 9.1 per cent per year. This dropped to 7.9 per cent for 1990–95. By 1996, the average inflation rate had gone down further to 7 per cent. The Philippines had the highest inflation rate in 1996: 8.4 per cent, while Malaysia had the lowest, at 3.5 per cent. These figures lie substantially below the inflation rate among developing countries overall, which was 13.7 per cent in 1996, 43.6 per cent per year in 1990–95, and 36 per cent per year in the 1980s. In fact, compared to Latin America, where annual inflation was as high as 195.6 per cent per year in the early 1990s, East Asia represented a region of remarkable price stability.

Underlying the low inflation rates in East Asian economies were government budgets that were close to balance. Any budget deficits had been comparatively small or had been severely curtailed in the years before the crisis. The Philippines, for example, had a budget deficit equal to 5.4 per cent of GDP in 1990. By 1996, this deficit had shrunk to half of one per cent. Indonesia, Malaysia and Thailand had all sustained budget surpluses during the 1990s; in

1996, Malaysia had a budget surplus of 3.9 per cent of GDP, Thailand's was 1.5 per cent, and Indonesia's was 1.0 per cent. The Republic of Korea had the greatest budget deficit in 1996 and it was equal to just 1 per cent of GDP and it followed a budget surplus in 1995.

Table 2.7 Inflation before the crisis: East Asia vs. the rest of the world, 1980–96

	Average annual increase of Consumer Price Index (%)		
	1980–89	1990–95	1996
East Asia*	9.1	7.9	7.0
Indonesia	9.6	8.7	7.9
Rep. of Korea	6.4	6.2	5.0
Malaysia	3.6	3.5	3.5
The Philippines	14.1	10.8	8.4
Thailand	5.7	5.0	5.9
Industrialized countries	5.5	3.3	2.2
Developing countries	36.0	43.6	13.7
Latin America	116.7	195.6	22.3

* The average for East Asia is a weighted average of the inflation rates of the five East Asian countries considered.

Source: International Monetary Fund 1998.

Currency values in the five East Asian economies had been remarkably stable for many years. This is no surprise as government authorities intervened heavily in currency markets to avoid any substantial fluctuations. The International Monetary Fund (IMF) catalogued the exchange rate arrangements in Malaysia and Thailand during the early and mid-1990s as pegged exchange rate regimes. Those in Indonesia, Korea and the Philippines were catalogued as floating regimes. In reality, however, all five countries intervened heavily in foreign exchange markets during the 1990s, seeking to sustain currency values within a narrow range. In Thailand, the central bank, every morning at 8:30 a.m., fixed the baht exchange rate against a basket of currencies dominated by the dollar, agreeing to exchange baht for foreign currencies within a close range of the established rate. In Indonesia's 'managed floating' regime, the exchange rate was in reality 'administratively set, and in no sense was a genuine float in which market forces determined day-to-day movements' (Hill 1996, p. 75). In the Philippines, the central bank often clarified that the exchange rate was market-determined, not fixed by the central bank. But although the peso was the most volatile of the five East Asian currencies, foreign exchange intervention by the Bangko Sentral ng Pilipinas was frequent, and sometimes heavy, seeking to keep currency fluctuations within a very narrow range. Malaysian and Korean monetary authorities also exercised considerable control of exchange rate movements.

Figure 2.1 displays the behavior of nominal exchange rates between the currencies of the five East Asian nations and the dollar, for the period of December 1987 to December 1996, before the crisis exploded. As can be seen, Thailand's baht had been fluctuating close to 25 baht per dollar since 1987. In the Philippines, the peso-dollar exchange rate remained stable around 25 to 27 pesos per dollar after 1990. There was also a narrow range of fluctuation for the Indonesian rupiah – between 1 900 and 2 100 rupiah per dollar. And for the Malaysian ringgit, the exchange rate remained close to 2.6 ringgit per dollar in the 1990s. Finally, in South Korea, the value of the won remained between 700 and 800 per dollar.

This exchange rate stability operated within the context of rapidly growing capital inflows. All five East Asian economies introduced major policy initiatives that acted to liberalize their financial markets in the 1980s and 1990s.[5] For some, this was a consolidation of earlier movements of liberalization. For instance, Indonesia had an open capital account since the 1960s, but kept tight controls on the domestic banking system, maintaining a regime of financial repression that was liberalized significantly only in the 1980s and 1990s. Lending and deposit interest rates were lifted in 1983, bank entry requirements were liberalized in 1988, and the regulatory and supervisory structure of stock markets was revamped in the late 1980s. In Thailand, on the other hand, both domestic and international financial transactions were tightly controlled until the late 1980s and early 1990s. Controls on deposit rates were lifted in 1989–90, restrictions on lending rates were eliminated in 1992, most controls on capital outflows were removed in 1991, and in 1993 the Bangkok International Banking Facility was established, allowing domestic and foreign businesses to borrow locally in foreign currency. In the Philippines, the Foreign Investment Act of 1991 for the first time allowed foreign investors to own 100 per cent of business enterprises in the Philippines in most sectors of the economy, supplanting restrictions which limited foreign equity participation to 40 per cent. In the Republic of Korea, financial markets were liberalized in the early 1990s, eliminating controls on interest rates, and allowing foreign capital to increase their access to domestic institutions.

Close to $263 billion in capital flowed to the five East Asian countries on a net basis in the period of 1990 to 1996. The capital influx accelerated in the mid-1990s, rising from $15 billion in 1990 to $67.3 billion in 1996. Table 2.8 shows the decomposition of the capital flows by country and by type of inflow. The Republic of Korea was the country with the greatest resource influx, equal

Indonesia: exchange rate, rupiah–dollar

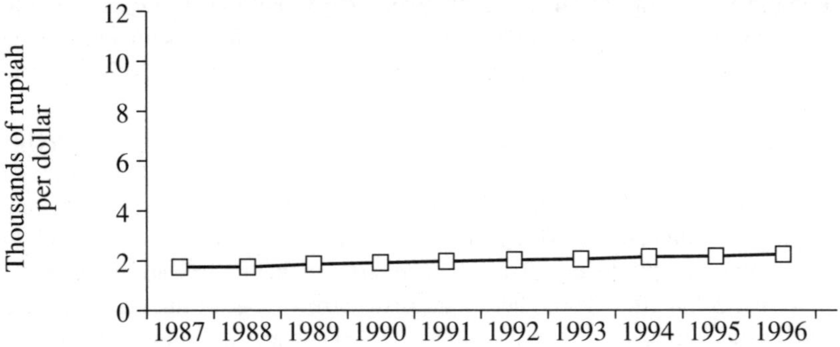

Republic of Korea: exchange rate, won–dollar

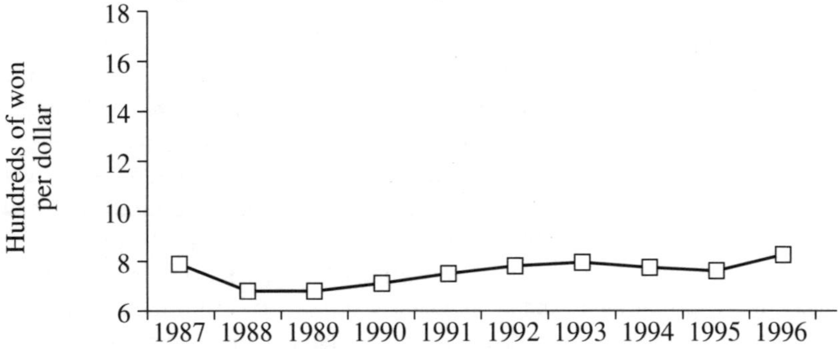

Malaysia: exchange rate, ringgit–dollar

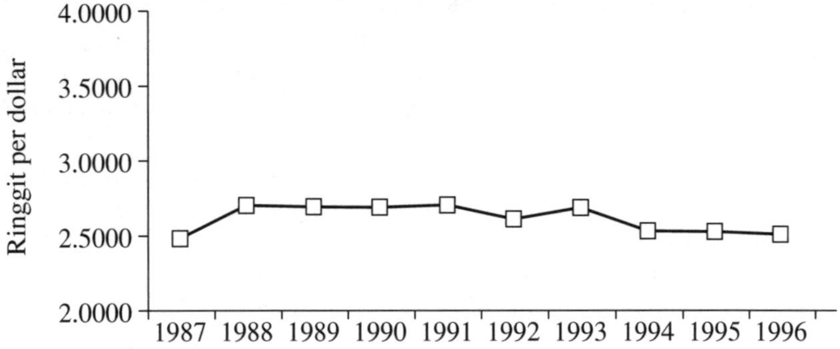

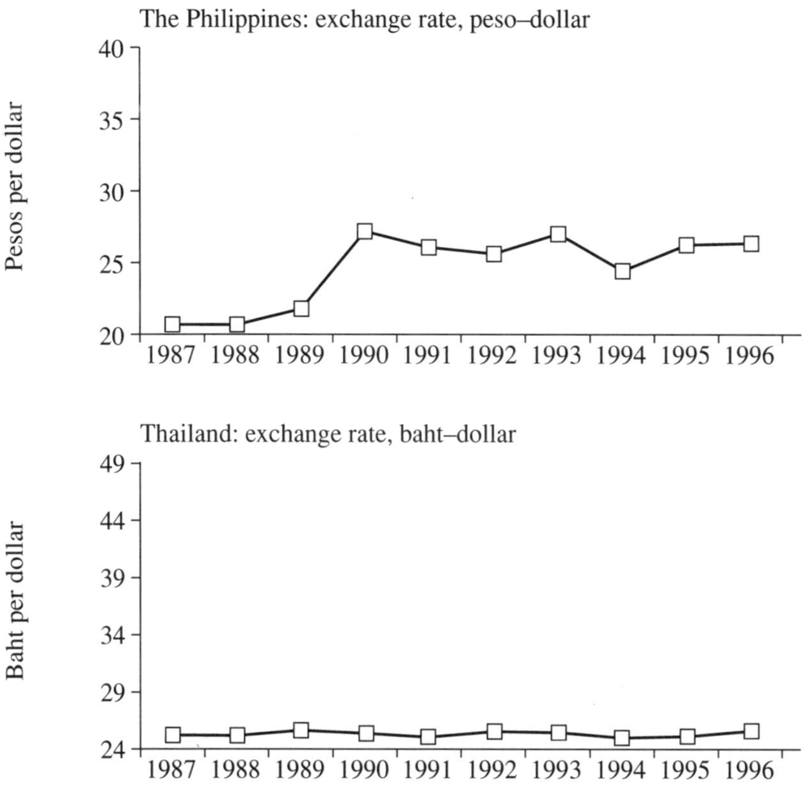

Source: International Monetary Fund 1998

Figure 2.1 Exchange rates in East Asia, December 1988–December 1996

to $70.9 billion from 1990 to 1996. The Philippines, on the other hand, was the country with the smallest inflow of capital, equal to $23.5 billion.

There was great diversity in the type of foreign capital entering East Asia. The largest category was Foreign Direct Investment (FDI), which constituted $78.5 billion on a net basis during the 1990 to 1996 period. However, the importance of FDI varied by country. In Malaysia, Indonesia, the Philippines and Thailand, FDI accounted for a substantial portion of net capital flows. But for Korea, net FDI inflows were not as important. For the latter, sales of private equities and bonds represented the most significant source of foreign capital. The commercial banking industry was another major source of funding. In 1990, only $2.2 billion entered East Asia on a net basis through commercial

Table 2.8 Capital flows to East Asia, 1990–96

	Net capital inflows (billions of US dollars)				
	1990	1992	1994	1996	1990–96
Indonesia	**5.9**	**8.0**	**9.6**	**15.6**	**62.6**
FDI	1.1	1.8	2.1	6.2	19.0
Portfolio equity	0.3	0.1	3.7	3.1	14.5
Bank lending	2.4	2.7	0.6	2.8	7.1
Private bonds	0.0	0.2	0.5	3.7	7.1
Other flows	2.1	3.2	2.7	–0.2	14.9
Republic of Korea	**1.4**	**7.8**	**17.0**	**20.4**	**70.9**
FDI	0.8	0.7	0.8	2.3	8.2
Portfolio equity	0.5	3.0	2.5	3.7	19.7
Bank lending	–1.2	1.5	5.8	7.7	17.7
Private bonds	0.2	2.6	8.5	6.7	27.1
Other flows	1.1	1.4	–0.6	0.0	–1.8
Malaysia	**1.2**	**6.1**	**8.7**	**12.0**	**53.8**
FDI	2.3	5.2	4.3	5.1	30.0
Portfolio equity	0.3	0.4	1.3	4.4	12.4
Bank lending	–0.2	1.4	1.7	1.2	9.1
Private bonds	–1.2	–0.4	1.2	2.1	4.3
Other flows	0.0	–0.5	0.2	–0.8	–2.0
The Philippines	**1.9**	**0.9**	**4.3**	**5.2**	**23.5**
FDI	0.5	0.2	1.6	1.5	7.2
Portfolio equity	0.0	0.3	1.4	1.3	6.5
Bank lending	–0.3	–1.4	0.0	–0.2	–2.5
Private bonds	0.4	0.0	1.0	2.5	5.7
Other flows	1.3	1.8	0.3	0.1	6.6
Thailand	**4.7**	**4.2**	**4.9**	**14.1**	**52.0**
FDI	2.4	2.1	1.4	2.3	14.1
Portfolio equity	0.4	0.0	–0.5	1.6	6.8
Bank lending	1.5	1.5	0.1	6.0	16.9
Private bonds	–0.1	0.5	3.8	3.8	11.9
Other flows	0.5	0.1	0.1	0.4	2.3

Source: World Bank 1999.

bank loans; by 1996 the corresponding figure was $48.3 billion. The magnitude of the lending boom varied by country. In the Philippines, the period of 1990 to 1996 was associated with a reduction of commercial bank loans. But in Thailand and Korea, commercial bank lending accounted for a significant fraction of net capital inflows, with a total of over $34 billion in loans flowing into these two countries alone between 1990 and 1996. Japanese, US, British, German and French banks were heavily involved in what literally became a frenzy of loan pushing. As Dennis Phillips, a spokesman for Commerzbank, a major German bank involved in the lending spree, puts it: 'There was a huge euphoria about Asia and Southeast Asia. It was the place to be' (O'Brien et al. 1998, p. D1).

As Table 2.8 presents, portfolio equity flows also exploded. While in 1990 there were only $1.5 billion in net flows of portfolio equity into the five East Asian countries, by 1996 this had increased to $14.1 billion. The growth of stock markets in the region reflects these figures. Stock market capitalization was minimal in the East Asian countries in the early 1980s, but by the early 1990s, these emerging stock markets were the darling of investors and the fastest-growing markets in the world. Table 2.9 shows that the country with the highest rate of growth in stock market capitalization was Indonesia, whose market capitalization increased, in real terms, by an astounding 2 952 per cent per year during the period of December 1988 to June 1997, just before the crisis erupted. In Thailand, market capitalization rose by 655.8 per cent during the same time period, in Malaysia it was 336 per cent, in the Philippines the annual growth was 66.4 per cent, and in Korea, where stock markets had started to

Table 2.9 The stock market in East Asia before the crisis, 1988–97

Country	Market capitalization* Dec. 1988	Market capitalization* June 1997	Real growth per year** Dec. 1988–June 1997 (%)
Indonesia	434 178	259 561 000	2 952
Rep. of Korea	64 543 684	136 229 883	18.4
Malaysia	63 193	714 170	336.3
The Philippines	88 592	1 961 893	66.4
Thailand	221 958	1 614 920	655.8

Notes:
* Nominal value, in millions of local currency.
** The increase in real capitalization is equal to the percentage increase in nominal capitalization adjusted by a stock market price index.

Source: International Finance Corporation 1998.

boom a few years earlier, the annual increase was 18.4 per cent. Although these high growth rates reflected the expansion of markets that had developed from very small sizes in the 1980s, their dynamism was unparalleled in the rest of the world.

Having examined a broad set of macroeconomic indicators for the East Asian economies in the period before the crisis emerged, we have failed to find evidence of the macroeconomic policy malaise that often surrounded economic crises in the past. These signs include acute public budget deficits, high rates of money supply creation, chronic inflation, capital flight and currency instability, among others. In seeking to understand the crisis, the next section describes its unfolding and the aftermath.

4. THE DEVELOPMENT OF THE CRISIS

Most accounts of the crisis place its start on 2 July 1997, when the Thai central bank let the baht float, after spending close to $23 billion to sustain its value in the face of massive capital outflows and frenzied devaluation expectations. Almost immediately, the other East Asian countries became the subject of intense capital flight. Central banks desperately intervened in foreign exchange markets, selling billions of dollars and other reserve currencies in order to buy their own currencies and avoid depreciation, but they failed in this attempt. The Philippine peso was the first one to follow the baht: the central bank of the Philippines decided to let the peso float on 11 July. And on 14 July, Malaysia's central bank also let the ringgit float. Indonesia was next, on 14 August, when the rupiah was allowed to freely float. The last country to be affected was the Republic of Korea, which finally let the won depreciate in value in November 1997 after months of capital outflows and failed foreign exchange market intervention.

What happened to currency values after the July–November debacle? The data presented in Table 2.10 shows that by December 1997 all five currencies had sharply depreciated in value. The Thai baht had depreciated by close to 80 per cent relative to its value at the end of May, from 24.8 to 44.8 baht per dollar. The Malaysian ringgit lost 52 per cent of its value between May and December 1997; the Indonesian rupiah depreciated by 110 per cent in the same time period, the Philippine peso dropped by 50 per cent, and the Korean won by 74 per cent. The rupiah went on to depreciate even more in the first half of 1998, going from a value of 2 432 rupiah per dollar in May 1997 to 9 400 in May 1998, a devaluation of 287 per cent in one year!

By the spring of 2001, some currencies had rebounded relative to their lowest values after the crisis, but as Table 2.10 displays all remained sharply devalued relative to May 1997. Some, such as the rupiah and peso, had not increased in value at all since the worst moment of the crisis.

Table 2.10 Currency depreciation in five East Asian Economies: 1997–2001

	Value of currency in dollars				
	30 May 1997	19 Dec. 1997	11 May 1998	3 March 1999	31 Jan. 2001
Indonesia (rupiah)	2 432	5 100	9 400	8 885	9 450
Rep. of Korea (won)	891	1 550	1 395	1 229	1 265
Malaysia (ringgit)	2.51	3.82	3.86	3.80	3.80
The Philippines (peso)	26.4	39.6	39.3	39.1	49.5
Thailand (baht)	24.8	44.8	38.6	37.7	42.8

Source: *Wall Street Journal*, various issues.

In the aftermath of the crisis, all five East Asian countries faced higher interest rates, stock market collapses, banking debacles, and a deepening recession. In the case of Indonesia, the interest rate (measured by the money market rate) increased from 13 per cent in January of 1997 to over 40 per cent by late December. In Korea, the interest rate (on overnight call money) rose from 13 per cent in early 1997 to 25 per cent by the end of December. In Thailand, the interest rate hike (of the one-month inter-bank rate) was from 9.2 per cent to 27 per cent in the same time period, and in the Philippines the 90-day Treasury bill rate jumped from 11.7 per cent to 19.3 per cent. Only in Malaysia did the interest rate fail to increase substantially, with the three-month inter-bank rate rising from 7.4 per cent in January 1997 to 10.1 per cent by the end of the year.

The stock market crashes that occurred in parallel to the currency crises not only dried up sources of capital for domestic investments but also acted to severely shrink the wealth of local investors. In Indonesia, the Jakarta Stock Exchange Composite Index dropped from a value of 696 at the end of May 1997 to 402 at the end of December 1997. For Korea, the Korea Stock Exchange KOSPI Index went down by 50 per cent, from 757 in May 1997 to 376 in December 1997. In Malaysia, the Kuala Lumpur Stock Exchange Composite Index declined from 1 105 at the end of May 1997 to 595 by the end of December 1997. The stock market crash in the Philippines, as measured by the Philippine Stock Exchange Composite Index, was from a value of 2 809 in May 1997 to 1 891 in December of that year. And in Thailand, the Stock Exchange of Thailand Index went from 566 in May to 373 in December. The International

Finance Corporation, which assesses world stock market performance, catalogued the five East Asian countries among the worst ten performers in 1997. The bourses have recovered since the end of 1997, but prices remain substantially below the levels before the crisis, except for Korea, whose stock market price index in mid-2000 substantially exceeded its value before the crisis in 1997.

With declining growth in the second half of 1997 and a full-blast recession in 1998, all five countries suffered from lower standards of living. This is reflected in the data presented in Table 2.11, showing the growth rate of real GDP for the period of 1996 through 1999 as well as forecasts for 2000. Strong growth in early 1997, before the collapse, allowed the countries to avoid sharply negative annual growth rates for 1997, but all of them had a drop of real GDP in 1998. The sharpest recessions occurred in Indonesia, where real GDP fell by 13.2 per cent in 1998, and in Thailand, where it fell by 10.4 per cent. The situation improved in 1999, with Korea leading the region with a strong 10 per cent growth, and with the Philippines, Malaysia and Thailand also displaying respectable growth. Only Indonesia showed no growth in 1999. All economies were expected to sustain at least moderate growth in the year 2000.

Table 2.11 Growth of real GDP in East Asia: before and after the crisis

	Annual rate of growth of real GDP (%)				
	1996	1997	1998	1999	2000*
Indonesia	8.0	4.7	–13.2	0.2	4.0
Rep. of Korea	9.1	5.0	–6.7	10.7	7.5
Malaysia	5.8	7.5	–7.5	5.4	6.0
The Philippines	5.7	5.2	–0.5	3.2	3.8
Thailand	9.0	–1.8	–10.4	4.1	4.5

Note:
* Forecast by Asian Development Bank.

Sources: International Monetary Fund 1998; Asian Development Bank 2000.

The recessions resulted in sudden increases of unemployment. In Korea, urban unemployment had been between 2 and 3 per cent before the crisis. This went up to 7.4 per cent in 1998 and peaked at 8.7 per cent in February 1999. For Indonesia, the crisis displaced approximately 3 per cent of the labor force between July 1997 and July 1998, with unemployment ranging from 10 to 14.8 per cent in early 1999 (Krongkaew 2000). In Thailand, the labor market condition before the crisis was very tight, with less than 2 per cent of the labor force unemployed. The crisis increased unemployment by 2.5 percentage points between early 1997 and early 1999. In Malaysia, open unemployment rose from close to 2 per cent in the period before the crisis to 4.5 per cent in early 1999. Unemployment in the Philippines had been substantially higher than in the other East Asian countries, reflecting its slower growth. In 1996, the average unemployment rate was 8.5 per cent, slightly below the average for 1993–95, which was 9.5 per cent. The crisis made the unemployment rate jump to 13.3 per cent by April 1998.

In some of the countries, the official unemployment figures do not show the full impact of the crisis because they do not reflect underemployment. In the Philippines, for instance, in addition to an unemployment rate of over 10 per cent, it is estimated that about one-third of the labor force is underemployed. In Indonesia, the informal labor market may comprise as much as 65 per cent of total employment. The social impact of the crisis was devastating. Low-income households bore the brunt of the crisis and social safety nets to deal with their worsening situation were not in place. Emergency public works programs, in the Philippines and Korea, helped to alleviate the crisis for some unemployed workers, but these programs reached only a small portion of the poor (World Bank 1998, 2000b). As Khun Bunjan, a community leader from the slums of Khon Kaen, in Thailand, bitterly commented: 'It was the rich who benefited from the boom ... but we, the poor, pay the price of the crisis. Even our limited access to schools and health is now beginning to disappear' (World Bank 1998, p. 73).

In Indonesia, where the crisis lingered compared to other countries, daily survival became the norm for between 40 and 100 million people in 1998. Food prices, in particular, spiraled upwards and a large segment of the population could no longer afford more than one meal a day. The price hikes were partly linked to an El Niño-related drought, but they were fueled by the elimination of price supports by the government, and the sharp inflation associated with the crisis. By early February 1998, inflation was running at a rate of over 200 per cent a year. And by October of that year the country was facing a major famine. It was estimated that more than 45 million Indonesians could no longer buy enough rice to meet their daily nutritional requirements. Despite emergency government programs, which gave vouchers to women to buy rice at a quarter of the market price, a large segment of the population struggled to avoid malnourishment or famine during this time period. The personal anguish over the situation was captured by the following *Wall Street Journal* report: 'We can no longer eat rice every day,' complains Mahfud, a 56 year-old teacher who, each day, earns less than the 30 cents now needed to buy a kilogram of the grain. In his village on the outskirts of Jember, most residents work all day for the government. But they spend countless hours in nearby fields trying to coax along vegetables they can trade for their staple food: rice' (Brauchli 1998, p. A1).

The financial and economic collapse of the five East Asian economies led them to seek the emergency assistance of the International Monetary Fund. Following its approach to the 1994–95 Mexican crisis, the IMF pulled together a $17.2 billion bailout package for Thailand in August 1997. The package included loans from the IMF, the World Bank, the Ex-Im Bank, the Asian Development Bank, a number of countries including Japan, Australia and China and, ironically as it turned out, Malaysia, Indonesia and the Republic of Korea. A second assistance package of $38 billion was put together for Indonesia in late October. In December, Korea reached an agreement with the IMF for a third massive bailout plan; this loan package was equal to $57 billion, the largest ever, surpassing the 1994–95 Mexico rescue package.

The role of the IMF in the aftermath of the crisis has been sharply questioned, not only in terms of the specific policy menu adopted by the IMF, but also in terms of the role of that institution in assisting economies in distress. For one, the IMF requested that the governments reduce government spending in order to raise the funds required to restructure financial institutions. But by shrinking government spending in a recession situation, the policy further aggravated the crisis. This reproduced the often-quoted mistake made by the United States in the 1930s, when President Hoover tried to balance the budget in the midst of the Great Depression. The IMF, in its quest for immediate public sector austerity, also acted to reduce subsidies and safety nets that adversely impacted on the poor. And IMF requests for the speedy closing and restructuring of ailing financial institutions may have worsened the situation by encouraging bank runs on healthy institutions. Federal Reserve Chairman Alan Greenspan, in a Congressional testimony, noted that the IMF 'misread the depth of the really fundamental problems that were involved in the crisis that evolved … I think their actions were somewhat misguided in the early stages' (as quoted in Wessel and Davis 1998). The IMF itself reversed course, after heavy criticism. For instance, in early 1998, it allowed Thailand to post a budget deficit, instead of a budget surplus, as had been in the original terms of agreement that led to the bailout. Similar leniency was also observed later with respect to Indonesia, after the social impact of the crisis reached enormous proportions.

The moral hazard attached to IMF bailouts has been raised as a major question surrounding IMF intervention in East Asia. By allowing creditors to be paid in full, the IMF:

> encourages those lenders and others to take excessive future risks. Banks that expect loans to be guaranteed by governments do not as carefully as they should look at the underlying commercial credit risks. And when banks believe that the availability of dollars to meet foreign exchange obligations will be guaranteed by the IMF, they will not look carefully at the foreign exchange risk of the debtor countries. (Feldstein 1998, p. 30; see also Calomiris 1998)

There is, however, a lack of empirical evidence on this issue.

The events of 1997 and 1998 constituted for many a surprising and unexpected development. Until the crisis, the five East Asian economies had been displayed, by both the private sector and international organizations, as showcases for the rest of the developing world. Given the strength of key fundamental variables displayed earlier, the question emerges: What went wrong?

5. THE ANATOMY OF AN EMERGING MARKET CRISIS: CAPITAL INFLOWS AND THE EXCHANGE RATE

Although the East Asian crisis was unanticipated in most circles, there were danger signs long before it exploded in July 1997.

Investors in stock markets in the five countries had been nervous about the economic situation in these nations for quite some time. This preoccupation was reflected in the stagnation of prices in the East Asian bourses in the years before the crisis. Table 2.12 presents the International Finance Corporation (IFC) Stock Market Price Index (in local currency) for the five East Asian countries during the period of December 1988 to June 1997. There is a clear split in the behavior of stock market prices before and after 1994. While there was a sharp increase of the IFC price index in the period from 1988 to the end of 1993 (for all countries except Korea), for the period of January 1994 to June 1997 the increase of the index sharply slowed down or even turned around, displaying price reductions. In Thailand, for example, the index dropped by 19.6 per cent a year in real terms between January 1994 and June 1997. For South Korea, the drop was equal to 4 per cent, and for Malaysia the reduction was 4.4 per cent. In Indonesia, stock market prices went up, but at a slower pace compared to earlier years. Although market capitalization continued to rise in the five East Asian economies until the crisis erupted (both domestic and foreign investors continued to plunge into the markets), the boom in prices had ended much earlier.

What explains the deflated stock market prices? There are a number of economic and political factors involved, the importance of which varies by country, but there is one major force that is common to all the economies involved: There was a growing perception that the East Asian currencies would be sharply devalued in the near future and that associated with this devaluation would be economic distress. Eventually, these expectations of devaluation would lead to massive capital flight in all five countries.

In Thailand, the capital outflows had started in 1996 and early 1997, long before the currency markets collapsed in July 1997. Speculation based on an expected devaluation of the baht aggravated considerably in May 1997. Hedge

Table 2.12 East Asian stock market prices before the crisis, December 1988–June 1997

	IFC stock market price index*			Annual real change (%)	
	Dec. 1988	Dec. 1993	June 1997	1988–93	1993–97
Indonesia	305	588	724	18.5	6.6
Rep. of Korea	907	866	745	–1.0	–4.0
Malaysia	357	1 275	1 077	51.4	–4.4
The Philippines	842	3 196	2 809	55.9	–3.5
Thailand	387	1 682	527	66.9	–19.6

Notes:
* In local currency.
Index base year: Philippines (1984 = 100), Indonesia (1982 = 100), Rep. of Korea (1980 = 100), Malaysia (1977 = 100), and Thailand (1984 = 100).

Source: International Finance Corporation 1998.

funds, which move billions of liquid dollars across the globe to speculate on future exchange rate adjustments, had entered the scene in a major way (Eichengreen and Mathieson 1999, pp. 8–9). A few years before, in 1992 and 1993, hedge funds had been a critical part of the speculative attack on, and collapse of, the exchange rate mechanism of the European Monetary System.[6] The Bank of Thailand, though, was intent on preventing a devaluation. During the 1990s, throughout a period that included major domestic political events (including a short-lived military coup), the central bank had tightly controlled the value of the baht, keeping it around 25 baht per dollar. The May speculative outburst put powerful upward pressure on the exchange rate, moving it close to 27 baht per dollar. The Bank of Thailand, in cooperation with other central banks in the region, intervened in foreign exchange markets to support the value of the baht. Short-term interest rates were raised and, in a surprise move, the Bank of Thailand ordered local commercial banks to stop lending baht to foreign residents, unless they could show that the transactions would not be used to speculate, thus effectively creating a two-tier foreign exchange market. Having millions of dollars tied-up in open baht positions, many speculators suddenly found themselves unable to borrow dollars except from the Bank of Thailand, whose short-term lending rate skyrocketed. As a result, hedge funds lost what is estimated to be $450 million in May 1997. Stanley Druckenmiller, chief investment officer at the Soros Fund Management, which handles one of the major global hedge funds, stated at the time: 'They [the Bank of Thailand] have taken a lot of profit we might have had. They did a masterful job of squeezing us out' (Henderson 1998, p. 105).

Unfortunately for the Bank of Thailand, the victory over hedge funds was only temporary. It was temporary because hedge funds and short-term currency speculators were not the only ones who were anticipating a baht devaluation. As other local and foreign investors acted on their own devaluation expectations, massive capital flight resumed shortly after this event. Embattled by the sustained attack on the currency, on Tuesday, 1 July, Thailand's Prime Minister Chavalit Yongchaiyudh came on television to restate that the baht would never be devalued. This echoed another momentous television statement made 15 years earlier by President José López Portillo of Mexico in 1982 when he declared that the peso would not be devalued and that he would defend its value 'like a mad dog.' Just as the peso was devalued shortly after López Portillo's statement, so did the baht, the next day.

What stimulated the expectations of devaluation of the baht and the other East Asian currencies as well? As was noted earlier, the value of these currencies had remained remarkably stable in the 1990s. Yet, as we also saw earlier, prices had been rising in the region, albeit at a moderate rate. Inflation was declining, but it was still about 8 per cent per year between 1990 and 1996. With exchange rates fixed and domestic prices rising, the prices of goods produced in East Asia increased relative to the prices of goods produced in other countries, implying a loss of price competitiveness in world markets. This loss of competitiveness is reflected in the changes of the *real exchange rate* in the East Asian economies during the 1990s. The real exchange rate of any given country is defined as the price of foreign goods relative to the price of domestic goods, both measured in local currency. A rise of the real exchange rate is linked to an increase of domestic competitiveness as it shows foreign goods becoming relatively more expensive. On the other hand, a reduction of the real exchange rate is linked to a decrease of domestic competitiveness, with domestic goods becoming relatively more expensive.[7]

Real exchange rates had been declining among all East Asian countries in the 1990s. Consider the case of Korea, which because of its strong fundamentals few had anticipated it could fall into the abyss it did in 1997 and 1998. The data show that the real exchange rate of the won relative to the dollar had persistently and sharply declined over a period lasting a decade.[8] Between 1985 and 1996, the won had appreciated in real terms by close to 30 per cent of its original value. In fact, the won also appreciated in *nominal* terms between 1985 and 1996, from 881 won per dollar in 1985 to 771 in 1995. The depreciation associated with the East Asian crisis moved the real value of the won in 1998 and 1999 back down to levels prevailing in 1984 and 1995.

Real exchange rates decreased in all five East Asian crisis countries during the period preceding the crisis, to a greater or lesser extent.[9] For Malaysia, the currency appreciated in real terms by approximately 15 per cent in the relatively short period between 1991 and 1996. In Indonesia, the rupiah appreciated by close to 11 per cent in the same time period. In the Philippines, the peso's real exchange rate declined by close to 30 per cent in the period of 1989 to 1996. Finally, in Thailand, the baht gradually but continuously appreciated by close to 15 per cent in the period of 1985 to 1996.

The persistent real exchange rate reductions (and the resulting loss of competitiveness of East Asian products in world markets) caused a fall in the exports of goods and services relative to imports in all of the five countries. As a result, trade and current account balance deficits grew. Table 2.13 presents the behavior of the current account balance in East Asia from 1985 to 1997, measured relative to GDP. In all five countries, the current account balance deteriorated during this time period and, in some, it moved from surplus to deficit. The country with the largest current account balance deficit before the crisis was Thailand, which had a deficit of 6.8 per cent of GDP during the 1990–95 period and 8.3 per cent in 1996.

Table 2.13 East Asian countries: current account of the balance of payments as a percentage of GNP

	1985–89 (%)	1990–95 (%)	1996 (%)	1997 (%)	1998 (%)	1999 (%)
Indonesia	–2.5	–2.4	–3.5	–2.3	4.2	2.9
Rep. of Korea	4.3	–1.3	–4.8	–1.9	12.6	6.0
Malaysia	2.4	–5.6	–4.9	–5.1	6.6	16.3
The Philippines	–0.5	–3.7	–4.6	–5.0	2.0	8.6
Thailand	–2.0	–6.8	–8.3	–2.0	12.8	11.0

Sources: World Bank 1995, 2000a.

The growing current account balance deficits displayed by the East Asian countries began to attract attention in some circles. In its annual outlook, completed before the crisis erupted, the Asian Development Bank expressed some concern over the situation: 'In 1996, most Asian countries experienced a sharp slowdown in export growth. This decline in export growth rates has generated yet another economic debate, with apprehensions being expressed regarding the ability of the Asian economies to continue their high performance because their competitiveness in the international markets is slipping.'[10] Similarly, in a conference on the major macroeconomic issues facing the member countries of the Association of South East Nations (ASEAN), held in Jakarta, Indonesia, on 5-7 November 1996, Michael Camdessus, then the

Managing Director of the IMF, examined the challenges facing East Asian economies. He observed:

> large net private capital inflows have tended to raise aggregate expenditures, increase inflationary pressures, and widen current account deficits in all major recipient countries. Yet, part of these inflows – especially those of a short-term nature – can be suddenly reversed, because of either changes in market sentiment about the recipient country, contagion effects, or changing financial conditions in other countries. Countries in such situations must thus pay particular attention to the sustainability of their external position. (Camdessus 1997, p. 20)

The growing current account balance deficits raised serious fears regarding the financial soundness of the economies, as they implied growing indebtedness. A current account balance deficit, that is, an excess of payments over receipts on current account, must be financed. There are basically two ways to finance it: a loss of international reserves on the part of the central bank or through external borrowing (see Rivera-Batiz and Rivera-Batiz 1994, ch. 9). How did the East Asian economies finance their current account balance deficits? In 1996, for example, the combined current account deficit for the five economies was $53.9 billion. How was this deficit paid for? As it turns out, it was financed entirely through external financing. In fact, throughout the early 1990s, the central banks of the five countries *accumulated* foreign exchange reserves, thus augmenting the amount of external borrowing the economies undertook during these years. In 1996, the external borrowing of the five countries amounted to $74.4 billion.

The accumulation of current account deficits in the 1990s and their financing through private capital flows made the East Asian economies the biggest debtors in the world by the end of 1996. The data presented in Table 2.14 show that all five countries were among the developing world's largest debtors. Furthermore, when the debt is calculated relative to the size of the economy, by dividing the external debt by GDP, one finds that three of the East Asian economies – the Philippines, Indonesia and Thailand – were at the top of the list of the world's most indebted countries at the end of 1996. Indeed, the Philippines had the highest debt-to-GDP ratio among developing countries (59.5 per cent), followed by Indonesia (58.3 per cent) and Thailand (53 per cent).

Although the five East Asian countries became more heavily indebted in the 1990s, they were already highly-indebted countries to begin with. The developing country debt crisis of the1980s had left all five countries among the top 20 debtors in the world in 1990. For some of them, the debt increased faster than GDP as the 1990s unfolded, while for others debt increased slower than GDP. For Thailand, the debt-to-GDP ratio jumped from 33.4 per cent in 1990 to 53 per cent in 1996. Similarly, in Korea, the debt-to-GDP ratio rose from 18.7 per cent in 1990 to 29.3 per cent in 1996. In the other three countries, however, debt-to-GDP ratios did not rise significantly in the 1990s and, for Indonesia and the Philippines, the ratio actually declined. In Indonesia, the debt-to-GDP ratio went down from 64 to 58.3 per cent in the period from 1990 to 1996 while for the Philippines it dropped from 69.4 per cent to 59.5 per cent. In Malaysia, the ratio slightly rose from 37.5 per cent in 1990 to 42.4 per cent in 1996.

Table 2.14 Biggest debtors in the developing world, 1996

	External debt (millions US$)	External debt/GNP (%)
Brazil	194 046	25.0
Mexico	167 469	50.6
China	150 541	18.3
Korea	142 070	29.3
Indonesia	132 816	58.3
Russian Federation	123 186	27.9
Argentina	105 388	35.4
Thailand	98 368	53.0
India	97 491	27.7
Turkey	79 747	44.0
Greece	55 299	44.7
The Philippines	50 120	59.5
Malaysia	41 967	42.4
Poland	41 628	31.1

Source: World Bank 1998.

Because indebtedness had been comparatively high in East Asia for some time, the massive borrowing undertaken in the 1990s gave rise to major concerns regarding the servicing of this debt, despite the miraculous economic growth. In addition, there were some major changes regarding the composition of the debt in the 1990s. First of all, the external debt was increasingly private debt, not public sector debt, as was the situation in the 1980s. Furthermore, an increasing share of the private debt was not being guaranteed by the government. In Indonesia, private, non-guaranteed debt rose from 17.4 to 37.9 per cent of all long-term external indebtedness between 1990 and 1996. In Korea, the increase was from 22.3 to 36 per cent, and in Malaysia from 11.9 to 32.5 per cent. For Thailand, which already had a substantial portion of long-term private debt in 1990 (36.8 per cent), the share increased to 68.3 per cent in

1996. Finally, in the Philippines, private, non-guaranteed debt rose from less than 5 per cent of all long-term external debt in 1990 to 15.4 per cent in 1996.

With the growing role of private debt, the significance of current public sector budgets on the financing of external debt payments declined sharply. What became more important was the health of the economy and, in particular, its financial system. Both of these were critical to the transformation of the external debt into productive investments. An economic downturn and/or a major mismanagement of investment funds into projects with low expected returns or high risks, could trigger a loss of investor confidence, leading to capital flight and a possible crisis. Worries about the future fiscal costs of such bailouts and the revenues they require, say in the form of inflationary taxes, become the topic of concern (see Burnside et al. 1998). These worries were magnified by two additional trends regarding external debt in the 1990s: the rise of short-term debt (in foreign currency) and commercial bank lending.

The experience of Latin American economies, from Mexico to Brazil, suggests that mismanagement of the maturity structure of debt lies at the core of financial crises. Growth of short-term debt has been a major common factor in many financial crises. In East Asia, short-term debt expanded substantialy in the 1990s. In Thailand, the share of short-term debt on the country's stock of debt increased from 21.3 per cent in 1986 to 68.3 per cent in 1996. In Korea, the share of short-term debt rose from 19.8 per cent in 1986 to 50 per cent in 1996. In Indonesia, the increase was from 9.1 per cent in 1986 to 25 per cent in 1996. And in Malaysia, it was from 12.1 per cent in 1986 to 28 per cent in 1996. Only in the Philippines did short-term debt remain constrained, equal to 19 per cent of all debt in 1986 and 20 per cent in 1996.

The growth of short-term debt constituted a major warning sign of potential troubles ahead. The absence of this type of debt had helped East Asian economies to survive relatively unscathed through the developing country debt crisis in the 1980s. This is the conclusion, for example, of Woo and Nasution in their analysis of Indonesia:

> there is a trade-off in external debt management between generally lower interest payments and predictability of debt-service payments. Short-term liabilities pay lower interest rates most of the time, but it is risky to rely on a strategy which rolls over a large amount of short-term debt every period. An unforeseen credit crunch would force the country to increase borrowing in order to cover its interest payments. If this credit squeeze were to persist ... the extra borrowing would be difficult to sustain as the situation increasingly smacked of a Ponzi game. (Woo and Nasution 1989, p. 115)

A second major issue regarding the external indebtedness of East Asian countries in the 1990s was the growing portion of the debt accounted for by commercial banks. In all five economies, bank lending became more significant. In the Philippines, the proportion of long-term debt accounted for by commercial bank loans skyrocketed from 6 per cent in 1990 to 31 per cent in 1996. In Korea, the increase was from 32.4 per cent in 1990 to close to 50 per cent in 1996. In Malaysia, bank lending rose from 30.6 per cent to 50 per cent of the stock of long-term debt. In Thailand, commercial bank debt increased from 47 to 55 per cent of all debt between 1990 and 1996, and in Indonesia, the corresponding change was from 32.2 to 37.2 per cent.

The rapid expansion of bank lending as a component of external debt was potentially troublesome because of the weak and imperfect state of the banking systems of these economies. Despite the squeaky-clean image of East Asia in the early 1990s, the reality was that all of the five East Asian countries had underdeveloped, imperfect financial systems and a history of banking crises, leading up to the period right before the crisis.[11]

The Philippines suffered from a series of crises in the period of 1981 to 1987. In 1986, 19 per cent of bank loans were non-performing. Three commercial banks, 128 rural banks, and 32 thrift institutions failed, and two other private banks were under intervention. Furthermore, the biggest commercial bank, the Philippines National Bank, and the Development Bank of the Philippines, both government-owned, became de facto insolvent and had to be bailed out. Although this crisis was partly caused by external factors (rising world interest rates and a global recession), by macroeconomic mismanagement (including substantial budget deficits), and by political uncertainty, the state of the banking industry itself was a major issue. The presence of bank-holding-company groups created dangerous, incestuous interrelations between lending institutions. When combined with bank supervisory weaknesses, excessive risk-taking, fraud and mismanagement, it was a prescription for trouble.[12]

Korea also had significant banking problems in the mid-1980s. The government had to provide emergency loans to troubled banks accounting for 24 per cent of commercial bank assets. Indonesia had its own difficulties in the 1990s; non-performing loans, which were concentrated in state-owned banks, were over 25 per cent of total lending in 1993. Malaysia had undergone a major banking crisis from 1985 to 1988, with non-performing loans estimated at 32 per cent of all loans in 1988. And Thailand had suffered a severe banking collapse from 1983 to 1987 in which more than 25 per cent of the country's financial assets were affected. Fifteen finance companies failed after a number of bank panics and runs developed (Lindgren et al. 1996, p. 33).

The weaknesses of the financial systems in the East Asian countries had been repeatedly noted by a wide array of analysts. In the case of Thailand, as early as 1991, Barry Johnston had observed:

> the emergence of distressed financial institutions in Thailand had its origins mainly in weak managerial practices and in inadequate legal, regulatory and supervisory frameworks for financial institutions. The indigenous private sector financial institu-

> tions were established by trading families and other powerful economic groupings and had a high concentration of ownership and, in several cases, of loan exposure to interrelated entities. Such institutions were not 'self-regulatory' in the sense that there was a lack of normal checks and balances between shareholders, directors and management, and this resulted in inherent management weakness. (Johnston 1991, p. 274)

Despite this assessment, it was a series of developments five years later that made clear that the Thai situation had not substantially changed since that time, giving fuel to the capital flight that led to the financial crisis.

In May 1996, Thailand was stunned to hear the revelation that the Bangkok Bank of Commerce, the nation's ninth largest bank, had close to 50 per cent of its assets (about $3 billion) in the form of non-performing bank loans, many of them made to acquaintances of the bank's president. Opposition parties in the country alleged that it was laxity and political partisanship on the part of the Bank of Thailand that explained this disaster. This was followed, in August, by allegations of government corruption in the granting of licenses to new banks, with bribes of $90 million involved. Both the governor of the central bank and the prime minister resigned, with Chavalit Yongchaiyudh, head of the New Aspiration party, becoming the new Prime Minister in elections held in November. More bad news surfaced in January 1997, when Thailand's largest finance company, Finance One, collapsed. It was apparent at this time that the Thai financial system was under serious stress, giving rise to the speculative capital outflows that would eventually lead to the currency crisis of May 1997.

The problems of the banking system in East Asia have been summarized by the World Bank, with the benefits of hindsight: 'the East Asian countries had some weaknesses in their banking systems including:

> low capital-adequacy ratios of banks; inadequately designed and weakly-enforced legal lending limits on single borrowers or group of related borrowers; asset classification systems and provisioning rules for possible losses, which fell short of international standards; poor disclosure and transparency of bank operations; lack of provisions for an exit policy of troubled financial institutions; and weak supervision. (World Bank 2000d, p. 35)

One might add that inadequate project evaluation and risk-assessment techniques were also serious problems. In part, the public sector bailouts of financial institutions in the earlier episodes of financial distress in the 1980s and early 1990s (noted above), acted to create a moral hazard incentives problem, as private institutions took excessive risks or mismanaged their portfolios on the assumption that they would be bailed out by the government in case of financial difficulties. The result of these problems was the expansion of lending to questionable projects that had small or negative short-term returns and relied on rosy assessments of risky long-term returns. Massive investments in infrastructure and in real estate were not carefully assessed in terms of their risk. For instance, at the time the crisis occurred, Malaysia was involved in seeking finance for a $4.55 billion dam/hydroelectric project in Bakun, a northern regional airport in Kedah, the Linear City in Kuala Lumpur, and a road linking three islands in the central range of the country's peninsula. In Kuala Lumpur stands the tallest building in the world, a 1 483-foot high tower completed just before the crisis began. In Thailand, the abandoned beginnings of a $1 billion elevated light-rail project on the outskirts of Bangkok is called Stonehenge by local residents and the skyline is dotted with the skeletons of unfinished buildings. Indonesia was at the verge of completing financing packages for a 60-mile long bridge between Indonesia and Malaysia. A syndicated loan was also being arranged to build the Jakarta Tower, which would have become the tallest building in the world. All these investments were made within the context of a real estate sector that was plagued by over-capacity and at the verge of a collapsing bubble.

Each of the forces discussed in this section may not have had the power to generate a crisis by itself, but all of them together were potentially explosive. A slowdown in domestic economic activity or a worsening current account balance, for example, could turn around the confidence of lenders and investors. Local commercial banks and financial institutions, which had borrowed abroad substantially, were then subject to the risk that nervous foreign lenders would not roll-over their short-term loans. With a large portion of bank assets tied-up in the form of long-term loans, the banks would encounter a liquidity crisis. The possibility of a bank run made the situation worse. And even though an expansion of central bank credit could temporarily avert a crisis, the fact that the short-term external debt was denominated in foreign currency meant that the central bank would lose international reserves in the process. This could eventually force a balance of payments crisis.[13]

6. THE AFTERMATH OF THE CRISIS: WHERE ARE WE NOW?

The current situation of East Asia provides ground for optimism, but the financial system remains fragile. Growth of GDP has picked-up in all five countries and current forecasts are for continued growth. Korea, in particular, has had a remarkable recovery, growing over 10 per cent in real terms during 1999 and with similarly high forecasts for 2000. The current account balance in all five countries is in surplus and exports have rebounded. The real currency depreciations in all five currencies are likely to provide an even stronger impetus to exports.

Despite these positive signs, the recovery continues to be delicate. Banks remain under-capitalized, even after a wide array of government policies seeking to inject capital into the financial system have been implemented. The exit of many financial institutions has left the sector much more concentrated than before. Many banks remain under state control and the public sector debt associated with the crisis keeps rising. Although Korea and Malaysia have been more aggressive in the restructuring of banks, other financial institutions in those countries remain in weak condition. Thailand has dealt more aggressively with finance companies, proceeding to deal with the banking system on a more gradual basis. Indonesia has made the least progress and most financial institutions remain under state control and insolvent (see Claessens et al. 1999 and Asian Development Bank 2000).

Non-performing loans continue to be a major difficulty, far over that encountered by Mexico and other Latin American countries in 1995 and 1996. Korea has been the most successful country in restructuring the financial sector. The Korean state agency in charge of taking over financial institutions and transferring, consolidating or liquidating claims on non-performing loans had been able to reduce the percentage of these loans in the financial system to about 10 per cent of all loans by the beginning of 2000. In Malaysia, the corresponding figure was 25 per cent. For Thailand, the ratio of non-performing loans to total loans was still 39 per cent at the start of 2000. In Indonesia, where the financial crisis has been particularly severe, non-performing loans constituted over 60 per cent of all loans in early 2000.

The impact of the East Asian crisis on capital inflows has been long-lasting. Net capital flows to the five East Asian countries are still negative and are expected to remain so during 2000 and 2001. The exorbitant fiscal cost of the financial and corporate restructuring has created a huge debt overhang. At the beginning of the year 2000, the external debt of the five countries, as a fraction of GDP, remained above the levels before the crisis. As a percentage of GDP, the external debt of Indonesia grew from 58.3 per cent at the end of 1996 to 149.4 per cent at the end of 1998 and 95.5 per cent at the end of 1999. In Malaysia, the corresponding percentage grew from 42.4 per cent at the end of 1996 to close to 60 per cent in 1998 and 55.3 per cent in 1999. In Thailand, the percentage of the debt relative to GDP increased from 53 per cent at the end of 1996 to 76.8 per cent by the end of 1998 and 61.5 per cent in 1999. In the Philippines, the percentage rose from 59.5 per cent in 1996 to 73.3 per cent in 1998 and 68 per cent in 1999. In Korea, the debt-to-GDP ratio rose from 29.3 per cent at the end of 1996 to 46.9 per cent in 1998 and 33 per cent at the end of 1999.

The danger in the coming years, however, lies in the growing budget deficits that have emerged after the crisis. They are linked to rising public indebtedness. Table 2.15 shows the general budget balance as a fraction of GDP for

East Asia, from 1997 to 1999. Note that, as we discussed earlier, all five countries had either surpluses or negligible deficits in 1996. However, by 1999, Indonesia had a budget deficit of 2.3 per cent of GDP, Korea's was 2.9 per cent, Malaysia's was 4.1 per cent, the Philippines 4.4 per cent and Thailand's deficit was 3 per cent of GDP. These budget deficits are likely to widen, as a result of the additional resources needed to complete bank capitalization plus the interest on the existing public debt (International Monetary Fund 2000).

Table 2.15 East Asian countries: the budget balance in the aftermath of the crisis

	General budget balance/GDP (%)		
	1997	1998	1999
Indonesia	–0.7	–1.9	–2.3
Rep. of Korea	–0.9	–4.0	–2.9
Malaysia	4.0	–1.0	–4.1
The Philippines	–0.8	–2.7	–4.4
Thailand	–0.9	–2.5	–3.0

Source: International Monetary Fund 2000.

7. POLICY IMPLICATIONS: THE POLITICAL ECONOMY OF EMERGING MARKET DISEASE

The analysis of the East Asian crisis developed in this chapter suggests the presence of a vicious cycle facing policymakers in emerging markets. Countries that have increased their domestic investment while liberalizing their capital accounts encounter a surge of capital inflows. These capital inflows allow increased investment rates and the rapid growth of national income. Yet, they also plant the seeds of a future downturn and, possibly, a crisis. The reason is that capital inflows generate upward pressures on the value of domestic currency. In countries with floating exchange rates, the value of the domestic currency would immediately rise, directly causing a real currency appreciation. Under fixed or managed exchange rates a real currency appreciation also occurs, through the inflationary impact of the capital inflows.[14] The result is an economic pattern that was seen in all East Asian countries in the first half of the 1990s: an economic boom (especially in non-traded goods sectors), moderate or low inflation, stable exchange rates, a real currency appreciation, and rising international reserves.

The seeds of the bust, however, have been planted in the boom period. As the value of the currency rises in real terms, the growth of domestic exports eventually slows down and the current account balance deteriorates. External debt accumulates and at some point investors will revise their local risk-assessments in the upward direction. This then leads to capital flight and currency depreciation. If the central bank stubbornly defends prevailing currency values, and its foreign exchange reserves are not enough to withstand the massive capital exodus, the country will eventually face a balance of payments crisis and the currency will have to be allowed to float.

The crisis is accelerated, and it's impact greater, if domestic financial institutions are fragile and do not have the ability to handle the credit crunch and the higher interest rates linked to the capital outflows. The situation is also worsened if price bubbles (in real estate or in domestic capital markets in general) have existed, which burst and generate even greater capital flight. Financial panics and bank runs linked to liquidity crises can also worsen the crisis and its aftermath (Sachs and Radelet 1998b; Chang and Velasco 1998, 1999). And if there has been over-investment, in the form of excessive lending to risky projects with low short-term returns, the crisis can freeze economic activity on a grand scale (McKinnon and Pil 1996). Finally, the presence of contagion effects can assist in transmitting the crisis to countries in the same region or suffering from similar economic circumstances (Eichengreen et al. 1996; Eichengreen and Rose 1998).

We have characterized this type of phenomenon as emerging market disease. Understanding it leads to a set of policy prescriptions, which we now examine in the context of the East Asian crisis. The sharp, real appreciation of all five currencies in East Asia, and the growing current account balance deficits, suggest that the currencies were overvalued by mid-1997. This was already the conclusion that the firm Goldman-Sachs had obtained in October 1996 from their model of real exchange rates, which indicated that the real exchange rate was overvalued in Indonesia, Thailand and the Philippines. Later, in 1997, before the crisis erupted, Goldman-Sachs added Korea and Malaysia to the list of countries with overvalued real exchange rates. More recently, Chinn (1998) used a purchasing power parity model of equilibrium exchange rates to determine that 'as of May 1997, the baht, ringgit and peso were overvalued.'

The fact that central banks delayed currency devaluations, which was a central factor in the crisis, is well-known. What has not been noted in the literature, though, and what the analysis of emerging market disease helps us understand, is that central banks face a disturbing trade off regarding currency values. Under the influence of capital inflows, emerging markets' equilibrium real exchange rates decline over time. In this situation, central banks would be ill-advised to devalue the currency, as it would only stimulate expectations of a revaluation. A devaluation would be called for only after the negative effects of a sustained real currency appreciation on the current account balance are imminent. At that time, capital flows may begin to reverse their direction and this is the moment when policy action is required. Clearly, in the East Asian economies, as in the case of Mexico in 1994, the exchange rate adjustments came too late. But in a situation where policymakers may be anticipating (perhaps unrealistically so) an improvement of the current account balance, the exact timing of the switch of the equilibrium exchange rate from currency appreciation to depreciation is uncertain.

What remains true, though, is that once capital outflows begin in earnest, and expectations of devaluation become widespread, the devaluations cannot be delayed. As Radelet and Sachs conclude:

> Had Thailand responded ... in early 1997 by floating the baht and moderately tightening monetary and fiscal policies, the Asian financial crisis could have been largely avoided. Thailand and Korea, of course, made the paramount mistake of trying to defend their exchange rate peg until they had effectively exhausted a substantial proportion of their foreign exchange reserves. (Radelet and Sachs 1998a, p. 37)

Since capital flows are at the center of the economic phenomena that are linked to emerging market disease, capital controls have surfaced in many policy discussions in the aftermath of the crisis. Most experts agree, however, that the introduction of widespread restrictions on capital flows has its own problems and can be counterproductive. The ample historical experience on the imposition of capital and exchange controls indicates that they are troublesome because they (1) lead to the formation of black markets, widespread evasion and corruption, and (2) delay the implementation of short-term policy reforms required to dissipate the symptoms behind the capital flight, such as a currency devaluation, budget deficit reduction and anti-inflation policies (Rivera-Batiz and Rivera-Batiz 1994, ch. 3). The existing research also suggests that controls on capital outflows have been unable to effectively stop massive capital flight and balance of payments crises (see Edwards 1989; Kaminsky and Reinhart 1999).

Despite the skepticism with controls on capital flows in general, many economists agree that emerging markets should consider adopting policies intended to reduce the volatility of short-term capital flows, particularly capital inflows. Even the IMF, which at one point considered amending the institution's charter to make the free flow of capital one of its major goals, has been more flexible on this issue in recent years. Michael Camdessus, as Managing Director of the IMF in 1996, encouraged East Asian countries to consider temporary controls on capital inflows, stating: 'because the greatest threat to instability is posed by more volatile short-term inflows ... the adoption of prudential requirements *vis-à-vis* short-term inflows ... has ... played a useful role. However, in our experience, direct quantitative controls on capital inflows rarely work for any sustained period' (Camdessus 1997, p. 23).

The imposition of direct taxes on short-term capital inflows, and indirect taxes, such as reserve requirements on short-term bank deposits, have been among the policies proposed by various economists (Calvo et al. 1995, p. 380). Chile represents the most visible case where this type of policy was implemented. Various high-profile economists have endorsed it. For example, in 1998, Joseph Stiglitz, then Chief Economist at the World Bank, in response to a question about what policies can be developed to deal with financial crises, stated: 'You want to look for policies that discourage hot money but facilitate the flow of long-term loans, and there is evidence that the Chilean approach or some version of it, does this' (*New York Times*, 1 February 1998; see also Eichengreen 2000).

Established in 1991 in the face of a surge of capital inflows, Chile imposed a minimum one-year requirement for the stay of foreign direct investment in the country. It also required that all other foreign funds flowing into the country include a deposit of 30 per cent in the form of no-interest accounts at the central bank for one year. The policy was phased-out by May 2000, when a long period of sustained capital outflows led policymakers to seek incentives (rather than disincentives) for capital inflows. Evidence on the effectiveness of the controls suggests that the policy was highly successful in switching capital inflows away from short-term flows (see Hernandez and Schmidt-Hebel 1999; Calvo and Reinhart 1999). On the other hand, a number of studies show that the controls only changed the composition, not the level, of capital inflows. They also do not appear to have controlled one of the key symptoms of emerging market disease: the real exchange rate appreciation linked to massive capital inflows. Finally, it should be realized that this type of policy is not without costs since it raises the cost of capital and, over time, may give rise to various tax-evasion schemes (Edwards 1999).

The final set of policy prescriptions we discuss here relates to financial fragility and the speed at which emerging markets liberalize the capital account. The severe impact of financial liberalization and massive capital inflows into imperfect, weak financial systems was a crucial factor behind the East Asian crisis.[15] Adequate regulatory and supervision systems, which define and monitor appropriate capital-adequacy ratios of banks; enforce legal lending limits on single borrowers or groups of related borrowers; require banks to hold an adequate fraction of liquid reserves; establish standards to follow in case of losses, provide for mechanisms to insure depositors and deal with possible bankruptcy of financial institutions; engage in strict audits of institutions and impose severe corporate and managerial penalties for the violation of rules, procedures and regulations; and assure greater disclosure and transparency of bank operations, are sorely needed in place before the capital account is opened to cross-border banking transactions (Caprio and Honohan 1999; Caprio and Klingebiel 1996). A sequencing of financial liberalization, where foreign direct investment (FDI) is opened-up before short-term capital flows and commercial bank lending transactions, may allow both policymakers and the private sector enough time for the institution-building required to intermediate effectively large inflows of capital.[16]

At this time, the five East Asian countries are embarked in a major restructuring process that will take time to be fully resolved. The external debt overhang and wide public sector deficits constitute serious public policy concerns. However, the basic fundamentals regarding physical and human capital accumulation in East Asia (as we discussed them in section 2 above) have not essentially changed. This suggests that economic growth will rebound in the region (as it is already doing). As confidence on this growth gathers momentum, capital inflows will return. Note, however, that the basic phenomena associated with emerging market disease have not disappeared. They are just dormant. Once capital inflows return, the disease will reawaken. Careful policy management, along the lines discussed in this concluding section, will need to be implemented to prevent a recurrence of the events in the past few years.

NOTES

1. See, for example, Chang and Velasco 1999, Corsetti et al. 1999a, 1999b; Goldstein 1998; Kaminsky and Reinhart 1998; Krugman 1998, 1999; Radelet and Sachs 1998a, 1998b; Rivera-Batiz 1999a, and Stiglitz 1998.
2. See Blejer and del Castillo 1998, Dornbusch 1997, and Edwards and Edwards 1987.
3. An analytical presentation of Dutch disease appears in Rivera-Batiz and Rivera-Batiz 1994, pp. 355–7.
4. The view that the so-called East Asian miracle was fueled by export-led growth, is presented in World Bank 1993. For a theoretical analysis of the links between trade and growth, see Rivera-Batiz 1996.
5. For an analysis of financial liberalization in the five East Asian countries, see Alba, Hernandez and Klingebiel (this volume), Callen and Reynolds 1997, Claessens and Glaessner 1997, Collins and Park 1989, Dekle and Pradhan 1997, Dohner and Intal 1989, Johnston 1991, Lindgren et al. 1996, Montgomery 1997, Montiel 1997, Nascimento 1991, and Woo and Nasution 1989.
6. For a discussion of the 1992–93 crisis of the European Monetary System, see Buiter et al. 1998.
7. Symbolically, the real exchange rate is represented by q, where $q = eP^*/P$, with e representing the nominal exchange rate (say, baht per dollar), P^* the price of foreign goods (measured say in dollars), and P the price of domestic goods (measured in baht). The real exchange rate q then depicts how expensive foreign goods are compared to domestic goods. An increase in q means foreign goods are relatively more expensive while a drop in q suggests that domestic goods are becoming more expensive.
8. In the Korean case, we use the symbol e to represent the dollar–won exchange rate (in dollars per won), P^* is the price level in the United States (we use the consumer price index), and P is the price level in Korea (measured by the Korean consumer price index).

9. We measure the real exchange rate of the currencies relative to the US dollar, so that the foreign price level P^* is the US price level (the US consumer price index).
10. Asian Development Bank 1997a, p. 10. The Bank, however, ends up dismissing the significance of the deficits.
11. For a comprehensive description of the banking and financial fragility in East Asia, see Delhaise 1998.
12. Nascimento 1991 and Dohner and Intal 1989 provide an analysis of the Philippine crisis in the 1980s.
13. See Chang and Velasco 1998, 1999 for an analysis of the role of international illiquidity on financial crises.
14. Although central bankers often seek to minimize this impact by sterilizing their purchases of foreign exchange through sales of bonds.
15. See, for example, the comprehensive analysis of Thailand by Alba et al., Chapter 5 in this volume.
16. See Rivera-Batiz 2000 for a discussion of the costs and benefits of FDI.

REFERENCES

Asian Development Bank (1995), *Asian Development Outlook, 1995 and 1996*, Oxford: Oxford University Press.

Asian Development Bank (1997a), *Asian Development Outlook, 1997 and 1998*, Oxford: Oxford University Press.

Asian Development Bank (1997b), *Emerging Asia: Changes and Challenges*, Manila: Asian Development Bank.

Asian Development Bank (2000), *Asia Recovery Report 2000*, Manila: Asian Development Bank, May.

Barro, Robert J. and Jong-Wha Lee (1994), 'Data Set for a Panel of 138 Countries,' mimeo, Department of Economics, Harvard University.

Barro, Robert J. and Xavier Sala-i-Martin (1995), *Economic Growth*, New York: McGraw-Hill.

Birdsall, Nancy and F. Jaspersen (1997), *Pathways to Growth: Comparing East Asia and Latin America*, Washington, DC: Inter-American Development Bank.

Blejer, Mario and Graciana del Castillo (1998), 'Déjà vu All Over Again? The Mexican Crisis and the Stabilization of Uruguay in the 1970s,' *World Development*, **26**: 449–64.

Bloom, David E. and John Williamson (1997), 'Demographic Transitions and Economic Miracles in Emerging Asia,' mimeo, Harvard Institute for International Development.

Brauchli, Marcus W. (1998), 'Indonesia's Struggles Become Elemental: A Shortage of Rice,' *Wall Street Journal*, October 20: A1, A8.

Buiter, Willem, Giancarlo Corsetti and Paolo Pesenti (eds) (1998), *Financial Markets and European Monetary Cooperation: The Lessons of the 1992–93 Exchange Rate Mechanism Crisis*, Cambridge: Cambridge University Press.

Burnside, Craig, Martin Eichenbaum and Sergio Rebelo (1998), 'Prospective Deficits and the Asian Crisis,' Washington, DC: Development Research Group, World Bank.

Callen, Tim and Patricia Reynolds (1997), 'Capital Market Development and the Monetary Transmission Mechanism in Malaysia and Thailand,' in John Hicklin, David Robinson and Anoop Singh (eds), *Macroeconomic Issues Facing ASEAN Countries*, Washington, DC: International Monetary Fund, pp. 184–230.

Calomiris, Charles (1998), 'The IMF's Imprudent Role as Lender of Last Resort,' *Cato Journal*, **17**: pp. 275–94.

Calvo, Guillermo and Carmen Reinhart (1999), 'When Capital Inflows Come to a Sudden Stop: Consequences and Policy Options,' mimeo, University of Maryland.

Calvo, Guillermo, Leonardo Leiderman and Carmen Reinhart (1995), 'Capital Inflows to Latin America with Reference to the Asian Experience,' in S. Edwards (ed.), *Capital Controls, Exchange Rates and Monetary Policy in the World Economy*, Cambridge: Cambridge University Press, pp. 339–82.

Camdessus, Michel (1997), 'Sustaining Macroeconomic Performance in the ASEAN Countries,' in John Hicklin, David Robinson and Anoop Singh (eds), *Macroeconomic Issues Facing ASEAN Countries*, Washington, DC: International Monetary Fund, pp. 19–28.

Caprio, Gerard and Daniela Klingebiel (1996), 'Bank Insolvency: Bad Luck, Bad Policy or Bad Banking?,' in M. Bruno and B. Pleskovic (eds), *World Bank Annual Conference on Development Economics*, Washington, DC: World Bank, pp. 32–44.

Caprio, Gerard and Patrick Honohan (1999), 'Restoring Banking Stability: Beyond Supervised Capital Requirements', *Journal of Economic Perspectives*, **13**: pp. 43–64.

Chang, Roberto and Andres Velasco (1998), 'The Asian Liquidity Crisis,' National Bureau of Economic Research Working Paper, No. 6796.

Chang, Roberto and Andres Velasco (1999), 'Liquidity Crises in Emerging Markets: Theory and Policy,' in Ben S. Bernanke and Julio J. Rotemberg (eds), *NBER Macroeconomics Annual 1999*, Cambridge, MA: MIT Press, pp. 11–57.

Chinn, Menzie D. (1998), 'Before the Fall: Were East Asian Currencies Overvalued?,' National Bureau of Economic Research Working Paper, No. 6491.

Claessens, Stijn and Thomas Glaessner (1997), *Are Financial Sector Weaknesses Undermining the East Asian Miracle?*, Washington, DC: World Bank.

Claessens, Stijn, S. Djankov and D. Klingebiel (1999), 'Financial Restructuring in East Asia: Halfway There?,' Financial Sector Discussion Paper No. 3, World Bank.

Clemente, Lilia (1994), 'Investing in Asia's Emerging Equity Market,' *Columbia Journal of World Business*, **29**: pp. 92–111.

Collins, Susan M. and Won-Am Park (1989), 'External Debt and Macroeconomic Performance in South Korea', in J.D. Sachs (ed.), *Developing Country Debt and the World Economy*, Chicago: University of Chicago Press, pp. 121–40.

Corsetti, Giancarlo, Paolo Pesenti and Nouriel Roubini (1999a), 'What Caused the Asian Currency and Financial Crisis?', *Japan and the World Economy*, **11**: 305–73.

Corsetti, Giancarlo, Paolo Pesenti and Nouriel Roubini (1999b), 'Paper Tigers? A Model of the Asian Crisis,' *European Economic Review*, **43**: 42–63.

Dekle, Robert and Mahmood Pradhan (1997), 'Financial Liberalization and Money Demand in ASEAN Countries: Implications for Monetary Policy,' in John Hicklin, David Robinson and Anoop Singh (eds), *Macroeconomic Issues Facing ASEAN Countries,* Washington, DC: International Monetary Fund, pp. 153–83.

Delhaise, Philippe (1998), *Asia in Crisis: The Implosion of the Banking and Finance Systems*, Singapore: Wiley & Sons.

Demirguk-Kunt, Asli and Enrica Detragiache (1998), 'The Determinants of Banking Crises in Developing and Developed Countries,' *IMF Staff Papers*, **45**: 81–109.

Diaz-Alejandro, Carlos (1985), 'Good-Bye Financial Repression, Hello Financial Crash,' *Journal of Development Economics*, **19**: 64–93.

Dohner, Robert S. and P. Intal (1989), 'Debt Crisis and Adjustment in the Philippines,' in J.D. Sachs (ed.), *Developing Country Debt and the World Economy*, Chicago: University of Chicago Press, pp. 169–91.

Dornbusch, Rudiger (1986), 'Stabilization Policies in Developing Countries: What Have We Learned?,' in R. Dornbusch (ed.), *Dollars, Debts and Deficits*, Cambridge, MA: MIT Press, pp. 151–65.

Dornbusch, Rudiger (1997), 'The Folly, the Crash and Beyond: Economic Policies and the Crisis,' in S. Edwards and M. Naim (eds), *Mexico 1994: Anatomy of an Emerging-Market Crash*, Washington, DC: Carnegie Endowment for International Peace, pp. 125–40.

Edwards, Sebastian (1989), *Real Exchange Rates, Devaluation and Adjustment*, Cambridge, MA: MIT Press.

Edwards, Sebastian (1998), 'Capital Controls are not the Reason for Chile's Success,' *Wall Street Journal*, April 3: A19.

Edwards, Sebastian (1999), 'How Effective are Capital Controls?,' *Journal of Economic Perspectives*, **13**: 65–84.

Edwards, Sebastian and Alejandra Cox Edwards (1987), *Monetarism and Liberalization: The Chilean Experiment*, Cambridge, MA: Ballinger.

Eichengreen, Barry (2000) 'Taming Capital Flows,' *World Development*, forthcoming.

Eichengreen, Barry and Andrew Rose (1998), 'Staying Afloat When the Wind Shifts: External Factors and Emerging-Market Banking Crises,' National Bureau of Economic Research Working Paper, No. 6370.

Eichengreen, Barry and Donald Mathieson (1999), 'Hedge Funds: What do We really Know?,' *IMF Economic Issues*, No. 19, September.

Eichengreen, Barry, Andrew Rose and Charles Wyplosz (1996), 'Contagious Currency Crises: First Tests,' in T.M. Andersen and K. Moene (eds), *Financial Liberalization and Macroeconomic Stability*, Oxford: Blackwell Publishers, pp. 1–23.

Feldstein, Martin (1998), 'Refocusing the IMF,' *Foreign Affairs*, **77**: 20–33.

Fischer, Stanley (1998), 'The Asian Crisis and the Changing Role of the IMF,' *Finance and Development*, **35**: 2–5.

Goldstein, Morris (1998), *The Asian Financial Crisis: Causes, Cures and Systemic Implications*, Washington, DC: Institute for International Economics.

Hanushek, E. and D. Kim (1995), 'Schooling, Labor Force Quality and Economic Growth,' National Bureau of Economic Research Working Paper, No. 5399.

Henderson, Callum (1998), *Asia Falling*, New York: McGraw Hill.

Hernandez, Leonardo and Klaus Schmidt-Hebel (1999), 'Capital Controls in Chile: Effective? Efficient? Endurable?,' Central Bank of Chile Working Paper, Santiago, Chile.

Hill, Hal (1996), The Indonesian Economy Since 1996, Cambridge: Cambridge University Press.

International Finance Corporation (1998), *Emerging Stock Markets Factbook 1998*, Washington, DC: International Finance Corporation.

International Finance Corporation (1999), *Emerging Stock Markets Factbook 1999*, Washington, DC: International Finance Corporation.

International Monetary Fund (1996), *World Economic Outlook*, Washington, DC: International Monetary Fund.

International Monetary Fund (1998), *World Economic Outlook*, Washington, DC: International Monetary Fund.

International Monetary Fund (1999), *International Financial Statistics Yearbook*, Washington, DC: International Monetary Fund.

International Monetary Fund (2000), *World Economic Outlook*, Washington, DC: International Monetary Fund, April.

Johnston, R. Barry (1991), 'Distressed Financial Institutions in Thailand: Structural Weaknesses, Support Operations, and Economic Consequences,' in V. Sundararajan and Tomas Balino (eds), *Banking Crises: Cases and Issues*, Washington, DC: International Monetary Fund, pp. 234–75.

Kaminsky, Graciela L. and Carmen M. Reinhart (1998), 'Financial Crises in Asia and Latin America: Then and Now,' *American Economic Review*, **88**: 444–48.

Kaminsky, Graciela L. and Carmen M. Reinhart (1999), 'The Twin Crises: The Causes of Banking and Balance of Payments Problems,' *American Economic Review*, **89**: 473–500.

Krongkaew, Mehdi (2000), 'Mitigating the Social Cost of Financial Crisis in East Asia: Experiences and Policy Lessons,' paper presented at the Workshop on Managing Capital Flows in a Volatile Financial Environment, World Bank Institute, Bangkok, February 21–24.

Krugman, Paul (1979), 'A Model of Balance of Payments Crises,' *Journal of Money, Credit and Banking*, **11**: 311–25.

Krugman, Paul (1994), 'The Myth of Asia's Miracle', *Foreign Affairs*, **73**: 62–78.

Krugman, Paul (1998), 'What Happened to Asia?,' mimeo, Department of Economics, Massachusetts Institute of Technology.

Krugman, Paul (1999), 'Analytical Afterthoughts on the Asian Crisis,' mimeo, Department of Economics, Massachusetts Institute of Technology.

Lindgren, Carl-Johan, Gillian Garcia and Matthew Saal (1996), *Bank Soundness and Macroeconomic Policy*, Washington, DC: International Monetary Fund.

McKinnon, Ronald and Huw Pil (1996), 'Credible Liberalization and International Capital Flows: The Overborrowing Syndrome,' in T. Ito and A. Krueger (eds), *Financial Deregulation and Integration in East Asia*, Chicago: University of Chicago Press, pp. 220–45.

Montgomery, John (1997), 'Indonesian Financial System: Its Contribution to Economic Performance and Key Policy Issues,' in John Hicklin, David Robinson and Anoop Singh (eds), *Macroeconomic Issues Facing ASEAN Countries*, Washington, DC: International Monetary Fund, pp. 231–52.

Montiel, Peter J. (1997), 'Exchange Rate Policy and Macroeconomic Management in ASEAN Countries,' in John Hicklin, David Robinson and Anoop Singh (eds), *Macroeconomic Issues Facing ASEAN Countries*, Washington, DC:International Monetary Fund, pp. 253–98.

Nascimento, Jean-Claude (1991), 'Crisis in the Financial Sector and the Authorities' Reaction: The Philippines,' in V. Sundararajan and Tomas Balino (eds), *Banking Crises: Cases and Issues*, Washington, DC: International Monetary Fund, pp. 175–233.

O'Brien, Timothy, Edmund Andrews, and Sheryl WuDunn (1998), 'Covering Asia with Cash: Banks Poured Money into Region Despite Warning Signs,' *New York Times*, 28 January.

Radelet, Steven and Jeffrey Sachs (1998a), 'The East Asian Financial Crisis: Diagnosis, Remedies and Prospects,' *Brookings Papers on Economic Activity*, No. 1, 1–74.

Radelet, Steven and Jeffrey Sachs (1998b), 'The Onset of the East Asian Financial Crisis,' National Bureau of Economic Research Working Paper, No. 6680, August.

Rivera-Batiz, Francisco L. (1996), 'The Economics of Technological Progress and Endogenous Growth in Open Economies,' in G. Koopmann and H.E. Scharrer (eds), *The Economics of High-Technology Competition and Cooperation in Global Markets*, Baden: Nomos Verlagsgesellschaft, pp. 31–62.

Rivera-Batiz, Francisco L. (1999a), 'The East Asian Financial Crisis: What Went Wrong?,' in Lin Guijun and C. Jayachandran (eds), *China in the Globalization of the World Economy*, Beijing: University of International Business and Economics Press, pp. 20–30.
Rivera-Batiz, Francisco L. (1999b), 'Education and Economic Development: The Case of East Asia,' Working Paper, Program in Economic Policy Management, Columbia University.
Rivera-Batiz, Francisco L. (2000), 'Foreign Direct Investment in Latin America: Current Trends and Future Prospects,' in United Nations, *Interregional Cooperation in Trade and Investment: Asia-Latin America*, Bangkok: United Nations Economic and Social Commission for Asia and the Pacific, pp. 161–91.
Rivera-Batiz, Francisco L. and Luis A. Rivera-Batiz (1994), *International Finance and Open Economy Macroeconomics*, Englewood Cliffs, NJ: Prentice-Hall.
Rivera-Batiz, Luis A. and Paul Romer (1991), 'Economic Integration and Endogenous Growth,' *Quarterly Journal of Economics*, **10**: 531–56.
Rodrik, Dani (1995), 'Getting Interventions Right: How South Korea and Taiwan Grew Rich,' *Economic Policy*, **21**: 53–107.
Romer, Paul M. (1990), 'Endogenous Technological Change,' *Journal of Political Economy*, **98**: S71–S102.
Stiglitz, Joseph (1998), 'Bad Private-Sector Decisions,' *Wall Street Journal*, February 4.
Sundararajan, V. and T. Balino (1990), 'Issues in Recent Banking Crises in Developing Countries,' IMF Working Paper, WP-90–19, Washington, DC, March.
Wessel, David and Bon Davis (1998), 'Limits of Power: How Global Crisis Grew Despite Efforts of a Crack U.S. Team,' *Wall Street Journal*, September 24: A1, A10.
Woo, Wing Thye and Anwar Nasution (1989) 'The Conduct of Economic Policies in Indonesia and its Impact on External Debt,' in Jeffrey D. Sachs (ed.), *Developing Country Debt and the World Economy*, Chicago: University of Chicago Press, pp. 101–20.
World Bank (1993), *The East Asian Miracle: Economic Growth and Public Policy*, Oxford: Oxford University Press.
World Bank (1995), *World Tables*, Baltimore, MD: Johns Hopkins University Press.
World Bank (1996), *Managing Capital Flows in East Asia*, Washington, DC: World Bank.
World Bank (1997), *Global Economic Prospects and the Developing Countries*, Washington, DC: World Bank.
World Bank (1998), *East Asia: The Road to Recovery*, Washington, DC: World Bank.
World Bank (1999), *Global Development Finance*, Washington, DC: World Bank.
World Bank (2000a), *Global Development Finance*, Washington, DC: World Bank.
World Bank (2000b), *Global Economic Prospects and the Developing Countries*, Washington, DC: World Bank.
World Bank (2000c), *World Development Report 1999–2000*, Oxford: Oxford University Press.
World Bank (2000d), *World Development Indicators 2000*, Washington, DC: World Bank.

3. An historical perspective on the East Asian crisis

Michael D. Bordo

As an economic historian of financial crises, the most obvious perspective that comes to my mind about the East Asian crisis is that we have seen it all before. In many ways I believe that there is a lot of truth to that statement but there are also some basic differences between the recent set of crises and those of the past. In what follows I will make comparisons between the crises of the previous golden age of globalization, the last quarter of the nineteenth century ending with World War I, and those in this decade. In many respects the crises of the inter-war period, like those of the 1960s, reflect systemic problems with the international monetary system and need a slightly different perspective than the East Asian crisis.

1. BACKGROUND: GLOBALIZATION IN HISTORICAL PERSPECTIVE

As background to our discussion of the crises of the past and of the present it is important to note that the present era of massive capital flows to emerging countries, of integration of financial markets and of greatly reduced barriers to international trade, has many similarities to the five decades before 1914 – the Victorian golden age. Some authorities agree that international financial markets were even more integrated before World War I than they are today. They were bound together by the corset of the gold standard. Capital flowed across borders undeterred by currency risk or exchange controls. Interest rates on government securities denominated in different currencies converged strongly. International capital movements, scaled by the income of the countries concerned, reached levels never matched subsequently. The integration of capital markets was reinforced by and in turn reinforced the integration of labor and commodity markets. International migration reached high levels and the growth of trade outstripped the growth of income.

Evidence for the golden age of capital market integration can be seen in the net flows of capital from the core countries of Western Europe (Great Britain, France, Germany, Netherlands, Belgium) to the overseas regions of recent settlement (the Americas and Australia). At its peak, the outflow from Britain reached 9 per cent of Gross National Product (GNP) and was almost as high in France, Germany, and the Netherlands (Bairoch and Kozul-Wright 1996). Private capital moved essentially without restriction. Much of it flowed into bonds financing railroads and other infrastructure investments and into long-term government debt. Figure 3.1 shows five-year moving averages of the mean absolute value of the ratio of the current account balance to Gross Domestic Product (GDP) for 12 countries: Argentina, Australia, Canada, Denmark, France, Germany, Italy, Japan, Norway, Sweden, United Kingdom, and the United States. The data are obtained from Bordo et al. 1998. Figure 3.2 shows current account balances for one large capital exporter, the United Kingdom, one large capital importer, Canada, and the largest 'emerging market,' the United States. A striking feature of these data is the size and persistence of current account deficits in the pre-1914 period, especially in Australia, Canada, Argentina, and the Nordic countries and of the current account surpluses of the UK and France.

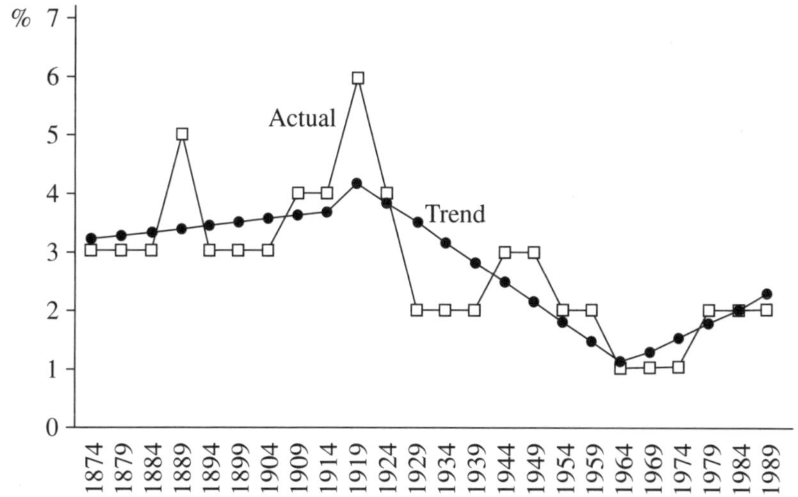

Source: Bordo et al. 1998.

Figure 3.1 External capital flows of selected countries, as percentage of GDP, five-year moving averages

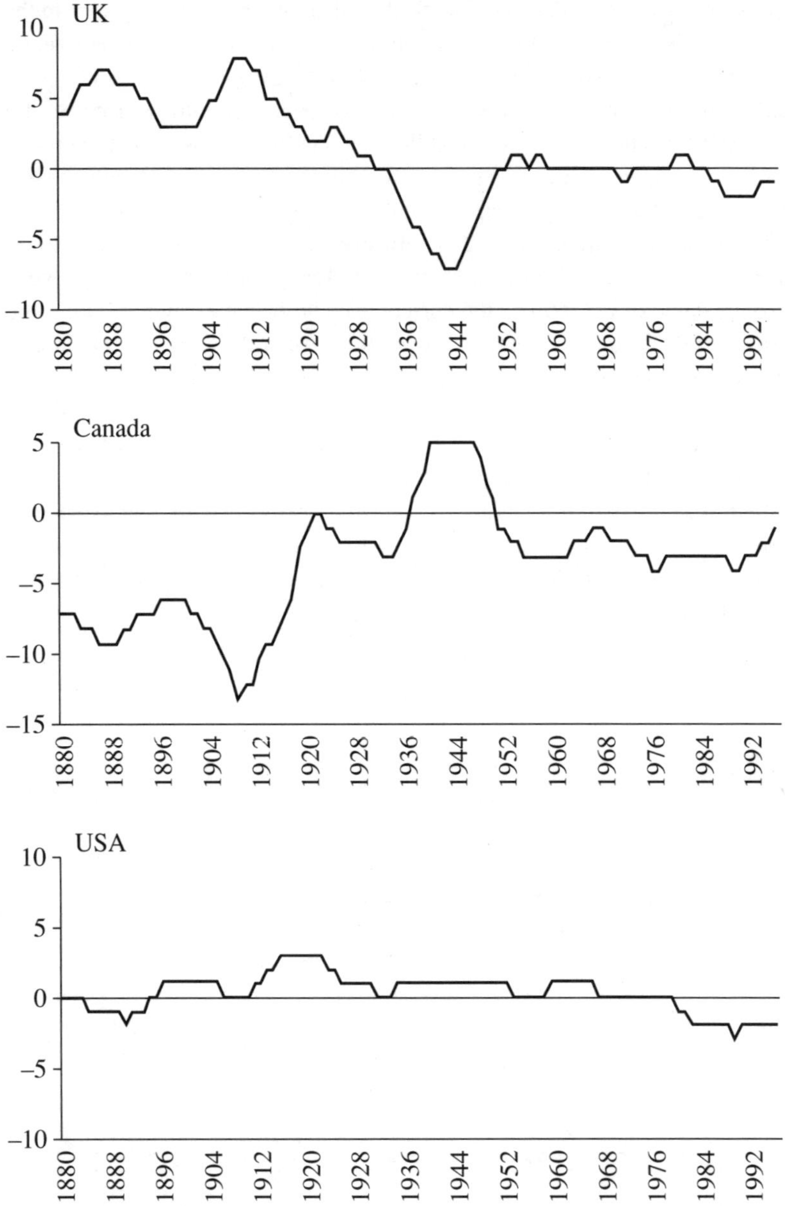

Source: Bordo et al. 1998.

Figure 3.2 Ratio of the current account to GDP, selected major countries

For comparison, Figure 3.3 shows the mean absolute value of the ratio of current account to GDP for 22 of today's emerging markets using data from the International Monetary Fund's *International Financial Statistics* for the period 1949 to 1996. The 22 selected countries, which had GDP that exceeded 30 billion dollars and were classified as indebted countries by the World Bank, are: Algeria, Brazil, Chile, China, Colombia, Egypt, Hungary, India, Israel, Korea, Malaysia, Mexico, Morocco, Pakistan, Peru, Philippines, Poland, Romania, South Africa, Thailand, Turkey and Venezuela. These countries were running current account imbalances under the recent managed float averaging 4.1 per cent of their GDPs, which is similar to the average for the prewar sample of 3.9 per cent which includes both capital importers and exporters.

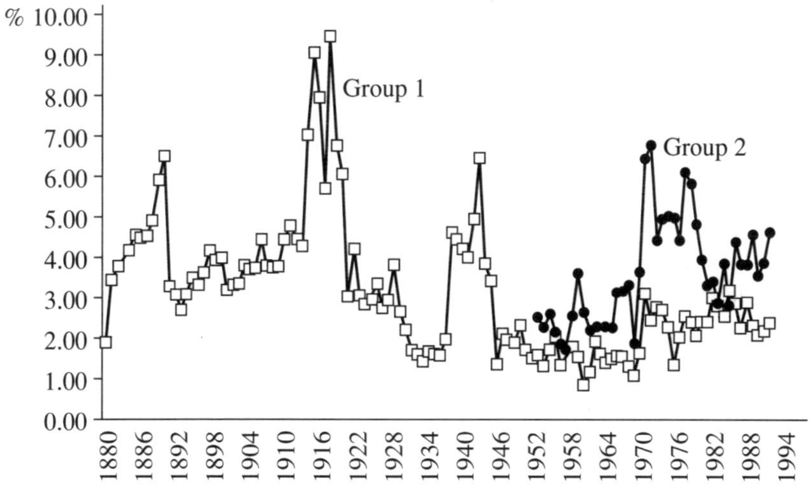

Source: Bordo et al. 1998

Figure 3.3 Ratio of current account to GDP, mean of absolute values

Net capital flows to emerging countries however are more variable now than they were then. Also the capital flows then were considerably more persistent than now. This is based on evidence in Bordo et al. (1998) using Phillips Perron Z tests and variance ratios. The greater persistence of current account deficits before 1914, or to put it another way: the lack of current account reversals, may provide some insights into recent events. Factors that could explain both the greater size and greater persistence of net capital flows before 1914 include the following:

1. The greater credibility of policymakers' commitment to stable monetary and fiscal policies as manifested in adherence to the gold standard, which I argue (Bordo and Rockoff 1996) acted as a 'good housekeeping seal of approval.'
2. The fact that most British investment went to former colonies where the British heritage was strong or commercial ties longstanding (e.g. Argentina). A similar story can be said for France. By comparison, today's capital recipients tend to be very different from the capital exporters.
3. Much of the capital flowing to the New World went to finance railroads and other infrastructure. This investment required a long-term commitment because of its very nature; the returns only accrued when the project was completed. Infrastructure investment in today's emerging countries does not dominate to the same extent.
4. Prewar investment went into export-related and natural resource-related projects that generated a stream of foreign exchange revenues sufficient to pay the money back – it did not give rise to balance of payments problems.
5. Greater flexibility in nineteenth century economies so that a shift in capital flows which implied the need to reallocate resources between sectors producing traded and non-traded goods could be easily accommodated.

Thus, today's globalized capital market may be inherently less stable and prone to reversals than in the golden age.

2. LENDING BOOMS AND BUSTS

Just as in the recent period, foreign capital flows to emerging markets were subject to booms and busts. The classic case is that of foreign portfolio investment to Latin America which went through four cycles before World War II. Carlos Marichal in his book *A Century of Latin American Debt Crises*, documents the fascinating record.

The first wave occurred in the 1820s when British capital flowed into the newly independent nations of Latin America to finance gold and silver mines and infrastructure. The boom led to massive speculation in the London Stock Market in many stocks of fictitious or dubious character culminating in a crash and banking panic. All the new states defaulted on their debt and did not regain access to foreign capital for decades until they renegotiated their debts and paid into arrears. After being burned in South America, British capital shifted to the USA into the securities of states financing canals and early railroads. When many states defaulted on their debts in 1842 at the nadir of one of the worst recessions of the nineteenth century, British capital pulled out of the USA for a number of years.

The second Latin boom was in the 1850s and 1860s to finance railroads. It ended with the crisis of 1873 and massive defaults. The third wave, shown very clearly in Figure 3.4, involved the massive flow of British portfolio investment to Argentina and Uruguay in the 1880s, again to finance railroads and infrastructure. The boom ended with a crash in 1890 and a debt moratorium. This triggered the Barings crisis in London. The famous investment house of Barings, that had underwritten many Argentine bonds, was revealed to be insolvent. A money market panic was prevented by the Bank of England's coordination of a lifeboat operation in which other banks, backstopped by the Bank of England (in turn buttressed by loans from the Bank of France), reflated Barings. Argentina was not rescued, it was cut off from British capital until it had renegotiated its debt and established a stable financial regime. British lending did not resume for years and in 1914, World War I permanently shut off the British spigot.

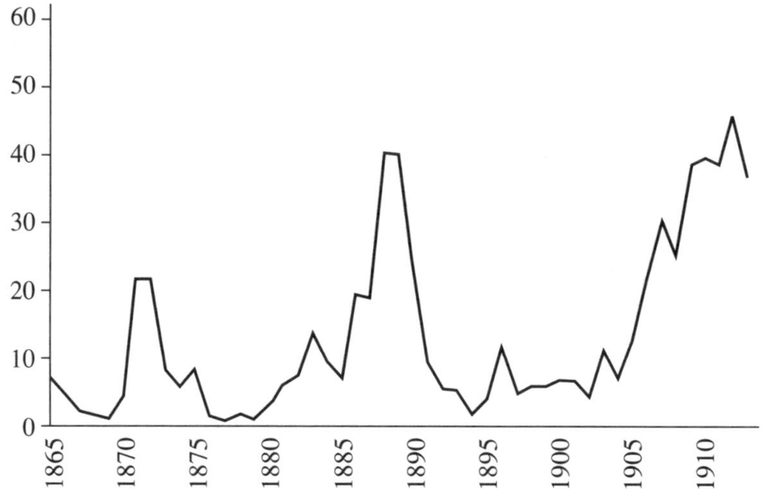

Source: Marichal (1999).

Figure 3.4 British portfolio investment in Latin America 1865–1913 (millions of pounds sterling)

The last historic wave of portfolio investment to Latin America was from the USA in the 1920s, largely into municipal infrastructure. That ended with the Great Depression and defaults by virtually every debtor country.

The lesson we learn from history is that there has always been optimism followed by pessimism in a world with imperfect and asymmetric information. Lenders are not fully informed about internal conditions in emerging countries, and borrowers may not put the funds made available to their best use. Moreover, in the pre-1914 era, adherence to the gold standard, by reducing currency risk, made lending attractive just as did pegging to the dollar in the recent period.

3. CONTAGION

What about contagion? Were the crises of the pre-1914 period characterized by the so-called contagious effects of the recent crises? The answer I believe is that contagion is a misnomer and the correct term is transmission. In the golden age, financial crises were transmitted across the world through the links of the fixed exchange rate gold standard. Crises associated with banking panics in the USA spread to England and the continent in 1857 and in 1893 and 1907. They also went the other way. They were transmitted via arbitrage in capital markets and via the current account. Virtually every crisis in Europe led to a worse event in the peripheral world.

There is evidence that shocks to important financial institutions in London from defaults in one country would lead to a restriction in lending to other borrowing countries. The evidence also suggests that the British investors as a whole were able to distinguish between solvent and insolvent borrowing countries. Thus Davis and Huttenback (1988) show how British capital alternated between the USA, Canada, Australia, Argentina, and other countries reflecting the ebb and flow of their prospects. The historical record suggests few instances of 'pure' contagion where lending to completely innocent parties was cut off.

4. THE DIFFERENCE BETWEEN NOW AND THEN

What is different in today's boom–bust episodes from earlier ones is the belief that domestic financial institutions are protected by an internal safety net and that foreign lenders will not suffer losses on their loans in hard currencies because funds to compensate them will be made available by the multiple international lending agencies and the monetary authorities of the advanced countries. In earlier times, losses were actually sustained by lenders, and by borrowers who were then cut off from further loans. Eventually, settlement of outstanding debts was reached, but at the cost of cessation of economic growth.

Moral hazard weakens incentives for lenders to monitor the performance of both the private and public sectors where they invest. By contrast, in earlier times, presumably both borrowers and lenders learned the hard lesson that caution paid. Thus although there were crises, although there were wealth losses and declines in income, the record suggests that the wealth losses from today's crises (seen in the size of the fiscal transfers to restructure banking systems and the international rescue packages), in which the market incentives of prudence in lending have been muted by moral hazard and the knowledge that big bailouts are forthcoming, may be much larger.

REFERENCES

Bairoch, Paul, and Richard Kozul-Wright (1996), 'Globalization Myths: Some Reflections on Integration, Industrialization, and Growth in the World Economy,' United Nations Conference on Trade and Development, Discussion Paper No. 113, March.

Bordo, Michael D. and Hugh Rockoff (1996), 'The Gold Standard as a Good Housekeeping Seal of Approval,' *Journal of Economic History*, **56**: 389–428.

Bordo, Michael D., Barry Eichengreen and Jongwoo Kim (1998), 'Was There Really an Earlier Period of International Financial Integration Comparable to Today?,' National Bureau of Economic Research Working Paper 6738, September.

Davis, Lance and Robert Huttenback (1988), *Mammon and the Pursuit of Empire*, Cambridge: Cambridge University Press.

Marichal, Carlos (1989), *A Century of Latin American Debt Crises*, Princeton, NJ: Princeton University Press.

Marichal, Carlos (1999), 'Latin America's Financial Crisis in Historical Perspective,' lecture presented to the IMF Institute Mini-Course *Financial Crises in Historical Perspective*, Washington DC, February 1999.

PART II

Causes and Consequences of the Crisis

4. The politics of moral hazard: The origins of financial crisis in Indonesia, Korea and Thailand

Stephan Haggard and Andrew MacIntyre

1. INTRODUCTION

While debate continues over the causes of the Asian economic crisis, there is growing consensus that weaknesses in the financial sector were implicated in its onset, propagation and depth. Inadequate supervision and prudential regulation of bank-dominated financial systems permitted high corporate leveraging and excessive risk taking (Krugman 1998; Caprio 1998).[1] Of the three countries considered here, all underwent bank-financed investment booms during which lending grew rapidly despite low and declining returns on capital. In all countries, these booms followed domestic deregulation that permitted new entrants, particularly weakly regulated non-bank financial institutions (NBFIs; finance companies in Thailand and Indonesia, merchant banks in Korea). Booms were further fueled by a particular regulatory failure that receives dominant attention in some accounts (Wade and Veneroso 1998): the mismanagement of capital account liberalization. Opening of the capital account left banks and firms with little experience in managing foreign exchange risks highly vulnerable to external shocks, particularly where liberalization favored short-term borrowing.

A final, more controversial issue is the extent to which these problems were the result of sins of omission, in the form of weak regulation, or of commission, in the form of explicit or implicit guarantees against losses that generated moral hazard. Such guarantees might have arisen as a result, *inter alia*, of industrial policy, cronyism and corruption, government fears about disruption of the payments system given the size of leading banks and companies ('too big to fail'), or deposit insurance (Chang 1999). These problems of moral hazard extended to foreign banks, which channeled lending through the domestic financial system in part because of implicit guarantees of stable exchange rates and even of repayment. Other accounts have made much of the additional moral hazard associated with the prospect of IMF lending in the eventuality of payments crises (Schwartz 1999).

In this chapter, we examine the government's management of emerging financial sector problems in order to assess these claims with respect to the role of moral hazard. Did mounting financial problems reveal that banks (both domestic and foreign) and their corporate clients expected the government to come to their rescue? If they did, and governments responded accordingly, then there would be merit to the moral hazard story. If governments did in fact have a credible no-bailout rule, then the claims for the significance of moral hazard would be exaggerated.

However, there is a third possibility: that there was *uncertainty* about what the government would do. This uncertainty might spring from a variety of political sources, but we focus on two. First, distressed banks and firms might doubt the credibility of the government's commitment to avoid bailouts, and thus engage in lobbying efforts to secure government support. Even if ultimately unsuccessful, these efforts could lead to a 'war of attrition' between the government and firms that delayed reform and rationalization, compounded the costs of adjustment, and reduced investor confidence (Alesina and Drazen 1991). We find evidence of these dynamics in all three countries. Second, broader institutional and political factors can reduce the capacity of the government to respond aggressively to crisis as well. In the two democracies, these factors included institutional arrangements, such as divided government in Korea, and characteristics of the party system, such as fragmentation in Thailand, which made coherent decision-making difficult. In authoritarian Indonesia, the problems included more fundamental uncertainty surrounding the viability of the government, and the complex of political property rights that went along with it.

Finally, some disclaimers. We do not present a general political theory of the politics of financial crises, nor do we claim causal sufficiency for the factors we highlight here. Our effort is primarily to underline the significance of political factors in the financial crises of the most seriously-affected countries. We are also aware of the risks of 20–20 hindsight; financial crises are difficult to foresee and manage for even the most politically cohesive and competent governments. However, it does appear that problems of moral hazard may be less important than politically-generated uncertainty in determining both the timing and intensity of the Asian financial crisis.

2. THAILAND

By late 1996 Thailand was coming off a remarkable economic boom, prolonged by the inflow of foreign capital. As real GDP growth slowed in 1996, two issues were of particular policy concern: the widening current account deficit (growing from an already-large 8.1 per cent of GDP in 1995 to 8.4 per cent in 1996) and unease about the health of the recently liberalized financial sector. In combination, these external and internal factors fueled growing speculation against the baht in the second half of 1996 (Bhanupong 1998; Warr 1998). Despite mounting concern over the apparent inevitability of some sort of currency depreciation, Thai authorities failed to address either of these problems in a credible way. Rather, they clung to a strategy of defending the pegged exchange rate, and ultimately fell victim to massive speculative attacks on 2 July 1997.

In the financial sector, the period of the late 1980s and early 1990s was one of dramatic liberalization (Vajragupta and Vichyanond 1998; Alba et al., Chapter 5, this volume). Beginning in 1989, the government liberalized interest rates and the scope of banks' activities widened considerably. The financial system had been dominated by a small group of 15 large commercial banks, but beginning in the 1970s, finance companies established a niche in the provision of consumer credit. With entry by new banks tightly limited, finance companies came to play an increasingly prominent role in the financial system. In the 1990s, a combination of legal changes and market pressures pushed them into more risky lines of business, including particularly the financing of real estate and share purchases.

On the external front, the government loosened capital controls in 1990 and initiated the Bangkok International Banking Facility (BIBF) in 1993. The initial objective of the facility was to promote Bangkok as a regional financial center (through offshore or so-called 'out-out' operations). Given a fixed exchange rate and substantial differentials between on- and offshore rates, the BIBF functioned in practice as a window through which domestic banks and corporates could borrow directly from abroad ('out–in' transactions). After 1993, international borrowing through the BIBF, particularly short-term borrowing, funded a rapid expansion of domestic credit. Despite some efforts to slow down the foreign borrowing boom after 1994 through the imposition of prudential controls, by 1996, foreign-funded domestic lending totaled 1.8 times the size of the country's monetary base.

Coupled with this increasingly vulnerable external position was a deterioration in asset quality. Finance companies' exposure to the property sector has received the most attention in subsequent analyses of the crisis, but over-investment in a variety of other industries ranging from petrochemicals and automobiles to private hospitals created substantial surplus capacity; government incentives were implicated in several of these sectors. Concern about non-performing loans and fear that the country's regulatory authorities (located in the Bank of Thailand) were not exercising adequate prudential oversight mounted in the mid-1990s, and the devaluation of the baht pushed the country into full-fledged financial crisis. By the second half of 1997 Thailand was beset with an estimated Bt1 trillion in bad debts held by banks and finance companies and the government had spent an estimated Bt430 billion in propping up failing financial institutions (roughly, $28.6 billion and $12.3 billion) (*Bangkok Post*, 14 August and 12 September 1997).

The question for political economy is how the government managed these emerging problems. We argue that political links between members of the government and financial institutions generated severe moral hazard problems by providing opportunities for failing financial institutions to protect themselves and to delay the process of financial restructuring. Where outright corruption was not implicated – and it frequently was – political forbearance towards the interests of the financial sector was.

Broader constitutional weaknesses compounded these problems. With some important differences, all of the democratically-elected governments prior to the crisis – Chaitichai, Chuan, Banharn and Chavalit – rested upon shaky multiparty coalitions, made up of internally weak and fragmented parties that not only provided opportunities for private interests to gain access to the policy process, but made that process extraordinarily contentious. Parliamentary majorities were constructed from a pool of approximately a dozen parties, and cabinet instability was a chronic problem. As leader of the governing coalition, the prime minister was vulnerable to policy blackmail by coalition partners, and in some cases individual ministers, threatening to defect in pursuit of better deals in another alliance configuration. The parties, in turn, were heavily reliant on national or provincial businessmen with strong personal as well as political interests in financial market (and other) economic policies.

These political barriers to coherent policymaking are highly visible in the management of Thailand's ailing financial sector. Early warning signs of the problems facing the country's financial institutions came as far back as 1991 when the Bank of Thailand (BOT, the central bank) detected irregularities in a struggling mid-sized bank, the Bangkok Bank of Commerce (BBC). Extending over several years, the BBC scandal was clearly important in denting the reputation of the central bank. More important for our purposes, however, is what the BBC saga reveals about the political constraints on coherent policy-making in Thailand.

A bank examination in 1991 revealed that 27 per cent of total assets at BBC were nonperforming (Nukul Commission 1998, para. 283). Subsequent examinations in 1993 and 1994 showed that the problem had only worsened, despite pressure on BBC from regulators to increase its capital. The Financial Institutions Development Fund (FIDF), established in 1985, had a wide range of powers at its disposal to assist and rehabilitate financial institutions whose collapse might have systemic effects, including write down of capital and replacement of management. However, the Fund also enjoyed substantial discretion and could support institutions through low-interest loans, deposits or purchase of convertible debentures and shares. After the 1994 examination, the government agreed to purchase a substantial stake in the bank through the FIDF, but without any write down of shareholder capital or reduction of management prerogatives. The central bank governor defended this action on the grounds that similar forbearance had been shown toward banks in the past! (Nukul Commission 1998, paras. 300 and 306).

As the extent of mismanagement at BBC became public in mid-1996 following disclosure by the opposition, there was a run on the bank. After having indulged BBC for an extraordinary period, the central bank finally took formal control of BBC, forcing the central bank governor to resign. Ultimately, a total of $7 billion was spent to keep BBC afloat. Although the FIDF recovered some of that money, the bailout set a dangerous regulatory precedent and severely damaged the reputation of the BOT, the FIDF and the regulatory process more generally. The Nukul Commission of inquiry sidestepped the issue of outright corruption, stating only that 'in a [sic] recent past, top BOT officials were inclined toward political interests' (para. 317). But several politicians within Prime Minister Banharn's Chart Thai party were known beneficiaries of large loans from BBC (*The Nation*, 13 March and 18 April 1997; Pasuk and Baker 1998, pp. 105–10, 259). The BBC saga came to life again under the Chavalit government when it emerged that criminal charges laid against several BBC executives had lapsed because Bank of Thailand officials had failed to act before the statute of limitations came into play in early 1997. Chavalit ordered the suspension of a deputy governor at the central bank and several other senior officials over the affair, but this did little to conceal the fact that politicians who were now members of his party maintained strong links to BBC.

In September 1996 Banharn's government collapsed after key coalition partners deserted him. After what was widely regarded as the country's dirtiest election, and having benefited from large-scale defections from Banharn's Chart Thai party, Chavalit's New Aspiration Party (NAP) narrowly emerged as the largest party in the parliament (*Far Eastern Economic Review*, 28 November 1996, pp. 16–22). Chavalit proceeded to construct a six-party coalition compromising most of the parties from the previous government. Nonetheless, he also signaled that he would appoint a cabinet built around an 'economic dream team' of highly respected technocrats, most notably Amnuay Viruwan as finance minister, to address the country's mounting economic difficulties.

The biggest area of concern in the financial sector was not the banks themselves, but the finance companies. By the end of 1996, Thailand's 91 finance companies (25 were pure finance companies and 66 performed both finance and securities functions) accounted for nearly 25 per cent of total credit (EIU 1998, pp. 31, 50). By the time the Chavalit government entered office, their difficulties were apparent to both domestic regulators and foreign investors:

the end of a prolonged property boom in late 1996; mounting nervousness about unhedged foreign liabilities given renewed speculative attacks on the baht; and the consequences of the central bank's misguided effort to help support the currency and dampen inflationary pressures through higher interest rates, an effort which only served to induce more foreign borrowing. By the end of 1996, six companies had requested assistance from the FIDF and the Fund had outstanding loans of about Bt30 billion (Nukul Commission 1998, para. 342).

Despite the effort to insulate economic policymaking from the vagaries of Thai politics, the logic of the country's political structure very quickly reasserted itself. On 5 February 1997 the first Thai company (Somprasong) defaulted on a foreign loan repayment. Late in the month, it was announced that the largest of the finance companies, Finance One, was seeking a merger with a bank to stave off collapse. By the end of February, FIDF assistance extended to 14 companies and totalled Bt50 billion (Nukul Commission 1998, para. 343). In the face of widespread fears of an impending financial implosion, finance minister Amnuay and central bank governor Rerngchai Marakanond suspended trading of financial sector shares on the stock exchange on 3 March and went on national television to announce a series of emergency measures designed to reassure nervous markets. The two key elements of the policy intervention were a requirement that all banks and finance companies make much stronger provision for bad loans and an announcement that ten of the weakest financial companies would have to raise their capital base within 60 days.

These measures did little to reassure financial markets, and when trading resumed the following day (4 March), financial shares fell heavily as depositors and creditors moved to withdraw funds. Underlying the market's nervousness were several factors, including doubts about the health of other finance companies and banks as well as about the government's ability to follow through with its restructuring plans. Such fears proved well founded. The original Ministry of Finance report showed that 18 finance companies and three banks faced difficulties, but the list was trimmed following direct intervention from the prime minister (Nukul Commission 1998, para. 368). Several senior members of Chart Pattana, the second largest party in the coalition, had controlling interests in some of the ten targeted institutions. Not only did they succeed in vetoing the plan and ensuring that no action was taken against the ten companies, but the very fact that they were permitted to remain open meant that – as with BBC – the central bank had to provide liquidity in order to keep them afloat in the face of runs by creditors and depositors. At the end of March, when 10 finance companies were suspended, FIDF assistance had been extended to 30 firms and totalled Bt130 billion.

The management of the financial market problems in March constituted a critical juncture in the development of the larger crisis in Thailand. Both Thai and foreign analysts expressed concern about the scale of the bad loan problem.

Amnuay and Rerngchai were unable to pursue the strict path favored by financial hawks: forcing shareholders to accept losses by allowing ailing institutions to fail. Nor were they prepared to permit foreign investors to take a controlling stake in these institutions. However, even the modest path they opted for – lifting capital adequacy provisions and singling out the weakest institutions for immediate attention – proved politically unattainable. These initiatives were effectively vetoed by other members of the ruling coalition, some with direct stakes in the institutions. Rather than risking the collapse of his new government by alienating Chart Pattana, Chavalit preferred to gamble on compromise and delaying measures.

The finance minister's inability to follow through on the modest plans he had outlined had a corrosive effect on investor confidence. Moreover, there were debilitating costs to delay. An unwelcome side-effect of injecting large-scale emergency funding into the ten failing finance companies was a substantial surge in the growth of monetary aggregates, which only served to sharpen the fundamental contradiction in the government's overall strategy with respect to the exchange rate. At the same time as it was pumping money into insolvent finance companies to keep them afloat, the central bank was also spending down reserves to prop up the exchange rate and avoid any substantial increase in interest rates. As was increasingly recognized by the markets, this was not a sustainable strategy. In mid-May the baht suffered its heaviest assault to date as both foreign investors and Thai nationals fled to the dollar (Siamwalla 1997, p. 2).

Frustrated by his inability to persuade the coalition's leaders in cabinet to move on more extensive financial sector reforms (as well as on other fronts, such as cutting more pork from the budget), Amnuay resigned from the government on 19 June. Within two weeks – on 2 July – the baht was cut loose, depreciating sharply and signaling the onset of the country's crisis.

However, the onset of the crisis did not, of itself, guarantee effective action. Upon taking office, Amnuay's successor, Thanong Badaya did seek to seize the initiative; on 27 June he announced the suspension of 16 finance companies (including seven of the original ten), giving them 30 days to implement merger plans. At the same time, however, the prime minister announced that no further finance companies would be closed, and that the government would guarantee the closed finance companies loans and deposits; both measures had profound implications for the FIDF, to which the remaining finance companies increasingly turned for support. Moreover, Thanong stumbled on the same obstacle as Amnuay: while he had won approval for the initiative, Chart Pattana leaders were again able to block its implementation. Not only did Chart Pattana succeed in preventing the closure or merger of the 16 finance companies, it also managed to persuade the central bank to continue injecting liquidity into the institutions. In late July, in the context of negotiations with the IMF, it was revealed that loans to the 16 finance companies totaled Bt430 billion, a figure that exceeded the total capital of the finance companies and equaled about 10 per cent of GDP.

A week later, on August 5, in an effort to restore confidence and to make a necessary policy prepayment on the IMF agreement,[2] Thanong, announced that a further 42 finance companies would be suspended. A total of 58, or two-thirds of the country's finance companies, had now been suspended. Like the earlier 16, this batch was given a short period in which to meet tough new capital adequacy rules, merge with stronger institutions, or go out of business. However, charges of corruption and conflict of interest surfaced with respect to the committee given the responsibility of reviewing the finance companies' rehabilitation efforts. These concerns led to further delays, and were only overcome in late August when Virabhongsa Ramangkura, a respected technocrat newly appointed as deputy prime minister in a hurried cabinet reshuffle in mid-August, installed Amaret Sila-on, the respected head of the Thai Stock Exchange, to oversee the process (*Bangkok Post*, 26 August 1997).

But as one section of the government was moving to force an overhaul of the financial sector, another was moving in precisely the opposite direction. With the deadline for deciding the fate of the suspended finance companies looming, the politics of reform intensified. In early October, the Association of Finance Companies vigorously courted Chart Pattana leader Chatichai as well as Prime Minister Chavalit seeking a relaxation of the criteria for rehabilitation. The IMF responded by publicly expressing concern that the independence of Amaret's screening committee not be undermined. Nevertheless, a week later he resigned after only a short tenure, declaring that he was being undercut by forces within the government (*Bangkok Post*, 12 October 1997). Further concessions were soon made to Chart Pattana and the finance companies. Announcing the creation of two new independent agencies to handle the evaluation and processing of the finance companies, Thanong also revealed that the deadline for their restructuring would now be extended (without a new date being set) and that loans earlier extended to the ailing finance companies by the central bank could be treated as equity. This move increased the probability that the public resources injected into these companies – which had continued to increase (*Bangkok Post*, 14 August 1997; Nukul Commission 1998, paras. 343–346) – would never be recovered (*Bangkok Post*, 14 October 1997). In another successful rearguard move, Chart Pattana succeeded in holding up the approval by cabinet of the plans for the two new agencies announced by Thanong until text was inserted in the decrees specifically reversing their independence from the government (EIU 1998, p. 13).

By this stage, however, the crisis was forcing broader political realignments. On 19 October finance Minister Thanong resigned over the reversal of a petrol tax a mere three days after it had been announced as part of the government's IMF-backed program. In the wake of maneuvering in preparation for the formation of an expected new government led by Chart Pattana and impending defections in Chavalit's own party, the crippled prime minister announced his resignation on 3 November. Thailand was in very deep disarray.

The crisis in Thailand began to abate in 1998 when a new government under Chuan Leekpai committed forcefully to implement the IMF program and established an independent Financial Restructuring Agency which moved vigorously to close all but two of the 58 finance companies and force a more general process of financial restructuring. The new government was able to make some progress on these issues during an initial honeymoon period when it benefited from a clear sense of national emergency. But as 1998 progressed it too found itself subject to pressures similar to those of its predecessors.

To summarize, politics in Thailand exerted a powerful influence over policymaking with respect to the financial sector. There are clear signs of moral hazard related to the way the FIDF interpreted its mandate (Nukul Commission 1998, paras. 329–40), but the problems ran deeper. First, politicians with direct interests in regulated financial institutions were able to influence the government's decision-making, delaying an effective response to the problem. Second, and relatedly, both intra-coalitional and intra-party conflict frustrated the efforts of reformers. These political failings contributed to the onset of the crisis directly by weakening confidence in the Thai financial sector, and deepened it once the devaluation occurred by further delaying adjustment until the change of government.

3. KOREA[3]

As in Thailand, the roots of Korea's financial crisis are to be found in an investment boom. Unlike Thailand, investment was heavily concentrated in manufacturing, and within manufacturing in heavy and chemical industries dominated by the largest conglomerates (chaebol) (Haggard and Mo 1999). During 1994–96, facility investment grew by 38.5 per cent a year, and as in the past, firms relied heavily on bank borrowing to finance it. Because of the size of the Korean groups, the politics of the crisis took a somewhat different form than in Thailand. Rather than attention focusing initially on the insolvency of banks and finance companies, it was the weakness of several large chaebol that triggered concerns about bank solvency.

Also as in Thailand, liberalization of both the domestic financial markets and the capital account constitute an important backdrop to the boom. Korea proceeded in a highly gradual fashion in liberalizing its financial sector; throughout the 1980s, steps in the direction of privatization, deregulation and liberalization were frequently followed by reassertion of government controls. Beginning in 1991, however, the Kim Young Sam government initiated a new financial liberalization package that included deregulation of interest rates. After 1994, the government lifted administrative controls on the important commercial paper market, which led to a rapid expansion of short-term financing. In a heavily politicized process, the government converted 24 relatively weak finance companies into merchant banks in 1994–96 in order to provide them new business opportunities. Merchant banks lent aggressively, engaged in a variety of speculative activities such as investment in Russian bonds, and subsequently proved themselves the Achilles heel of the financial sector.

Liberalization of the financial market was not limited to the domestic front; in the name of globalization and entry into the OECD, the Korean government eliminated a number of barriers to Korean banks and firms borrowing abroad. The result was a sharp increase in foreign indebtedness, which stood at $78.4 billion at the end of 1995, $104.7 billion at the end of 1996, and $161.8 billion in November 1997, when the currency crisis broke. The composition of Korea's debt proved a particularly serious problem. Liberalization of the capital account took a perverse form, initially favoring short-term over longer-term borrowing. At the time the crisis broke, over half of the country's debt (54.9 per cent) was short-term, which naturally created tremendous vulnerability to investor panic.[4] Failure to roll-over short-term debt on the part of American, European and Japanese banks was one of the precipitating causes of the crisis.

The question of the role of moral hazard in Korea's financial crisis has been a hotly contested one. Leipziger (1998; pp. 3), for example, argues that with an average debt–equity ratio on the part of the top 30 chaebol of 363 per cent in 1996, 'it became clear that domestic lenders were quasi-equity partners in industry.' He infers that this high leveraging was itself evidence of moral hazard, since 'no respectable banker should have been lending to the chaebol under these circumstances were they not assured that Government would make sure that losses were managed in the event of a downturn.' He also notes that banks had access to overdraft facilities at the Bank of Korea. However, Chang (1999) has pointed out that this inference is not so obvious. Industrial policy had peaked in Korea in the late 1970s, and been gradually dismantled over the 1980s; government direction no longer constituted a justification for counting on government support in the case of failure. Moreover, Chang documents that in fact a number of chaebol had been allowed to fail during the 1990s.

With some important modifications, our argument with respect to Korea parallels our discussion of Thailand. First, there is one important case of corruption – the Hanbo Group – which shows that at least some managers believed that they could gain access to credit through bribery. However, Hanbo's expectations proved misguided; unlike in Thailand, vigorous political competition, in the form of an impending election campaign, made it impossible for the government to come to Hanbo's rescue. However, the emergence of additional companies facing difficulty raised uncertainty about the government's true intentions, and whether it could in fact be blackmailed to come to firms' support. A protracted battle over support for Kia proved a seminal event in the unfolding of Korea's crisis, generating substantial uncertainty in the market even before the contagion from Hong Kong's stock market collapse in October that is generally seen as a precipitating factor in the crisis.

As in Thailand, the difficulties associated with the play of interests were compounded by broader institutional and political factors. The impending presidential election scheduled for December fragmented the ruling party and made it difficult to initiate important financial sector reform measures. The poor performance of the incumbent Kim Young Sam government, and the potential strength of the reformist opposition candidate, Kim Dae Jung, in capitalizing on that record, created divisions within the ruling party as presidential hopefuls and legislators sought to distance themselves from the government. These political factors blocked the passage of an important set of financial reforms and contributed to a more general uncertainty about the capacity of the government to respond to the crisis.

Any account of the onset of Korea's financial crisis must begin with the Hanbo scandal which broke in January. Although there were several failures of smaller chaebol in the second half of 1996, Hanbo was the country's fourteenth largest industrial group. The group was emblematic of the deeper problems among Korea's industrial groups. Hanbo had diversified rapidly into a number of capital-intensive activities, and banks finally balked at continuing to support the group's construction of a massive greenfield integrated steel facility. The government denied allegations of impropriety following the announcement of Hanbo's collapse. However, a series of subsequent bribery arrests and, above all, the arrest, National Assembly testimony, and conviction of the president's son, Kim Hyun Chul, revealed that prominent politicians had used their positions to influence lending to the group.

The disposition of the Hanbo case sent mixed signals about the government's intentions with respect to failing enterprises. The government made no effort to save Hanbo's management; the firm was effectively nationalized through the injection of new money. When two more of the top-30 chaebols folded – Sammi in March and Jinro in April – the government sought to orchestrate a more concerted response to the problem. On 18 April, 35 commercial and state banks announced an 'anti-bankruptcy' pact, under which they would continue to extend credit to any top-50 chaebol at risk and defer debt payments for 90 days, but only if the company was 'basically sound' and came up with a 'self-rescue' package of measures including layoffs, sale of assets and organizational consolidation. Since the anti-bankruptcy pact necessarily called the position of the banks into serious question, the government had to supplement the concerted lending and rescheduling effort with a new initiative to inject liquidity into the financial system through the purchase of non-performing assets. However, unlike the operation of the FIDF, this effort appeared to carry some conditionality with it. Market response to the plan was positive, and the stock market rallied sharply. However, beginning in July, Korean financial and foreign exchange markets entered a period of marked turbulence and uncertainty, and the government's management of the Kia bankruptcy was clearly a major cause. The Kia crisis broke on 23 June, when Kim Sun-Hong, chairman of the group, appealed directly to the government for assistance in persuading creditors not to call maturing loans. Kia differed from other chaebol in being both more focused – primarily on automobiles and linked sectors – and having wider ownership; unions were in fact one of the company's largest shareholders. On 15 July, the group's creditor banks placed it under the anti-bankruptcy pact on the basis of a rescue plan that included a reduction in the number of affiliates, real estate sales and layoffs.

What ensued was a highly politicized battle over the future of Kia, in which Kia's management sought to blackmail the weakened government into providing support. Refusing to resign, the group's chairman quickly denounced the loan package as inadequate and mobilized support for the company from suppliers, employees, competitors and the public at large through a 'Save Kia' campaign (*Korea Newsreview*, 26 July 1997, p. 16.) On 4 August, the banks postponed their final decision on the bailout package until 29 September and withheld further lines of credit in the interim.

Because of the high concentration of both the financial and corporate sectors, and the extraordinary leveraging of the latter, the difficulties of three or four major groups were enough to push the entire commercial banking sector into technical insolvency. On 25 August, the government announced measures to shore up the financial system, with a target of providing at least $8 billion of liquidity for the banking system (*Korea Newsreview*, 30 August 1997, pp. 24–5). At the same time, the government began to signal its impatience with the open campaign for intervention and support that Kia was waging, and with the entire anti-bankruptcy pact on the grounds that the uncertainty and delay over the future of the firm was itself becoming a major source of financial market uncertainty. The government began to send stronger signals that it wanted Kia's creditors to let the firm go bankrupt when the 29 September deadline passed.

The Kia management was unwilling to submit to court receivership (*pasan*), however, under which existing management would be replaced, and exploited an important loophole in Korean bankruptcy law to avoid it.[5] After having moved four subsidiaries toward court protection, Kia management filed for court protection for nine more on 22 September. One powerful weapon the government maintained in trying to force the creditors toward the receivership option was the threat that the government would not guarantee the foreign obligations – $687 million – of the firm if it sought court protection. Meeting on 25 September, Kang Kyung Shik and representatives of Kia's creditors announced their intention to seek receivership for the firm. At the final meeting of the creditors on 29 September, the creditors delivered an ultimatum: no further credit would be extended. Nonetheless, it took a full month, until 22 October, before the government intervened to definitively settle the Kia issue by ousting management and effectively nationalizing it.

Thus, by late October, the Korean banking system had been severely damaged not simply by the string of corporate bankruptcies themselves, but by a highly politicized and uncertain process which left the ultimate disposition of Kia and its creditors in limbo for months. Korea's tottering financial system was thus already on the verge of collapse when the shock from Hong Kong hit on 23 October. On 1 November, the Haitai Group announced it was unable to stave off bankruptcy, and Moody's and Standard & Poor's downgraded the credit rating of Korean banks on 3 November. Foreign banks began to refuse to roll over the short-term foreign debt of Korean financial institutions, the foreign press began to issue reports that the Bank of Korea's foreign exchange reserves were evaporating, and pressure on the exchange rate mounted, culminating in the effective devaluation of 21 November.

While the Hanbo scandal, anti-bankruptcy pact, and conflict over Kia were taking place, the government faced an additional set of problems in trying to initiate a broader package of measures to strengthen financial regulation. In the wake of the Hanbo scandal, the president initiated a Financial Reform Commission. Recognizing that any institutional restructuring would prove highly contentious within the bureaucracy, the Commission decided to proceed in two steps; first, to propose a series of regulatory measures that could be implemented immediately, and only then address the more difficult questions of institutional reform. The fate of this reform effort also had some influence on foreign perceptions of the government's capacity to act; to understand its fate requires further explication of the government's political weaknesses in 1997.

Following the Hanbo scandal, Kim Young Sam began to distance himself from the party and the party's nomination process. Lee Hoi Chang captured the nomination on 21 July, but he was unable to win a majority on the first ballot and only garnered 60 per cent on the second. Following his nomination, Lee showed a substantial lead in the polls and appeared on his way to victory in December. However, his popularity plummeted when it was revealed that his two sons had avoided military service for being underweight, quickly opening a debate within the party on whether he should be replaced. Another presidential hopeful, Rhee In Je, left the ruling party and launched his own campaign on 13 September, taking many of Kim Young Sam's supporters in the NKP with him and ironically strengthening Lee Hoi Chang's control of the party. Lee's chances were improved by the formation of an alliance with another candidate, Cho Soon, but Kim Dae Jung's position was also strengthened by an unlikely alliance with conservative candidate Kim Jong Pil; the combination of the ruling party's blunders and the alliance of the two Kims opened the possibility in the early fall that Kim Dae Jung might actually win the presidency.

In sum, the political background to policymaking in this period includes a severely weakened president and a divided ruling party headed by a candidate desperately trying to differentiate himself from the incumbent. Although National Assembly elections are not concurrent with the presidential elections in Korea, ruling party legislators naturally had concerns about the party's fate as well, and were disinclined to take actions that would damage the party in the run-up to the presidential elections.

In the meantime, the Financial Reform Commission had moved ahead with its more contentious institutional reform proposals, which involved three key features: increasing the independence of the Bank of Korea (BOK) from the Ministry of Finance and Economy (MOFE), but also stripping regulatory powers out of both the BOK and MOFE and locating them in an independent regulatory agency.[6] As the Financial Reform Commission itself did not have the power to draft legislation, the initiative had to pass through the MOFE, which had a strong interest in limiting the diminution of its powers; a first version of the bill effectively scuttled much of the Commission's reforms. A second version more in line with the Commission's intentions was ultimately submitted, but with few politicians seeing any gain from it, the ruling party and opposition agreed to postpone the legislation until after the elections.

However, with the crisis looming in late October and early November, the question of financial reform again received attention, in part at the insistence of the IMF; in secret discussions with the Korean economic team, IMF managing director Camdessus expressed explicit concern about the importance for the markets of passing the financial reform legislation and of guaranteeing that all presidential candidates would back the package.

At the end of the second week of November, it appeared that the package of financial reform bills was headed for passage. A subcommittee under the National Assembly's Finance and Economy Committee passed the package by a vote of 6–2 and passed it to the full committee for a vote on 14 November. However, one of the contentious issues in the reform package was the Financial Supervisory Board (FSB), which would consolidate a number of existing regulatory agencies, and whether it would be under the direct control of the prime minister or the minister of Finance and Economy, where the National Assembly believed it would have more oversight powers. The labor unions representing the Bank of Korea and the four agencies targeted for elimination were particularly opposed to the potential impact on agency employees. Bank of Korea workers demonstrated in front of New Korea Party headquarters on 13

November, and employees of the Securities Supervisory Board and the Insurance Supervisory Board protested in front of the National Assembly and Bank of Korea on the 14th (*Korea Herald*, 15 November 1997). The employees all threatened to strike immediately after the National Assembly passed the reform legislation, and a group of former central bank governors held a press conference to voice their opposition to the bills.

In principle, the ruling party could have passed the bills on its own, but Lee Hoi Chang's supporters were rightly concerned about the political cost of doing so. Kim Dae Jung did not want to alienate labor right before the election and could easily make an issue of the legislation; the ruling party thus preferred to consult with the opposition to secure their support. However, the opposition had few incentives to cooperate. If they signed on, they would be associated with potentially costly reforms, while if they postponed their assent, any negative economic effects of postponing the reform package would most likely rest at the feet of the president and the ruling party candidate, Lee Hoi Chang. Finance Minister Kang Kyung Shik and his staff tried in vain to persuade the National Assembly to pass the financial reform legislation on the last day of the session, but the Finance and Economy Committee didn't bother to send the bills to the floor for debate. As a result, Kang had failed to deliver the reforms as promised; for markets already increasingly unsettled by a number of other developments this was but one additional piece of bad news.[7]

We do not mean to dismiss the underlying sources of Korea's financial crisis in the overleveraged chaebol, a precipitous opening of the capital account, and shocks emanating from abroad, particularly in late October. Yet how the markets responded to these problems depended on investors' views of the government, and over the first three quarters of 1997, government behavior generated substantial uncertainty. First, and contrary to a pure moral hazard story, the Korean government did not rush to firms' and banks' rescue and in fact let a number of major firms fail. But there was initially substantial uncertainty about how the government would respond, which itself invited tests such as that posed by Kia. Even though the government ultimately stared Kia down, the prolonged period of uncertainty surrounding that case generated increasing doubts about the government's intentions.

These were compounded by larger political milieu which made it difficult for the government to initiate reform. By November, it is doubtful that passage of the reform legislation would have been able to reverse Korea's fortunes. However, the failure reflected a more fundamental stalemate in Korean politics of which investors and analysts were aware; that intra- and inter-party conflict in anticipation of the election was making it difficult for the government to respond effectively to the crisis. Only with the election of Kim Dae Jung was the government able to initiate the far-reaching financial and corporate reforms the country required.

4. INDONESIA

Of all the countries swept up in the Asian financial crisis, Indonesia's case is the most dramatic. This is particularly true given the fact that prior to the crisis, the country's key macroeconomic indicators provided few early warnings of impending crisis (Hill 1998; Radelet and Sachs 1998; World Bank 1998b). The current account deficit was substantial, with evidence of overvaluation, but the deficit was less than half of Thailand's and with no tell-tale signs of capital flight or speculation against the currency as there had been prior to the fall of the baht. Nor were there the signs of an asset bubble or overinvestment visible as in Korea and Thailand. And although there were clearly weaknesses in Indonesia's financial sector, through the third quarter of 1997, they were not seen as urgent or pressing problems. Nor is there a case to be made that the external crisis emanated from the financial sector, as was at least in part the case in Thailand and Korea. It is more plausible to argue that contagion from Thailand contributed to triggering the banking collapse not vice versa. Indeed, as late as the third quarter of 1997, financial reform was not seen as a pivotal issue for investor confidence. And yet by the fourth quarter of 1997 the situation had changed dramatically and the Indonesian banking system was in very deep distress.

In looking at the rapid collapse of the Indonesian financial sector, we focus on two factors. First, we follow a number of other commentators in noting a series of misguided (if well-intentioned) government policy actions that served to dramatically increase the banking sector's problems. However, these policy problems were compounded by the same type of uncertainty we have seen in the foregoing cases. Conflicting signals about the strength of the Suharto guarantee, compounded by broader institutional weaknesses, generated deep uncertainty among both crony and non-crony banks and firms, and paved the way for the rapid collapse of confidence within the banking sector.

The background to Indonesia's financial difficulties includes the combination of domestic financial liberalization and weak prudential regulation visible in Korea and Thailand. From having a very heavily regulated, small, and state-dominated financial sector, banking in Indonesia grew extremely rapidly in the decade prior the regional financial crisis (Cole and Slade 1996; Chant and Pangestu 1996; MacIntyre 1993). Crucial to this rapid change were two major rounds of financial deregulation in 1983 and 1988 which dramatically lowered the barriers for both local and foreign entrants to the banking sector. One result of this deregulation not evident to the same extent in Thailand and Korea was that industrial groups were able to acquire banking operations, with corresponding problems of intra-group lending. Recognizing these problems, Bank Indonesia (the central bank) introduced a series of additional reform packages from 1989 onwards to strengthen the prudential framework.

Yet quite apart from issues of straightforward corruption and cronyism, to which we return below, the central bank and finance ministry had limited capacity to monitor and enforce the new regulations. As former central bank governor Soedrajad Djiwandono (himself fired during the crisis for resisting Suharto) lamented, while the number of banks had doubled in the 1990s the size of the commercial bank supervisory staff at Bank Indonesia remained unchanged (author interview, 14 January 1999). Weak monitoring and enforcement capabilities meant that intra-group lending ceilings, capital-adequacy ratios, and limits on lending to the real estate sector were all susceptible to violation, with the attendant growth of non-performing assets.

Two contrasts with the other cases are also notable. Because commercial bank licenses were relatively easy to obtain (between 1988 and 1993 the number doubled, to 240) finance companies or merchant banks played a much less prominent role in the financial system than in Thailand or Korea. The fact that it was commercial banks rather than just NBFIs that were afflicted in Indonesia meant that the crisis had a much more profound effect on the payments system. A second difference is the extent to which foreign borrowing was intermediated through the financial sector. Because Indonesia had long had a fairly open capital account, corporations were able to borrow offshore directly. When the rupiah fell, the corporate sector was directly exposed, which fed back into the domestic banking sector.

As in the other cases, it has been argued that moral hazard problems lay at the heart of the financial crisis in Indonesia; indeed, Indonesia is held as the quintessential case of crony capitalism, in which direct political ties between Suharto's government and banks produced an assumed guarantee against failure.[8] As long-term observers of the Indonesian financial sector, David Cole and Betty Slade put it:

> in the 1990s the 'Suharto connection' became the 'guarantee' or collateral underlying the viability of many enterprises and financial institutions, most obviously in banking and securities markets. Any financial regulator who attempted to apply prudential rules to such connected financial institutions or transactions ... was removed from his position. Politics and connections dominated. (Cole and Slade 1998, p. 65)

The power and value of a genuine Suharto connection were widely understood. This was starkly illustrated in 1990 when Bank Duta, a private bank housing the substantial deposits of several shadowy political foundations controlled by Suharto himself lost nearly half a billion US dollars in foreign exchange speculation. Bank Duta was promptly rescued by two other large corporate groups with very close financial ties to Suharto, which in turn were quickly rewarded with other forms of state largesse (Schwarz 1994, p. 112).

It is important to remember, however, that the inner circle of Suharto family principals and core business associates was actually fairly small. Although the web of connected firms that fanned out from them was extensive, in any given sector only a small number of players were close enough to enjoy a bankable guarantee. Indeed, in principle, it cannot be otherwise as it is virtually axiomatic that a client- or crony-firm enjoys a privileged position that is valuable precisely because of its *scarcity*. The banks of Suharto family members or core-business associates do indeed constitute classic illustrations of moral hazard. But, as we shall see, the normally risk-free operating environment of crony financial institutions was called into doubt from late 1997 on as Suharto began sending mixed signals about the strength of their 'guarantee.'

That the great majority of banks could not count on the safety net enjoyed by the few strongly Suharto-connected banks is demonstrated clearly by the collapse of Bank Summa, just two years after the Bank Duta episode. Bank Summa was owned by the Astra group, the second largest industrial conglomerate in Indonesia. Despite its early association with Suharto, the Astra group had consciously distanced itself from the Suharto circle. When massive mismanagement caused Bank Summa to collapse, no assistance from the government was forthcoming and the Bank was forced into liquidation at enormous cost to the parent company (Cole and Slade 1996, pp. 136–7). If the Bank Duta experience illustrated the fail-safe guarantee of a Suharto connection, the Bank Summa experience illustrated that in the absence of a Suharto-connection anything could happen, even to a very large company.[9]

Indonesia's initial response to regional contagion was to widen the band within which the rupiah traded, and when this proved inadequate, to cut the rupiah completely free. As McLeod (1998a, 1998b) has argued, from this point the government proceeded to make a series of very damaging policy missteps. When the rupiah continued to fall sharply, not only did the central bank begin intervening sporadically in the currency market (thus undercutting the notion of a clean float), it also adopted an extremely contractionary monetary and fiscal stance in a bid to attract capital back into the country and support the currency. Although these orthodox measures were widely applauded at the time and served briefly to help slow the fall of the rupiah, it soon became apparent that they represented overkill, and effectively served to push the rupiah lower still.

As interest rates spiked sharply higher, lending to the property and construction sectors dried up and firms struggled to meet their dramatically increased repayment obligations. The same, of course, was also true for the many borrowers with unhedged dollar-denominated loans who were caught by the rupiah's fall. With assets in the property sector sharply devalued and with more borrowers defaulting on their loans, in part precisely because of the tight squeeze on liquidity, the banking sector was soon in serious difficulty.

Two months after floating the rupiah, in early October, the government turned to the IMF. The fourth quarter of 1997 – the period after the arrival of the IMF – proved to be pivotal. Up to this point, the government had demonstrated determined and focused policy action, albeit in a direction that had the unintended effect of making the situation worse. The IMF did not bring much that was new to the equation: it injected a small amount of additional capital,[10] but no markedly different ideas. The broad thrust of IMF advice with respect to macroeconomic policy was to maintain austere fiscal and monetary policy settings to support the currency. A number of sectoral adjustment measures cut deeply into core Suharto family and crony business operations. With respect to the banking sector, the diagnosis was to stop the downward spiral by closing insolvent banks so that confidence in the banking system as a whole would be restored and the flow of deposits and interbank lending might resume. These priorities fitted easily with the existing approach of senior economic technocrats within the government, who saw this as a sensible way of tackling the problems at hand and, coincidentally, as a golden opportunity to force difficult new economic reforms on Suharto.

Notwithstanding the logic behind this strategy, it failed in each and every respect, including with respect to the banking sector (see, *inter alia*, Radelet and Sachs 1998; McLeod and Garnaut 1998; as opposed to IMF 1999). More important for our purposes, however, were the powerfully conflicting signals that soon emerged from the government in its effort to implement the Fund program. Uncertainty centered on the value of a Suharto connection, and whether crony banks and firms would be saved or not. The uncertainty that resulted had clear consequences for investor confidence, both local and foreign.

Consistent with the desire to demonstrate its commitment to reform, the government moved very speedily to announce a number of policy measures, including the abolition of a number of crony import monopolies. On 1 November, 16 small banks (several controlled by relatives or cronies) were closed. On 3 November further major tariff cuts in industries affecting crony firms were announced, and Indonesia agreed to abide by the WTO's dispute settlement procedure with respect to its controversial national car project controlled by a Suharto son. The administration promised a review of 'strategic industries' falling under the portfolio of technology minister B.J. Habibie and the wholesale and distribution sectors were opened to foreign investors. These measures were impressive both for their speed and for the apparent willingness of the president to allow the privileges of allied business to be cut back.

However, at the very same time that Suharto was unleashing these reform initiatives, he was also taking rearguard actions which pulled in precisely the opposite direction. On 1 November, amidst the flurry of IMF-related initiatives, Suharto quietly signed a decree giving the green light to 15 big-ticket investment projects that had been postponed in September in the name of fiscal restraint. All of the rescued projects belonged to relatives or close cronies. By the end of the week, the president's second son and his half-brother declared in a public tirade that they would be suing the central bank governor and the finance minister for closing their banks. Although the decision to close these banks was not reversed, within two weeks the president's son announced that he had taken over another small bank and would transfer all the assets of his closed bank into the new one, making public mockery of the decision to close the bank in the first place.

The commitment to tight monetary policy was also called into question when the government allowed banks to borrow from the central bank's special liquidity credit facility to ease their acute operational difficulties. This gave rise to two problems. First, the borrowing resulted in a substantial increase in the money supply and the rapid upward revision of inflationary expectations. Second, as with the backsliding on structural reforms, it called into fundamental doubt the government's commitment to reining in crony privileges. Crony banks consumed the great majority of the emergency liquidity credit operation, with the Salim group's Bank Central Asia (BCA) soaking up Rp35 trillion (roughly US$7 billion in late 1997 prices), support equivalent to more than 500 per cent of its capital (*Jakarta Post*, 1 October 1998).[11] As was later publicly confirmed, crony banks immediately misappropriated the credits, siphoning them out of the country and even speculating against the rupiah.

The government's management of the emerging banking crisis was deeply unsatisfactory for Suharto-linked investors and non-Suharto-linked alike. For Suharto cronies, the prospect of having their banks closed, monopoly rents jeopardized, and lucrative infrastructure projects shelved was profoundly threatening; their business empires rested on such opportunities and the subsequent flows of credit that followed. Particularly worrying were the reputational costs: the value of these individuals to potential business partners was their ability to deliver a political connection and the value of that connection was now being called into doubt.

For non-Suharto-linked investors the situation was, if anything, even worse. The promises and actions which worried the cronies were of course a source of encouragement for non-cronies; they suggested that – as in major economic crises in past decades – Suharto would do whatever was necessary to restore confidence. Notwithstanding subsequent critiques of the macroeconomic elements of the technocrat/IMF agenda, at the time of its announcement the program was seen as promising an improvement of the business environment. However, as cronies fought to maintain their privileges, the resulting policy backsliding and outright reversals generated deep uncertainty as to Suharto's commitment to reform.

In short, both categories of investors were afflicted by the government's ambiguous policy actions. Crony investors could not be sure that their connection protected them. Non-crony investors could not be sure crony connections to Suharto had been weakened to the extent that a fairer business environment might emerge. Faced with this mounting uncertainty, the common reaction was to withhold investment and relocate liquid assets abroad. As indicated by the exchange rate, capital flight grew in momentum through November and December and became a torrent in January in response to a budget which only heightened uncertainty about the government's intentions.

But by this point, the damage to investor confidence was nearly irreversible, and larger institutional uncertainties came into play. Indonesia's political framework under Suharto was so massively centralized that sudden and strong policy action in almost any direction was possible. But because there were no institutional checks on executive authority by the president, decisive policy action could undertaken – and reversed – with relative ease (see MacIntyre 1999a, 1999b). Thus, while this institutional framework could underpin the rapid structural reforms of the 1980s, it could also produce the extreme policy fluctuations that proved so destructive to investor confidence in 1997 and 1998. Although the authoritarian nature of Suharto's regime enabled him to cling to office for several more months, the economic dislocation resulting from the exodus of capital produced sufficient social hardship to trigger a political backlash and the fragmentation of the political elite surrounding Suharto. On 21 May he finally stepped down, ushering in a new political era.

To summarize, three arguments have been advanced in this discussion of the Indonesian case. First, moral hazard is clearly part of the story of Indonesia's financial collapse, but the extent of moral hazard is neither as straightforward nor as widespread as many of the sweeping claims on the subject would suggest. Moral hazard pertained only to a small group of investors; there was ample evidence that others would not, in fact, be protected. Second, the course of economic policy in Indonesia in 1997 and 1998 reflected an underlying struggle over the strength and value of a political connection to Suharto; uncertainty over these political property rights generated broader policy and market uncertainty and lack of confidence. Finally, these effects were compounded by the very nature of authoritarian rule, which made highly capricious policy possible.

5. CONCLUSIONS

This chapter has as its objective an evaluation of the claim that moral hazard was at the center of the Asian financial crisis. We found evidence of moral hazard in all three cases: in Thailand's FIDF, in Korea's forbearance toward bank excesses, in Indonesia's cronyism. However, we also found that the nature of these guarantees was often highly ambiguous and contested. In Thailand, reformers made efforts to limit government commitments to poorly managed banks and finance companies, but without success. In Korea, both Hanbo and Kia, although for different reasons, thought that they would be supported, but weren't. Similar ambiguities in policy are visible in Indonesia, where Suharto's commitment to protect cronies proved highly uncertain.

We argue that this uncertainty is a crucial element in the onset and depth of the financial crises, as investors come to question the nature of government's policy commitments. In the cases just cited, conflicts among claimants, or between claimants and the government, generated this uncertainty. However, in each case we have isolated broader political factors – although not common ones – that induced uncertainty with respect to the government's stance toward the financial sector, ranging from Thailand's party system, to the breakdown of party coherence in Korea due to electoral competition, to the authoritarianism of the Suharto regime.

The implications of this review for policy appear straightforward; that credible commitments not to come to the assistance of firms is an important antidote to uncertainty over government intentions. But this policy advice, often given, is nearly circular – credible policy is credible – and begs the deeper political and institutional issues that breed moral hazard and policy uncertainty in the first place. Clearly, one important finding is the importance of increasing transparency and reducing corruption. Exposing the nature of private political commitments in itself is likely to generate opposition to their cost. Yet where corruption and cronyism are rooted in broader institutional structures, such as fragmented party systems or authoritarian rule, addressing financial market policy and corruption may not be enough, and more fundamental constitutional changes may be required to generate more coherent policy.

ACKNOWLEDGEMENTS

The authors gratefully acknowledge research grants from the International Center for the Study of East Asian Development (Kitakyushu, Japan), the Smith Richardson Foundation, the Institute on Global Conflict and Cooperation (University of California) and the Korean Research Fund. We also thank our colleagues at the Graduate School of International Relations and Pacific Studies in the Asian Financial Crisis Reading Group.

NOTES

1. Among the oft-cited regulatory failures were low capital-adequacy ratios; weak, and weakly enforced, lending limits to related managers and enterprises; permissive asset classification systems and provisioning rules; and in general, poor disclosure and transparency of bank operations (World Bank 1998a, pp. 34–5). These problems compounded the effects of weak institutional development of the banks themselves, which tended to lend on the basis of collateral and personal relationships rather than cash flow.

2. The IMF's $17.2 billion package was unveiled in Tokyo on 11 August.
3. The narrative in this section draws on Haggard and Pinkston 1999.
4. Capital account liberalization favored short-term debt over long, which substantially increased the country's vulnerability to shocks.
5. Under Korean law, firms may file for court 'protection' or 'mediation' (*hwa ui pob*). Under this procedure, management maintains its rights and if three-quarters of creditors agree, debt payments can be postponed and new credits extended. Banks may have an incentive to go along with this option since court receivership implies liquidation and certain losses.
6. The following is based on interviews with staff of the Financial Reform Commission and the Ministry of Finance and Economy.
7. On the initial failure of the IMF program, see Graham 1998.
8. The literature on Indonesia's modern political economy groans under the weight of accounts of clientelism and preferential treatment of favored firms (Robison 1986; MacIntyre 1994; Winters 1996).
9. In late 1996, Bank Indonesia Governor Soedradjad had been given approval by Suharto to close six struggling banks falling below prudential benchmarks. In the face of heightened political protest, Suharto directed that the action be held over until after the completion of the parliamentary elections in the second quarter of 1997 – after which events were overtaken by the crisis (interview, Soedradjad Djiwandono, 14 January 1999).
10. Notwithstanding the talk of an IMF package of up to US$43 billion for Indonesia, in practice only $3 billion was released to the government during this critical period, and this with no apparent clear purpose other than to support the currency – even though such an amount was so small as to be almost irrelevant for this purpose.
11. It is unclear exactly how much money was released through this liquidity credit operation. According to the *official* figures, the total may have reached Rp92 trillion, in which case BCA would have consumed more than a third on its own.

REFERENCES

Alesina, Alberto and Allan Drazen (1991), 'Why are Stabilizations Delayed?,' *American Economic Review*, **81**: 1170–88.

Bhanupong Nidhiprabha (1998), 'Economic Crises and Debt-Inflation Episodes in Thailand,' *ASEAN Economic Bulletin*, **15**: 309–18.

Caprio, Gerald (1998), 'Banking on Crisis: Expensive Lessons From Recent Financial Crisis,' Mimeo, World Bank Development Research Group, June.

Chang, Ha-Joon (1999), 'The Hazard of Moral Hazard: Untangling the Asian Crisis,' paper presented at the American Economic Association Meeting, New York, 3–6 January.

Chant, John and Mari Pangestu (1996), 'An Assessment of Financial Reform in Indonesia, 1983–90,' in Gerard Caprio, Izak Atiyas, and James Hanson (eds), *Financial Reform: Theory and Experience*, New York: Cambridge University Press, pp. 223–76.

Cole, David and Betty Slade (1996), *Building a Modern Financial System: The Indonesian Experience*, Melbourne: Cambridge University Press.

Cole, David and Betty Slate (1998), 'Why has Indonesia's Financial Crisis been so Bad?,' *Bulletin of Indonesian Economic Studies*, **34**: 61–6.

EI (Economist Intelligence Unit) (1998), *Country Profile: Thailand*, London: Economist Intelligence Unit.

Graham, Edward M. (1998), 'Korea and the IMF: What Went Wrong during the First Weeks Following the Bailout?,' *Cambridge Review of International Affairs* **11**: 31–54.

Haggard, Stephan and Robert Kaufman (1995), *The Political Economy of Democratic Transitions*, Princeton, NJ: Princeton University Press.

Haggard, Stephan and Jongryn Mo (1999), 'The Political Economy of the Korean Financial Crisis,' paper presented at the International Studies Association Meeting, Washington DC, 20–24 February.

Haggard, Stephan and Daniel Pinkston (1999), 'The Politics of the Korean Financial Crisis,' unpublished ms., University of California, San Diego.

Hill, Hal (1998), 'Southeast Asia's Economic Crisis: Origins, Lessons, and the Way Forward,' paper presented to the ISEAS 30th Anniversary Conference, Singapore, 30 July–1 August 1998.

IMF (1999), *IMF-Supported Programs in Indonesia, Korea, and Thailand: A Preliminary Assessment*, Washington, DC: International Monetary Fund.

Krugman, Paul (1998), 'Saving Asia: It's Time to Get Radical,' *Fortune*, 7 September, pp. 75–90.

Leipziger, Danny (1998), 'Public and Private Interests in Korea: Views on Moral Hazard and Crisis Resolution,' Economic Development Institute of the World Bank Working Papers.

MacIntyre, Andrew (1993), 'The Politics of Finance in Indonesia: Command, Confusion and Competition,' in S. Haggard, C. Lee and S. Maxfield (eds), *The Politics of Finance in Developing Countries*, Ithaca, NY: Cornell University Press, pp. 123–64.

MacIntyre, Andrew (1994), 'Power, Prosperity and Patrimonialism: Business and Government in Indonesia,' in A. MacIntyre (ed.), *Business and Government in Industrialising Asia*, Ithaca, NY: Cornell University Press, pp. 244–67.

MacIntyre, Andrew (1999a), 'Political Institutions and the Economic Crisis in Thailand and Indonesia,' in T.J. Pempel (ed.), *The Politics of the Asian Financial Crisis*, Ithaca, NY: Cornell University Press, pp. 143–62.

MacIntyre, Andrew (1999b), 'Political Parties, Accountability, and Economic Governance in Indonesia,' in I. Marsh, J. Blondel, and T. Inoguchi (eds), *Party Systems, Democracy, and Economic Governance in East Asia*, Tokyo: United Nations University Press, pp. 261–86.

McLeod, Ross (1998a), 'Indonesia,' in R. McLeod and R. Garnaut (eds), *East Asia in Crisis: From Being a Miracle to Needing One*?, London: Routledge, pp. 31–48.

McLeod, Ross (1998b), 'The New Era of Financial Fragility,' in R. McLeod and R. Garnaut (eds), *East Asia in Crisis: From Being a Miracle to Needing One?*, London: Routledge, pp. 333–51.

McLeod, Ross and Ross Garnaut (eds) (1998), *East Asia in Crisis: From Being a Miracle to Needing One*?, London: Routledge.

Muhaimin, Yahya (1991), *Bisnis dan Politik: Kebijaksanaan Ekonomi Indonesia 1950–1980*, Jakarta: LP3ES.

Nukul Commission (1998), *Analysis and Evaluation on Facts Behind Thailand's Economic Crisis*, (English edition), Bangkok: *The Nation*.

Pasuk Phongpaichit and Chris Baker (1998), *Thailand's Boom and Bust*, Bangkok: Silkworm Books.

Radelet, Steven and Jeffrey Sachs (1998), 'The East Asian Financial Crisis: Diagnosis, Remedies, Prospects,' *Brookings Papers on Economic Activity*, **1**: 1–90.

Robison, Richard (1986), *Indonesia: The Rise of Capital*, Sydney: Allen & Unwin.

Schwarz, Adam (1994), *A Nation in Waiting: Indonesia in the 1990s*, Sydney: Allen & Unwin.

Schwartz, Anna (1999), 'Asian Banking Crisis in the 1990s: All Alike?,' in C.G. Kaufman (ed.), *Research in Financial Services: Private and Public Policy*, Greenwich: JAI Press, pp. 25–48.
Siamwalla, Ammar (1997), 'Why Are We in this Mess?,' J. Douglas Gibson Lecture, School of Policy Studies, Queen's University, Ontario, October 15.
Vajragupta, Yos and Pakorn Vichyanond (1998), *Thailand's Financial Evolution and the 1997 Crisis*, Bangkok: Thailand Development Research Institute.
Wade, Robert and Frank Veneroso (1998), 'The Asian Crisis: the High Debt Model vs. the Wall Street–Treasury–IMF Complex,' *New Left Review* **228**: 3–22.
Warr, Peter (1998), 'Thailand', in R. McLeod and R. Garnaut (eds), *East Asia in Crisis: From Being a Miracle to Needing One*?, London: Routledge, pp. 49–65.
Winters, Jeffrey (1996), *Power in Motion: Capital Mobility and the Indonesian State*, Ithaca, NY: Cornell University Press.
World Bank (1998a), *East Asia: The Road to Recovery*, Washington, DC: World Bank.
World Bank (1998b), *Indonesia in Crisis: A Macroeconomic Update*, Washington, DC: World Bank.

5. Financial liberalization and the capital account: Thailand 1988–97[1]

Pedro Alba, Leonardo Hernandez and Daniela Klingebiel

1. INTRODUCTION

The 1980s and 1990s were critical times for Thailand's development. After an initial period of instability in the early 1980s, Thailand's economy expanded at an average pace of 9 per cent p.a. during 1987–96, while the number of households below the poverty line dropped from 32.6 per cent in 1988 to 16.3 per cent in 1996.[2] During this period, Thailand's economy also underwent deep structural changes, including the liberalization of its financial sector and the integration of its economy with global financial and product markets. For example, trade as a ratio to Gross Domestic Product (GDP) increased from 54 per cent in 1980 to 76 per cent in 1990, and further to 84 per cent in 1996.[3] With regard to financial integration, according to the World Bank (1997a), Thailand went from being a country only partially integrated in 1985–87 to one of the most integrated emerging market economies in 1992–94. Indeed, this period was also one during which Thailand received very large and sustained inflows of foreign capital, averaging some 9.4 per cent of GDP per annum during 1988–96.

The management of the economy during this period of rapid structural change and large capital flows that started in 1988 was a major challenge for the Thai authorities. Overall, the key economic objective remained to achieve rapid growth and poverty reduction through an export-based growth strategy that required maintaining competitiveness through a flexible exchange rate policy and improvements in technology, human capital and infrastructure. In order to attain this objective, the authorities faced, among others, two macro-policy and institutional challenges during the period 1988–96:

- Avoiding macroeconomic overheating in the face of massive capital inflows and growing financial integration that reduced the effectiveness of monetary policy; and

- Reducing the vulnerability of the financial sector (which had just emerged from crisis) to domestic and external shocks while liberalizing the sector and opening up to potentially volatile capital flows.

The purpose of this chapter is to document these challenges and the policy responses of the Thai authorities, in particular those that regard macroeconomic management and the financial sector in the context of growing financial integration and liberalization. Given the ongoing deep financial and economic crisis in Thailand, it is obvious – with the benefit of hindsight – that the policies and institutional improvements implemented by the Thai authorities during the 1980s and early 1990s were insufficient.[4] Hence, this chapter also tries to distill lessons on how developing countries can best deal with these challenges and avoid similar crises. It will not, therefore, focus on the management of the crisis, which has been the object of several recent contributions (that is, Radelet and Sachs 1998); the period of analysis in the chapter is 1987–96, and in only limited instances 1997, and does not include 1998.

The chapter concludes that the crisis was fundamentally a private sector debt crisis, rooted in private behavior regarding the magnitude of investment, its composition and how it was financed. Indeed, unlike the Latin American debt crisis, the Thai crisis was not caused by excessive sovereign borrowings. Liberalization of both financial markets and the capital account of the balance of payments, starting with weak initial conditions (particularly in the financial sector), and not accompanied by a strengthening of the institutional and regulatory framework, led to a rapid build-up of fragility in both the financial and corporate sectors. Coupled with a deficient macro-policy mix, liberalization led to a rapid build-up of currency and maturity mismatches that rendered Thailand vulnerable to a reversal in capital flows and culminated in the crisis of 1997–98.

The remainder of the chapter is organized as follows. Section 2 examines the initial conditions of the macro- and micro-economy at the outset of the capital inflow period in 1987/88. It assesses whether macro and micro conditions were favorable to opening up to foreign capital flows, and analyses the institutional environment and incentive framework for financial and corporate institutions at the onset of the capital inflow period. Section 3 shows how the financial sector and capital account were liberalized during the late 1980s and early 1990s. Section 4 explores the consequences of capital account and financial sector liberalization, both the macroeconomic effects – large private capital inflows and the built up of macro-financial vulnerabilities – and the micro-effects: increased vulnerability in the financial and corporate sector. Based on this analysis, section 5 assesses whether and to what extent the macro-policy mix and financial sector policy measures, pursued by the government during the capital inflow period, avoided overheating of the economy and strengthened the institutional and incentive framework in the financial and corporate sectors. Finally, the concluding section summarizes the results of the analysis and provides some lessons for the future.

2. INITIAL CONDITIONS

This section studies the initial macro-conditions under which the liberalization of the financial sector and the opening of the capital account took place, to assess whether the overall macroeconomy was benign. It also analyses the weaknesses in the institutional and incentive framework of the financial and corporate sector at the onset of the capital inflow period. In particular, it will explore:

- the existence of imbalances at the macro level;
- the structure, conditions, and incentive framework of financial institutions; and
- corporate governance, monitoring and performance in the real estate sector.

A. The Macro Environment

Following trends evident since 1975, the early 1980s were characterized by large macro imbalances fueled by rapid domestic credit expansion and loose fiscal policy. Domestic demand pressures and an inflexible exchange rate policy led to an appreciation of the real effective exchange rate, a faltering export performance and a large current account deficit of over 7 per cent of GDP in the late 1970s and early 1980s. In addition, the Thai economy was negatively affected by several external shocks in the late 1970s and early 1980s. These included the second oil shock in 1979, and a decline in Thai export commodity prices that, combined, resulted in a large deterioration in the terms of trade (TOT) equivalent to 8 per cent of GDP (Kochhar et al. 1996).

The stabilization program of 1984–87

In response, Thailand implemented a macro stabilization program during the period of 1984–87. The program combined a large devaluation of the nominal exchange rate in late 1984 with tighter financial policies. Its main features were as follows:

- The baht was devalued by nearly 15 per cent in nominal effective terms and then pegged against an undisclosed basket that weighted heavily the US dollar. As the dollar lost value vs. the yen during the second half of the 1980s, the baht, in turn, continued to depreciate in nominal terms vs. other East Asian currencies. These changes, in combination with the tight financial policies, reversed the appreciating trend of the real effective exchange rate (REER) during the early 1980s and led to a lasting real depreciation of the baht, which by 1987 had depreciated by 25.5 per cent compared to its level in 1984.

- Monetary policy was tightened starting in 1985. Real credit growth declined significantly in 1985 and 1986 as compared to the previous three years,[5] while real interest rates increased to their highest levels in the 1980s (Kochhar et al. 1996).
- Fiscal policy, however, was adjusted only with a one-year lag with the adoption of the 1985/86 budget in late 1985. Following a period of large deficits and no clear trend for the fiscal stance, between 1985/86 and 1987/88 the central government's fiscal balance went from a deficit of 5.3 per cent of GDP to a surplus of 0.7 per cent. Hence, fiscal policy became sharply contractionary starting in 1986.

Structural reforms

While limited progress was achieved in implementing structural reforms in Thailand during the 1980s, the overall structural context was benign relative to other middle income countries. In the areas of trade, investment and competition policies, and the state enterprise sector, micro distortions were not large to start with and hence did not represent a major impediment to growth during this time period. In Thailand, the private sector has traditionally been the main actor in economic activity and government policy has generally been supportive of the business environment (see for example, Robinson et al. 1991; Kochnar et al. 1996).

With regard to trade policy, despite early intentions already announced in 1981 to promote exports rather than import substitution, progress was rather mixed. While export taxes were largely eliminated during the 1980s, efforts to reduce import tariffs were frustrated by the need to strengthen fiscal revenues, leaving the average effective protection levels broadly constant at about 60 per cent (Kochhar et al. 1996). While moderate on average as compared to other developing countries, effective protection varied widely across industries, favoring final and manufactured goods over intermediate, capital and agricultural products. Some import substituting sectors such as automobiles benefited significantly from tariff and non-tariff barriers (NTBs). Battacharya and Linn (1988) found, however, that NTBs were less widespread in Thailand than in many other East Asian economies, but that they were not diminished during the 1980s. The anti-export bias of the trade regime was also reduced by the introduction of investment incentives aimed at export promotion. In addition, during this time period the authorities successfully strengthened the operations of the various duty drawback schemes and VAT refunds available to exporters (Robinson et al. 1991).

The Thai economic reform program was perceived to be successful: the strong macro adjustment combined with relatively benign structural policies led to a sharp correction in external imbalances and a strong recovery in growth. The program initially had a negative impact on investment and growth as a result of rising interest rates; the output gap peaked in 1996 at about 9 per cent of GDP. By 1987, however, the investment rate was increasing and real growth had recovered to an unprecedented 9.5 per cent, while inflation had quickly declined to low single-digit levels. On the external side, as a result of the initial contraction in income growth combined with the sustained real depreciation, exports boomed and there was a large adjustment in the current account of almost 8 percentage points of GDP between 1983 and 1986.

B. The Financial System

At the end of 1987, with the ratio of financial assets to GDP at 98.9 per cent, Thailand's financial system was deep compared to other emerging market economies with similar per-capita income. Much of this monetization took place at the beginning of the 1980s and was mainly due to the fact that an increasingly large share of private savings was channeled into accumulation of financial assets.[6] The monetization of the economy led to a complementary rise in credit. Credit to the private sector stood at 59 per cent of GDP at the end of 1987, up from 41 per cent in 1980. The Thai system was also bank-oriented, with more than 67.5 per cent of financial assets in banks, and with limited financial intermediation through mutual funds and other types of institutional investors. Bond and stock markets remained relatively underdeveloped, with oustanding bond market issues accounting for only 11.5 per cent of GDP at the end of 1989, and stock market capitalization amounting to 35.5 per cent (World Bank 1995).

Structure of the financial system

As of 1987, Thailand's formal financial system consisted of commercial banks, finance companies, credit foncier companies, government savings banks, private and government insurance companies, and a number of sectorally and functionally specialized financial institutions. Commercial banks were the central players in the system, absorbing 80.9 per cent of deposits and accounting for 73.1 per cent of total financial system assets.[7] Finance and securities companies accounted for 9.5 per cent of total system deposits and 12.7 per cent of total financial system assets. Specialized government banks had captured 9.5 per cent of total financial system deposits and 14.2 per cent of total financial system assets.[8]

Commercial banks At the beginning of 1988, commercial banks assets equal to 943 billion baht (or 72.5 per cent of GDP) were held by 15 domestic commercial banks and 14 foreign banks. Although the number of foreign banks was almost equal to the number of domestic banks, they together accounted for around only 5 per cent of commercial banking assets.[9] Their small market share was the result of tight government restrictions, which severely limited their activities and hampered their ability to compete with domestic banks.[10] Thailand's banking industry was concentrated and characterized by an oligopolistic market structure. The largest bank, Bangkok Bank, had a market share of 28 per cent at the end of 1988. The bulk of the commercial banking system assets were accounted for by four banks, one of which is government-owned (Krung Thai Bank). Their combined market share amounted to 63 per cent of total banking system assets (end 1988 figures).[11] These four banks also dominated the interbank loan market since they were the main supplier of liquidity for smaller and foreign banks. In addition, they were the leading players in foreign exchange transactions and thus could exert a degree of control on the supply of foreign exchange. The oligopolistic structure and the lack of the threat of new entry (the last time a domestic banking license was granted was in 1965) hampered innovation and diversification in the financial system.

Commercial banks financed their activities mostly via time deposits, which at the end of 1987 commanded an average share of about 70 per cent of total banking system deposits, followed by savings deposits that accounted for about 30 per cent of banking system deposits. At the end of 1987, commercial banks were relatively independent from foreign funding: borrowing from abroad accounted for only 3.9 per cent of total liabilities.

Commercial banks focused their activities on straight-out lending activities: non-interest income only amounted to 18 per cent of the net operating income in 1987 (World Bank 1990). As a result, at the end of 1987, loans as a ratio of total assets amounted to 73 per cent and were dominated by overdrafts, which accounted for an average of around 65 per cent of bank credit. In their lending activities commercial banks tended to rely more on collateral rather than on evaluation of project viability, borrower creditworthiness, or cash flows. Regarding the scope of permissible activities, banks were not allowed to engage in any securities activities including brokerage of bonds and equities.

Finance companies Finance companies constituted the second largest segment of the financial system and were the most important non-bank financial institutions. At the end of 1987, this segment was characterized by a large number of companies with a wide size range. Of the 93 institutions 26 were affiliated with private Thai commercial banks, and a further 12 with the government-owned Krung Thai Bank.[12] These affiliated companies were created to provide specialized services that banks were not allowed to provide (e.g., securities business) or as specialized and innovative providers of high-margin high-risk consumer finance. In contrast to banks, finance companies faced stiff competition not only from other finance companies but also from banks, that once services proved successful at the finance company level, started to introduce similar services. Moreover, finance companies faced a credible threat to entry as, in contrast to the banking sector, new institutions entered the market. While finance companies were typically smaller and more efficient than banks, given the number of players involved in the thin market, and the propensity of banks to introduce competing services, finance companies' margins were constantly under pressure.

Unlike commercial banks, finance and securities companies were not allowed to take direct deposits from the public, and funded their operations primarily through the issuance of large-denomination promissory notes[13] (52 per cent of total liabilities at the end of 1987), as well as credit from commercial banks (19 per cent) and funding from other financial institutions (9.2 per cent). At the end of 1987 foreign lending funds were of marginal importance as they only comprised 1.4 per cent of total liabilities.[14]

Similar to commercial banks, finance companies derived the largest share of their income (58 per cent in 1988) from lending activities, while 13 per cent came from hire purchase business, 12 per cent from securities trading, 10 per cent from dividends on investments, and 7 per cent from other sources. While securities and finance companies could engage in securities business, they were not allowed to offer overdraft facilities, credit cards and credit facilities related to trade finance, provide foreign exchange services, and set up branches. Due to commercial banks' (funding) cost and other regulatory advantages, finance companies tended to seek profits by allocating a major share of their portfolio into high(er) risk areas, including construction and real estate (18.3 per cent), margin loans and hire purchase (9.1 per cent) and personal consumption (25.5 per cent).[15]

Regulatory and incentive framework of financial institutions

Interest rate controls and requirements for lending to priority sectors Because of the dominant role of the banking sector, bank interest rates were the most important indicators of the cost and price of capital. At the end of 1987, the two most important rates – the deposit and lending rates – were subject to ceilings imposed by the Bank of Thailand (BoT). BoT also attempted to affect the allocation of bank credit across sectors via three policy measures: (1) the requirement that commercial banks had to lend 20 per cent of their previous year's deposits to the agricultural sector – any shortfall had to be deposited at the Bank for Agriculture and Agricultural Cooperative at a rate that was below the interbank rate; (2) the exemption of lending to priority sectors from capital requirements; and (3) access to preferential refinancing at BoT for lending such as promotion of exports, small scale industry, and agricultural production.

The external incentive framework The regulatory and supervisory framework, along with accounting rules, disclosure requirements, and the existence of a deposit insurance scheme, play a crucial role in defining the incentive framework in which financial institutions operate. In particular, the extent to which excessive risk taking is curbed by regulation, or penalized by the supervisory authority as well as by the market, greatly influence the behavior of financial institutions. There are three potential groups that can monitor bank managers, namely the owners, the market, and supervisors.

At the end of 1987, the incentive framework of banks and finance companies appeared relatively weak and may have been ineffective in aligning owners/managers' incentives with prudent banking. For example, the disciplinary effect of capital-to-assets requirements were limited due to the level and definition of capital adequacy requirements. While 8 per cent appears to be in line with the capital adequacy ratio imposed on banks in developed markets, it appears low relative to the high-risk operating environment in which Thai financial institutions operated. Moreover, despite the fact that the minimum level for capital is based on a narrow definition for capital, BoT permitted 31 exemptions for different classes of assets, including certain categories of risky, priority sector loans. In 1989, total exemptions from capital adequacy computation accounted for approximately 40 per cent of total assets. By permitting these exemptions BoT used capital adequacy as a tool of economic regulation to encourage directed credit rather than as a buffer to absorb unusual losses (World Bank 1990). These capital adequacy guidelines were further weakened by prudential norms on asset quality which effectively led to an overstatement of capital.[16] Furthermore, financial institutions were allowed to accrue uncollected interest income for up to 12 months, thereby overstating income and capital. Finally, regulations aimed at limiting excessive exposure to a single related entity or connected group of entities were weak and ceilings on exposure to particular 'risky' sectors (to sectors which are prone to boom and bust cycles: e.g., real estate) were non-existent.

Table 5.1 contains a summary of prudential regulations that Thai banks and finance companies were subject to. It illustrates one important point: in spite of the fact that finance companies tended to engage in riskier activities due to their regulatory constraints, finance companies were subject to less stringent prudential requirements than banks. For example, while commercial banks' capital-to-asset ratio was set at 8 per cent, finance companies had to hold only 6 per cent of capital against their risky assets.

Market discipline In Thailand, market discipline was not only hampered by a partial implicit guarantee on financial system deposits – a legacy of the resolution of the 1983–87 financial crisis (see below) – but also by loose financial accounting and disclosure. Furthermore, the role of a limited number of families in the ownership of both financial and non-financial institutions limited the scope for market oversight. Indeed, each of the major banks was associated, through cross-ownership and control, with a variety of non-financial companies as well as with at least one, and usually more than one, finance company. It has been estimated that ten families as of end-1987 controlled 46.2 per cent of the market capitalization of all listed firms, of which 39.6 per cent were in financial institutions, 60.9 per cent in non-financial companies.[17] Weaknesses in the governance of financial institutions may encourage lending to risky sectors or unviable projects. Moreover, a bank's relationship with enterprises which are part of its industrial financial group may not be conducted at arms-length and fair market prices.

Enforcement through supervision/regulatory forbearance. The Bank of Thailand had inadequate powers to intervene and close weak and insolvent institutions. This severely curtailed enforcement of the prudential regulatory framework as the ultimate sanction for non-compliance – intervention and closure of an institution – was not a credible threat. Enforcement actions were also hampered by the fact that the authority to license banks lay with the Ministry of Finance while the BoT was the supervisory authority. Any action related to the withdrawal of a license thus needed to be approved and coordinated with the Ministry of Finance. And finally, bank closures had been a very rare occurrence in Thailand. The last time supervisors forced a bank to close its doors was in 1965.

Performance and condition of financial institutions

Table 5.2 summarizes selected performance indicators for commercial banks and finance companies prior to financial sector liberalization and the opening of the capital account. As the table shows, the financial sector was still recovering from the 1983–87 crisis as reflected in relatively weak returns on assets and equity. Since financial institutions were subject to lenient interest accrual norms – they were allowed to accrue interest for up to 12 months (six months) for secured (unsecured) loans – these performance indicators most probably overstate profits. Moreover, the financial sector continued to experience portfolio problems as mirrored in a relatively high ratio of non-performing loans to total loans which amounted to 7 per cent for commercial banks. Similarly, a number of finance companies and several banks were still supported by the BoT via various measures (World Bank 1990).

Table 5.1 Thailand: Prudential regulatory requirements for commercial banks and finance companies, 1990

	Commercial banks	Finance companies
Limits on ownership	• Shareholding to one person limited to 5 per cent but nominee shareholding is permitted	• Shareholdings limited to 10 per cent of shares outstanding
Level of minimum capital adequacy requirements	• 8 per cent of risk assets for on-balance sheet items; however, a number of exemptions apply which effectively reduce minimum capital adequacy ratio considerably • 20 per cent in relation to amount of avals, acceptance bills, and loan guarantees outstanding	• 6 per cent of risk assets for balance sheet risks • 25 per cent for off-balance sheet contingent liabilities
Loan classification requirements (number of days before loan is classified as non-performing)	• 180 (uncollateralized) • 360 (collateralized)	• 180 (uncollateralized) • 360 (collateralized)
Provisioning requirements for loans classified as nonperforming	• 50 per cent on doubtful • 0 on substandard	• 50 per cent on doubtful • 0 on substandard
Limit on risk exposure:		
– Liquidity requirement	• 7 percent of deposits	• n.a.
– Foreign exposure limit	• Open foreign exchange position limited to 20 per cent of capital	• n.a.
– Single exposure limit	• 25 per cent of bank's capital fund • 50 per cent for contingent exposures	• 30 per cent of finance company's capital fund • 40 per cent including contingent liabilities
– Loans to insiders	• Loans to directors prohibited	• n.a.

Table 5.2 *Thailand: Performance indicators of commercial banks and finance companies (in per cent)*

	Commercial banks		Fincos	
	1987	1988	1987	1988
ROAE	14.5	15.5	9.25	8.537
ROAA	0.8	0.9	0.51	0.7
NPL/total loans	7.0	—	—	—
Provision for loan losses/total loans	0.7	0.8	—	—
Capital/asset ratio	5.6	5.9	—	—
Loan/deposit ratio	96.2	94.2	116.6	115.7

Source: World Bank 1990.

Resolution of the 1983–87 banking crisis

As it has been implicit in the analysis above, to a great extent the weaknesses of Thailand's financial system lay in the 1983–87 crisis and its resolution. In this section we briefly summarize the main features of this crisis, its causes and the way it was resolved.[18]

Causes and scope of the financial crisis In 1983–87, Thailand experienced a financial crisis that was associated with a slowdown in the economy, high world interest rates, and fraud and mismanagement on the part of several finance companies and banks. The crisis originated in the finance company segment of the financial system, which was poorly supervised and had engaged in heavy speculations in shares and real estate and affected institutions that together accounted for 25 per cent of total financial system assets. A total of 24 finance companies were subsequently closed, and nine others merged into two new companies. The crisis led the Bank of Thailand to create the Financial Institutions Development Fund (FIDF) in 1985 – a separate legal entity under the BoT with a mandate to provide liquidity support to financial institutions. The FIDF established a special support scheme – the 'April 4 Lifeboat Scheme' – which provided soft loans to 13 finance companies and eight commercial banks in exchange for an equity stake.

Treatment of depositors Depositors of commercial banks were largely bailed out, thus creating – reinforcing – expectations of an implicit insurance guarantee for that market segment. Depositors of 25 finance companies that participated in the 'lifeboat-scheme' were also bailed out. The only depositors to suffer any losses (in the form of forgone interest and illiquidity) were the creditors of the 24 finance companies that were closed. Thus, despite the lack of an explicit deposit insurance scheme, the resolution of the mid-1980s crisis reinforced the belief that depositors and banks would be bailed out if their investments proved unprofitable.

Treatment of financial institutions' shareholders and management Shareholders of insolvent financial institutions did see a (temporary) dilution of their investments, but they were not completely eliminated as shareholders.[19] While the chief executive officers of the failed and restructured institutions were removed, senior management was left in place. This allowed the weak banking culture to remain intact, and made the overall rehabilitation of the financial sector more difficult. Moreover, despite the fact that the financial crisis of the mid-1980s was caused by poor risk management and lending practices, relatively low average operating expenses in the aftermath of the crisis seem to suggest that financial institutions invested insufficiently into upgrading the skill base of their staff and their risk management practices.[20]

C. The Corporate Sector

At the end of the 1980s, both corporate governance and disclosure systems were weak, and capital markets played a limited role in the governance of firms and exhibiting at least three interrelated problems: (1) concentrated ownership; (2) weak information standards; and (3) poor protection of minority shareholders.[21]

Concentrated ownership One of the salient features of the corporate sector in Thailand is the dominance of family control over business operations. Thai firms were (are) generally closely held and managed by majority – often family – interests, while a relatively limited number of families controlled many of the corporations listed on the stock exchange. The concentration of ownership can be largely attributed to the relative youth of Thailand's corporates as ownership concentration is common in emerging market economies. Nevertheless, while ownership concentration can have advantages,[22] empirical evidence suggest that concentrated ownership structures may impede the development of professional managers that are required as firms mature and become more complex, and may lead to increase risk-taking by firms (in particular if ownership links between financial and non-financial firms exist) as other stakeholders (creditors and employees) share in the downside risk. Moreover, in order not to lose control, large shareholders have incentives to dilute market pressures for improved disclosure and protection for minority shareholders.

Weak information standards In Thailand in the late 1980s, the scope for market monitoring was limited as disclosure was weak and accounting standards and practices were not up to international practice, thus limiting investors' ability to monitor corporate performance (Alba et al. 1998b). Standards for financial statement disclosures, asset classification, marketable securities, loss recognition and debt restructuring needed improvement. As (large) firms – at the individual firm level as well as at the country level – had easy access to financing, firms and insiders had little to gain from improving disclosure and corporate governance.

Protecting minority shareholders An important factor influencing external financing patterns is the degree of protection from abuse by corporate insiders that is provided by legal and regulatory mechanisms to outside investors. There is growing international evidence that the quality and efficacy of these protection mechanisms influence whether and at what costs outside investors are willing to fund corporations. La Porta et al. (1998) suggest that poor protection mechanisms will limit the availability of external finance for firms, as well as raise the cost of funds to compensate for increased level of expropriation. The quality of protection mechanisms depends on a variety of factors such as the treatment of investor rights in the company, bankruptcy and securities legislation, the efficacy of legal enforcement, and the content and enforcement of capital market regulation, including listing rules and disclosure. While shareholders in Thailand appear better protected than shareholders in Latin America, the enforcement of minority shareholder rights was undermined by a weak judicial system. According to one of the legal sub-indices reported by La Porta et al. (1998), the efficiency of the financial system in Thailand is the second worse among the 49 countries in their sample.

Performance In 1988, Thai corporates which were listed on the stock exchange showed high profitability as their real return on assets (ROA) amounted to about 11 per cent. It was significantly higher than ROAs that German (4.3 per cent) or US companies (4.7 per cent) were reporting. Moreover, operational margins and real sales growth, two alternative measures of profitability, seem to support the notion that Thai corporates were quite profitable at the end of the 1980s. In 1988, (listed) Thai companies also had – relative to companies in developed countries – high operational margins (22 per cent versus 14.1 per cent for US companies and 13.2 for German companies) and saw their real sales grow by 12 per cent, the highest for East Asian companies and twice as fast as German or US companies (Claessens et al. 1998).

D. Initial Conditions: Summary

As outlined above, initial conditions in the macro and structural environment were benign in Thailand at the onset of the capital inflow period. In contrast, conditions in the financial and the corporate sectors were less favorable. Not only was the financial sector still weakened from the crisis (in terms of profitability and capital position of individual institutions) earlier in the decade, but the overall incentive framework in which financial institutions operated remained deficient, and the regulatory and supervisory framework was not considerably strengthened in the aftermath of the crisis. Moreover, the scope for moral hazard on the side of financial institutions was significant since the potential for market oversight was limited due to poor disclosure and quality of financial information, a concentrated ownership structure and cross-ownership links between financial and non-financial entities. In addition, incentives for market oversight were reduced because depositors were bailed out in the last financial sector crisis. On the corporate sector side, while profitability remained strong, the governance of corporates was weak, creating incentives for risky investment and over-diversification.

2. LIBERALIZATION OF THE CAPITAL ACCOUNT AND FINANCIAL SECTOR IN THE EARLY 1990s

Against the macro and micro background analysed in the previous section, the Thai government embarked on a program to further open the capital account and liberalize financial markets in the late 1980s and early 1990s. The main policy measures in these two areas are presented below.

A. Liberalization of the Capital Account

Already in 1985, Thailand maintained relatively open current and capital accounts, with liberal treatment of foreign direct and portfolio investments, although exchange controls still applied to the repatriation of interest, dividends and principal of portfolio investment. Foreign borrowing by Thai residents was allowed but subject to registration at the BoT. Starting in 1985, both current and capital account transactions were significantly liberalized. By the end of 1994, Thailand was free of foreign exchange restrictions on current account transactions, and had a very open and favorable regime for foreign investment. Foreign investors were still subject to some restrictions on foreign ownership, in particular with regard to companies listed on the Stock Exchange of Thailand (SET), and to severe restrictions on real estate. Thai investment overseas, in particular by financial intermediaries and banks, was also restricted. Following Johnston et al. (1997), major milestones in the liberalization process between 1985–96 were the following:

- *Current account transactions*: IMF article VIII obligations were assumed in May 1990.

- *Portfolio investment*: With regard to tax treatment, during 1986 the authorities reduced tax impediments to portfolio inflows, in particular for purchasing Thai mutual funds. This was followed in 1991 and 1992 by improvements in the tax treatment of dividends, royalty payments, capital gains, and interest payments on foreign debentures. In 1990, three mutual funds were created to attract foreign investment, and in 1991 repatriation of investment funds, interest and loan repayments by foreign investors was fully liberalized.
- *Foreign direct investment*: In addition to amendments in the Investment Promotion Act to promote more foreign investment, in 1991 the government authorized 100 per cent foreign ownership of firms that export all their output. Also, direct investment by Thai residents overseas was gradually liberalized in 1991 and 1994.
- *Foreign exchange system*: The most important change was the establishment in 1993 of the Bangkok International Banking Facility (BIBF), an offshore financial market which enjoyed tax and regulatory advantages aimed at fostering the development of Bangkok as a regional financial center (see Box 5.1). Other liberalization measures adopted during the 1985–96 period included: subjecting non-resident baht accounts at domestic commercial banks to lower reserve requirements and gradually eliminating restrictions on purchases of foreign exchange by residents and transfers of baht overseas.

B. Liberalization of the Financial System

In 1990, the Thai government promulgated a comprehensive financial reform plan with the stated goal of 'coordinating, synchronizing several aspects of the reform with the ultimate objectives to enhance competitiveness, flexibility, efficiency, and stability of the financial sector' (see Wibulswadi 1995). The main components of the reform program are summarized in Table 5.3.

Dismantling of interest rate controls Among the most important actions included in the reform program were the dismantling of interest rate controls over the period 1989 to 1992. Ceilings on commercial bank deposit rates were removed during 1989–91. In June 1992, ceilings on finance and credit foncier companies' deposit and lending rates, and on commercial banks' lending rates were removed. However, on October 1993, given the gap in interest rates (and spreads) between prime and non-prime borrowers, BoT began to require banks to declare their minimum lending rate (MLR – the rate on term credits to large customers), its minimum retail rate (MRR – the rate on small prime customers), and the widest margins charged above these rates. The initial 'formula' for the MRR was set so as to reflect commercial banks' total cost of funds given the

BOX 5.1 THE BANGKOK INTERNATIONAL BANKING FACILITY

The Bangkok International Banking Facility (BIBF) was established in March 1993 to facilitate the growth of international banking business in Thailand. As of the third quarter of 1996, 49 banks had been granted BIBF licenses, including Thai commercial banks and foreign banks with and without local branches in Thailand. The main operations of BIBF banks on the liability side are deposits or borrowing in foreign exchange from abroad, mainly through foreign inter-bank transactions and inter-office borrowings. On the asset side, their main activities are lending in foreign currency to Thai residents (out-in) and non-residents (out-out). BIBF institutions also engage in other standard off-shore banking activities such as loan syndication and foreign exchange transactions in third country currencies, and are also authorized to undertake investment banking activities.

BIBF banks are treated as residents by the Bank of Thailand for purposes of the BOP. As result, BIBF funding activities are counted as capital inflows under the BOP. While this should not affect the volume of inflows since normally the two sides are matched, it can affect the maturity structure of Thailand's external debt. To the extent that BIBF out-in lending to Thai firms is replacing other sources of short- and *long-term* foreign capital, the maturity structure of Thailand's external debt will shorten since most BIBF funding is short-term. And by reducing borrowing costs and indirectly easing access to foreign capital markets for smaller and less well-known Thai firms, the establishment of the BIBF may have increased the magnitude of short-term capital flows.

BIBF institutions benefited from several important tax advantages. Among the most important are a reduced corporate income tax (10 per cent rather than 30 per cent) and exemption from several sales taxes (3.3 per cent of turnover), stamp duties, and the permanent establishment tax. With regard to withholding taxes, all out-out transactions were exempt, while for out-in transactions the rate is 10 per cent, compared to 15 per cent for countries that do not have a double taxation agreement with Thailand. Most importantly, cross-border borrowings within the same institution were exempt from withholding taxes. Finally, unlike other deposit or deposit type instruments, short-term (under 12 months) BIBF monetary instruments were not subject to the 7 per cent cash reserve requirements, favoring a short-term maturity structure.

Source: Bank of Thailand: 'Analyzing Thailand's Short-term Debt,' *Bank of Thailand Economic Focus* Vol. 1, Number 3, July–September 1996.

Table 5.3 Thailand: Overview of financial sector liberalization measures

	Interest Rate Controls
1987	Removal of separate interest rate ceiling for lending to priority sectors.
1989	Removal of interest rate ceiling on time deposits of commercial banks with maturity > 1 year.
1990	Removal of interest rate ceiling on time deposits of commercial banks with maturity < 1 year.
1991/January	Removal of interest rate ceiling on savings deposits at commercial banks.
1991/June	Removal of interest rate ceiling on finance companies' and credit foncier companies' borrowing, deposits and lending.
1991/June	Removal of interest rate ceiling on commercial bank lending.
1993/Oct	Commercial banks required to announce minimum retail rate calculated from actual costs of deposits and operating costs as reference lending rates for retail prime borrower.
	Controls on finance companies' funding side
1990	Removal of requirement on minimum denomination of promissory notes that finance companies can issue.
1992	Receive permission to issue certificates of deposit.
1995	Receive permission to issue bills of exchange or certificates of deposit denominated in foreign currencies, with maturity of over one year, to overseas investors or commercial banks authorized to undertake foreign exchange transactions.
	Controls on Portfolio Composition
1991	Broadening definition of 'targeted rural credits' under the rural credit requirement to include credits for crop wholesaling and industrial estates in rural areas.
1992/Jan	Further relaxation of rural credit requirements via: i. broadening definition to include credits for farmers' secondary occupation, and credits for agricultural product wholesaling and exporting; ii. changing small industry definition from 5 million baht net assets outstanding to 10 million baht; iii. excluding interbank deposits from deposit base under rural credit.

	Expanding the scope of activities of finance companies/commercial banks
1987	List of authorized business for commercial banks and finance companies was broadened to include: i. custodial services; ii. loan syndication; iii. advisory services regarding mergers and acquisition; iv. feasibility studies.
1992/March	– Commercial banks allowed to operate as: i. selling agents for debt instruments issued by the government and state enterprises; ii. information service; iii. financial consulting services. – Finance companies allowed to operate as: i. selling agents for debt instruments issued by the government and state enterprises; ii. information services; iii. sponsoring services, preparing necessary documents for companies applying for listing on SET. – Securities companies allowed to operate: i. custodial services; ii. registrar and paying agents for securities; iii. information services; iv. sponsoring services.
1992/June	Allowing commercial banks to operate the following business: i. arranging, underwriting and dealing in debt instruments; ii. secured debenture holder representative; iii. trustee of mutual funds; iv. securities registrar; v. selling agents for investment units.
1994/Sept	Allowing commercial banks to invest in any business, or in its shares, of not more than 10 per cent of the total amount of shares sold.

Source: Bank of Thailand, Financial Institutions and Markets in Thailand, 1998.

deposit rates plus the banks' operating costs. Deposits banks also had to declare the rates for general and large deposits (see World Bank 1997b).

Relaxation of portfolio restrictions and expanding the scope of activities Also important in the reform program were those measures that eliminated restrictions on the scope of activity and portfolio of financial institutions. First, prior requirements on portfolio composition of commercial banks were relaxed (by expanding the definition of agricultural credits in which commercial banks are expected to lend to no less than 20 per cent of their deposits). Second, to bolster the competitive position of financial institutions, finance companies were authorized at end-1991 to conduct leasing business. In March 1992, finance companies were authorized to act as selling agents for government bonds, to provide economic, financial, and investment information services, and to advise companies seeking listing on the Stock Exchange Thailand (SET). Third, in 1992, commercial banks were allowed to expand their areas of operation to include issuance, underwriting, and distribution of debt securities, to act as supervisors as well as selling agents for mutual funds, and to become securities registrars. Finally, reserve requirements were converted into liquid asset requirements allowing banks to invest up to 3 per cent in government paper.

3. CONSEQUENCES OF THE LIBERALIZATION OF THE CAPITAL ACCOUNT AND THE FINANCIAL SECTOR

The liberalization of the capital account and the financial sector resulted in a rapid build-up of vulnerability, with both macro and micro manifestations.

On the macro side, the liberalization program resulted in a surge of private capital inflows and rapid credit growth. The increased foreign borrowing and rapid credit growth resulted in high leverage at the economy-wide level as well as an asset price bubble.[23] In turn, this led to a rapid increase in foreign exchange exposure and a shortening of the maturity structure, rendering the economy vulnerable to reversals in capital inflows and downturns in economic activity. One micro manifestation of the economy-wide borrowing binge was the rapid build-up of leverage and the increased foreign exchange exposure of the corporate sector. Similarly, as a result of the lending boom and coupled with the practice of collateral based lending, banks and finance companies became more vulnerable to economic shocks in the 1990s by: (1) lending excessively to sectors or firms whose debt service capacity was particularly susceptible to shocks; and (2) reducing their own capacity to absorb negative shocks, especially by exacerbating currency and maturity mismatches, by mispricing loans, and by underprovisioning for future potential losses. This build-up of vulnerability is analysed in greater detail below.

A. Surge in Capital Inflows

Together with Malaysia, Thailand is one of the countries that received the largest capital inflows in the East Asia region, indeed in the world, relative to GDP.

Private capital flows were already significant in the early 1980s, but declined in 1985 and 1986 as a result of the uncertainties surrounding the macro adjustment. As can be seen from Figure 5.1, private capital flows to Thailand surged in 1988, when there is a clear structural break in the data. Between 1987 and 1990, inflows increased to some US$11.1 billion, where they stabilized until 1993. In 1994 and especially 1995, inflows surged once again, surpassing US$21 billion in 1995, but declining sharply in 1996. Between 1988 and 1996, Thailand received the staggering cumulative amount of US$100.3 billion in capital inflows.

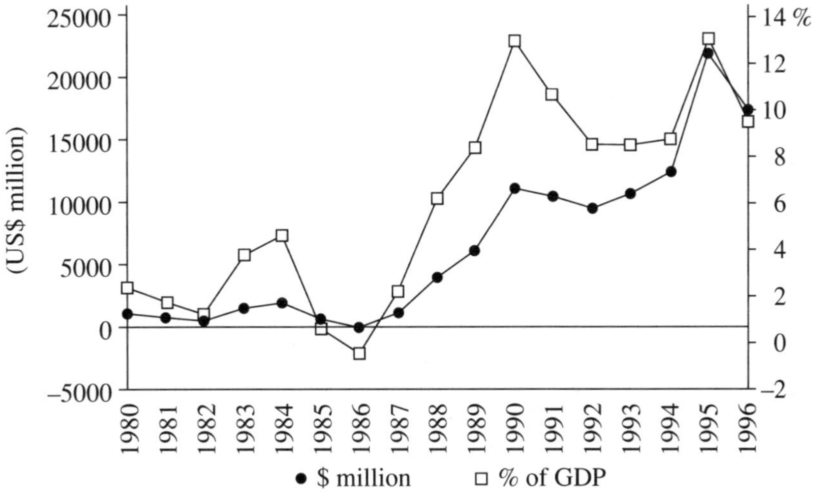

Source: Bank of Thailand.

Figure 5.1 Thailand: Total private capital flows (net)

Measuring capital flows as a percentage of GDP does not make the story different (see Figure 5.1). Again, the data suggest a structural break in 1988, when flows increased rapidly until 1990, reaching 13 per cent of GDP. After stabilizing at about 8 per cent of GDP in 1992–94, there was a second surge in 1995 when flows again surpassed 12 per cent of GDP.

Main components of capital inflows The Bank of Thailand classifies capital flows into non-bank and bank flows. The latter are resident banks borrowing from overseas sources (either from financial institutions or by issuing debt instruments), and, starting in 1993, a separate category for borrowing by BIBF banks (see Box 5.1). The non-bank categories are the following:

- *Foreign direct investment*: Including both net FDI inflows and outflows (Thai direct investment overseas);
- *Portfolio capital*: Distinguishing between fixed income and equity flows, and including direct investments by foreign residents in domestic instruments and Thai sovereign and corporate issues overseas (e.g., eurobonds, American Depositary Receipts);
- *Non-resident Baht accounts*: Capital inflows deposited by non-residents in domestic currency accounts in local banks mainly for investing in domestic securities;
- *Trade credits*: A minor component; and
- *Other borrowing*: Presumably mostly composed of syndicated borrowing by domestic corporates from overseas financial institutions.

Bank intermediation Banks and finance companies played a key role in intermediating capital inflows in Thailand. Their net foreign liabilities rose from 6 per cent of domestic deposit liabilities in 1990, to one third by 1996. During the overall period of 1988–96, bank borrowing accounted for 37 per cent of total inflows. But this average number hides a large difference between the initial phase of the inflow and the final four years, 1993–96. Bank borrowing played a relatively minor role during 1988–92, accounting for only 10 per cent of total flows, but increased sharply to 60 per cent during 1993–96. This occurred as a result of the establishment of the BIBF and was due mainly to two reasons: first, as outlined above, BIBF institutions were granted considerable tax advantages; and second, many Thai firms who could not directly access overseas capital markets were able to borrow from BIBF Thai banks. As a result, foreign bank loans through the Bangkok International Banking Facility soared from US$8 billion in 1993, its first year in operation, to US$50 billion in 1996, with US$30 billion of out-in transactions and 20 billion of out-out transactions (Kawai and Iwatsubo 1998).

Non-bank capital inflows There are three salient facts regarding the composition and trends of non-bank net capital inflows:

- The composition of non-bank capital flows to Thailand over the full period 1988–96 was relatively balanced: Net foreign direct investment (22 per cent), portfolio flows (25 per cent), non-resident baht deposits (29 per cent) and other loans (20 per cent) all account for similar amounts.
- Again, however, the averages hide significant changes over time. Most importantly, other borrowing accounted for some 41 per cent of non-bank inflows over the initial period 1988–92, but during 1993–94, there was a net *outflow* of capital under this category. The data suggest that Thai firms used bank lending to refinance their direct borrowings from foreign

financial institutions, especially since the establishment of the BIBF (Figure 5.2). In 1995–96, however, as explained below, the authorities implemented several measures to reduce the magnitude of bank, in particular short-term, inflows and net direct external borrowing by firms again became positive.

- The average figures also hide changes in the relative importance of the other non-bank capital inflow categories during the 1990s. First, during 1988–92 foreign direct investment accounted for a much larger proportion (42 per cent) of non-bank capital inflows (excluding other borrowing) than during 1993–96 (17.5 per cent). The Bank of Thailand believes that part of this decline was due to a 'significant rebooking of FDI though BIBF' (i.e., the refinancing and new borrowings of overseas affiliates of FDI companies, previously classified as FDI, through BIBF). Second, the relative importance of portfolio flows, especially debt instruments, increased from 14 per cent to 44 per cent between the two periods.

Increased reliance on foreign capital and the shortening of the maturity structure During the 1990s, the Thai economy increased its reliance on foreign capital, which is reflected in an increase of the share of foreign debt on total debt from 59.1 per cent in 1988 to 94.1 per cent at the end of 1997. At the same

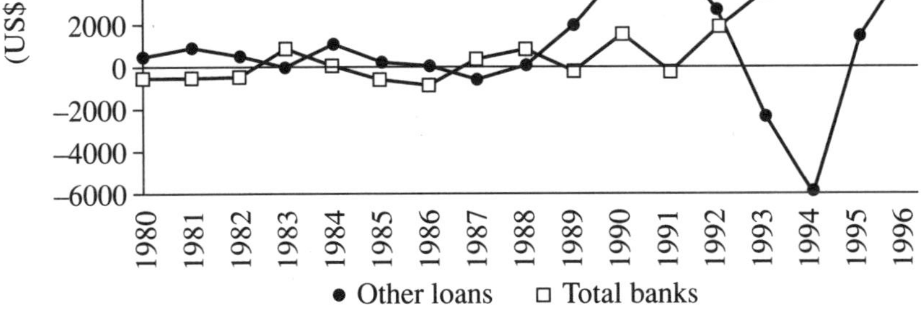

Source: Bank of Thailand.

Figure 5.2 Thailand: Intermediation of corporate foreign borrowings

time, changes in the composition of capital inflows during the 1990s increased the proportion of short-term and potentially more volatile inflows in total private capital. Important aspects of this were the large increase in BIBF inflows, the decline in FDI both in absolute and relative terms, and the increase in portfolio flows. Funds intermediated through non-resident (N/R) baht accounts, believed to be mainly invested in short-term liquid domestic debt instruments, as well as in the stock market, have remained important throughout the whole period.

These trends also led to a rapid build-up of private short-term debt. The Bank of Thailand estimates that short-term external debt quadrupled between 1990 and 1995, from US$10 billion to US$41 billion (Table 5.4), and doubled as a ratio to GDP from 12 to 24 per cent.

Table 5.4 Thailand: Private external debt (end of period: billion US$)

	1990	1993	1994	1995	1996
Medium and long-term	7.4	15.4	20.2	25.1	36.2
Non-bank	7.3	12.7	13.7	16.9	23.2
Bank debt	0.1	2.7	6.5	8.2	13.0
BIBF	0.0	1.4	3.0	3.8	n.a.
Other	0.1	1.3	3.5	4.4	n.a.
Short-term	10.1	22.7	28.9	41.0	37.6
Non-bank	6.2	12.3	7.4	7.3	8.7
Bank debt	3.9	10.4	21.5	33.7	28.9
BIBF	0.0	6.4	15.1	23.7	n.a.
Other	3.9	4.0	6.4	10.0	n.a.
Total Private	17.5	38.1	49.1	66.1	73.8
As % of GDP	21	30	34	39	41
Bank (% of total)	23	34	57	63	57
Short-term (% of GDP)	12	18	20	24	21
Short-term (% of total)	58	60	59	62	51

Note: n.a. = not available.

Source: BOT.

Commercial banks were heavily involved in the growth of external debt. As Table 5.4 shows, commercial bank debt as a share of total private external debt rose sharply from 23 per cent to 63 per cent between 1990 and 1995. Banks were also closely connected to the short-term debt build-up, in particular since the establishment of the BIBF in 1993. The US$30 billion increase in short-term debt between 1990 and 1995 is fully explained by bank borrowing. The growing reliance of banks on foreign funding for their activities is reflected in the fact that foreign liabilities, as a percentage of total liabilities, rose from 5.4 per cent (1988) to 6.4 per cent (1992) to 17.4 per cent (1996).[24]

B. Rapid Growth of Credit

The liberalization of the capital account coupled with the liberalization of interest rates (after 1992), led to a lending boom in the first half of the 1990s. Total credit outstanding grew on average 22 per cent per annum in real terms over 1988 to 1995. The loan portfolio of finance companies grew at an even faster pace – on average 30 per cent in real terms per annum during these years, compared to 20 per cent for commercial banks. Overall, loan growth on average outpaced the growth of GDP 1.8 times (or 2.3 times in the case of finance companies) (World Bank 1997b). Finance companies' credit grew fastest in 1992, with loans growing three times faster than GDP, but the rate of growth has been declining since. Compared to commercial banks, finance companies had a stronger incentive to lend because of a signal of the Bank of Thailand suggesting that the size of their credit portfolio would be an important determining factor for the award of a much coveted banking license, i.e., the bigger they are (in terms of asset size) the greater the chances of receiving a banking license.

Rising leverage ratios The rapid growth of credit was reflected in a rising credit to GDP ratio, which increased from 60 per cent in 1987 to 142 per cent in 1996 (see Figure 5.3). The expansion of credit relative to GDP implied two problematic domestic trends. First, the gearing of the economy increased by an average of 20 per cent per year over 1990–97. Second, an increasing share of loans from the financial sector was for the accumulation of non-productive assets, which is reflected in decreasing returns on capital investment. One measure of return on capital investment is the incremental capital-output ratio (ICOR), which compares the increases in investment relative to the increases in GDP. A rising ratio implies that investment is becoming less productive, or of lower quality. The ICOR rose steadily in Thailand from 2.8 in 1988, to almost 5 in 1991, to reach 6.2 in 1996. (see Armstrong et al. 1998) Also, the rising domestic debt level created an environment of declining liquidity, as interest expenses consumed greater amounts of income. Between 1988 and 1996, average interest expenses of the business sector increased 2.5 times as a proportion of GDP, reaching 19 per cent. This greatly exceeded the corresponding interest burden in Malaysia, which was 10.6 per cent, as a fraction of GDP, in Indonesia, where it was 11.2 per cent and the Philippines, with 10.6 per cent.

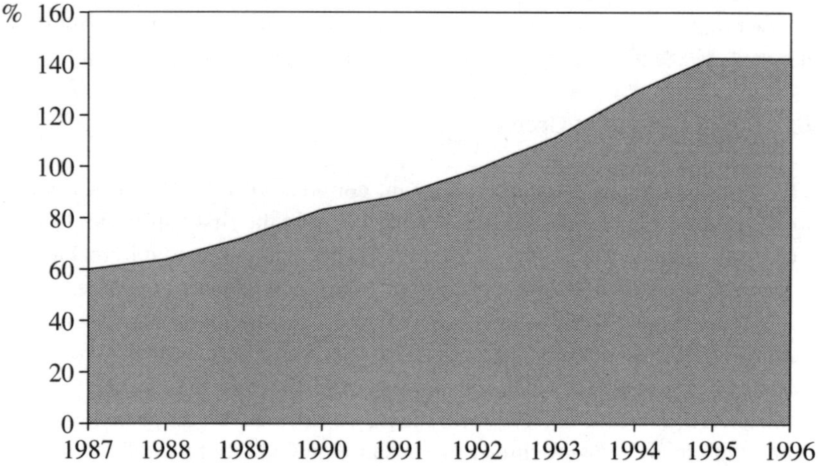

Figure 5.3 Thailand: Credit to GDP ratio, 1987–96

Increased leverage of the Thai corporate sector Firms in Thailand expanded quickly between 1988 and 1996 (as reflected in a rapid increase in fixed assets), in particular in the years immediately prior to the crisis. During 1994 to 1996, the fixed assets of Thai firms grew at 30 per cent per year (Alba et al. 1998a). The asset expansion resulted in severely unbalanced liability structures for many firms and much of these new assets were financed through bank debt. As outlined above, from the late 1980s onward, (financial and) non-financial corporations built up risky forms of leverage in the form of short-term foreign currency debt. The large rate differentials between domestic and international interest rates created incentives for unhedged foreign currency borrowing, especially at short maturity, which carried the lowest rates (the spread between local and international rates was on average 4.1 per cent in Thailand) (World Bank 1998). The stability of the baht and the perceived low risk of devaluation encouraged an open position, ignoring the associated risk of exchange rate depreciation.

During the 1990s, debt to equity ratios of Thai corporates increased significantly: the median value rose from 1.6 in 1988 to 2.3 in 1996. During the same period, the maturity structure of debt shortened considerably. The share of long-term debt almost halved, decreasing from 58 to 31 per cent over that period of time. At the same time, foreign indebtedness increased considerably. By 1996, the median value of foreign debt amounted to 80 per cent in Thailand, and 42 per cent (median value) of the Thai corporations' total debt was denominated in foreign currency, the bulk of which carried short maturities (30 per cent).[25]

Moreover, Alba et al. 1998b show that firms with more concentrated ownership tended to have higher leverage ratios. These authors find that firms recording the highest increase in leverage – an average of 53 per cent – between 1992 and 1996, were those where the top-five owners' concentration was 60 to 80 per cent. In contrast, firms with more dispersed ownership (below 40 per cent of shares belonging to the top five owners) show an increase in leverage of only 19 per cent, on average. Furthermore, the authors find some support for their hypothesis that 'firms with relatively worse performance got a disproportionately large share of financing in the period immediately preceding the crisis.'

By end-1996, hence, Thailand's firms were highly susceptible to liquidity and interest rate shocks. As a result of high leverage, even small shocks to interest rates, the exchange rate or operational cash flow would greatly affect the ability of these companies to service their debt. The high share of short-term liabilities made them further vulnerable to sudden swings in international investors' confidence and to the possibility of being unable to borrow from international capital markets to roll over short-term debt or meet other current debt service obligations.

C. The Deterioration in the Risk Profile of Financial Institutions

The lending boom was associated with a significant deterioration of the risk profile of Thai financial institutions during the period 1990–96. In particular, Thai banks and finance companies became more exposed to credit risk as the quality of their portfolios deteriorated, in part because the lending boom and enhanced competition in the financial sector led to lending to riskier firms and without proper credit assessments. Banks and finance companies also became more exposed to maturity mismatches. This deterioration in the risk profile is explained below in more detail.

Impact of the lending boom The rapid credit growth that took place in the early 1990s strained the expertise of financial institutions in screening, selecting and monitoring loans. As is common in many recently liberalized systems, the skills required to evaluate risky investment projects and monitor the borrower during the life of the loan may have been in short supply in a banking system in which directed and collateral-based lending were the primary activities for many years. Moreover, as deposit growth did not keep pace with loan growth, the already high loan to deposit ratio for finance companies and commercial banks increased further: Commercial banks' loan to deposit ratio increased from 96 per cent in 1988 to 112 per cent in 1995 and from 116 per cent to 138 per cent for finance companies, respectively (World Bank 1997b). The increase in this ratio also resulted from the fact that the financial system (especially commercial banks) substituted higher yielding loans assets with low margin cash or government bonds, which was reflected in rising loan to deposit ratios. Loan to deposit ratios well above 100 per cent made banks and finance companies susceptible to a sudden change in investor confidence and depositor withdrawals.

Lending to risky sectors Commercial banks and finance companies did not only increase their share of risky assets on their balance sheets but also expanded their exposure to 'higher risk' in the non-tradable sectors of the economy (see Table 5.5). This was even more the case for finance companies which expanded rapidly their lending activities in the real estate sector (from an average of 15 per cent in 1988 to 24 per cent in 1996, with some finance companies real estate exposure exceeding 40 per cent), and to loans to consumers.[26] These 'official' figures, however, are likely to be understated because of existing loopholes in the categorization of loans.[27] Market estimates have put the overall exposure of Thai financials in the real estate sector at 30 to 40 per cent.

Table 5.5 Thailand: Sectoral breakdown of lending activities (percentage of total lending)

	1988		1996	
	Commercial banks (%)	Fincos (%)	Commercial banks (%)	Fincos (%)
Agriculture, forestry, and mining	7.1	1.3	3.9	0.9
Manufacturing	25.8	21.8	26.8	15.3
Construction	4.3	3.5	4.6	3.7
Real estate business	6.3	14.8	9.1	24.3
Imports	5.3	2.8	3.2	1.7
Exports	8.3	1.3	4.2	0.8
Wholesale and retail trade	18.9	12.7	17.8	7.8
Public utilities and services	7.3	7.3	10.6	7.6
Banking and other financial business	6.3	9.1	7.5	11.0
Personal consumption	10.3	25.5	12.3	27.0
Total	100.0	100.0	100.0	100.0

Source: Bank of Thailand.

Competition and the customer base Under the BIBF umbrella, 19 new licenses were granted to 19 foreign banks in 1993. The increasing possibilities for AAA companies to borrow off-shore and the establishment of BIBFs increased the competitive pressure in the Thai financial marketplace, especially in the prime borrower and multinationals segments. As a result, finance companies and commercial banks (although to a lesser extent) lost their 'good' customers as these now had more funding alternatives. Nevertheless, due to their aggressive lending practices, finance companies managed to increase their overall market share quite substantially from 12.7 per cent to 21.8 per cent of total financial system assets over 1988 to 1996.

Increase in market risk for finance companies Most commercial banks limited their interest rate risk exposure by extending floating rate loans to their customers, hence transforming interest rate risk into credit risk. Finance companies, typically extended fixed rate loans to their customers and increased the maturity mismatch between their assets and liabilities considerably after 1992. Figure 5.4 shows that, although the bulk of loans extended by finance companies were short-term (less than one year), the average maturity of their liabilities was much shorter than that of their assets (about 56 per cent of their borrowings had a maturity of less than three months in 1996, up from 30 per cent prior to 1992).

Performance of banks and finance companies Commercial banks outgrew their weak performance of the 1980s during 1988 to 1995. Profitability as measured in return on assets and equity increased considerably in the early 1990s. Profitability was high because: (1) of a restructuring of the typical balance sheet (as a ratio to total assets, earning assets increased from 79 per cent in 1988 to 85 per cent by 1995), (2) lower effective tax rates (BIBF loans were taxed at 10 per cent instead of 30 per cent), and (3) an increase in other income (mainly earnings from securities business).[28] The increase in interest margins can largely be attributed to the liberalization of interest rates in 1992. A slowing of the economy, along with a sharply increased off-shore borrowing by banks and new issues of bank capital, filled the banks with liquidity. Meanwhile, the abolition of interest rate ceilings allowed banks to increase their lending rates and decouple them from the deposit rates. Nevertheless, as mentioned before, interest income may be overstated as a result of the lenient interest accrual norms. Moreover, despite the increase, net interest rate margins of banks during this period appear quite low compared to other countries. While net interest rate margins are a rough index of bank (in)efficiency, low margins do not necessarily imply that banks are operating efficiently. For example, low margins may reflect a higher loan to default ratio or may indicate that banks are mispricing credit risk by setting margins too low.[29]

While (accounting) earnings and profits improved during the 1990s, they began to drop in 1996. In 1995, the value of the return on assets and equity

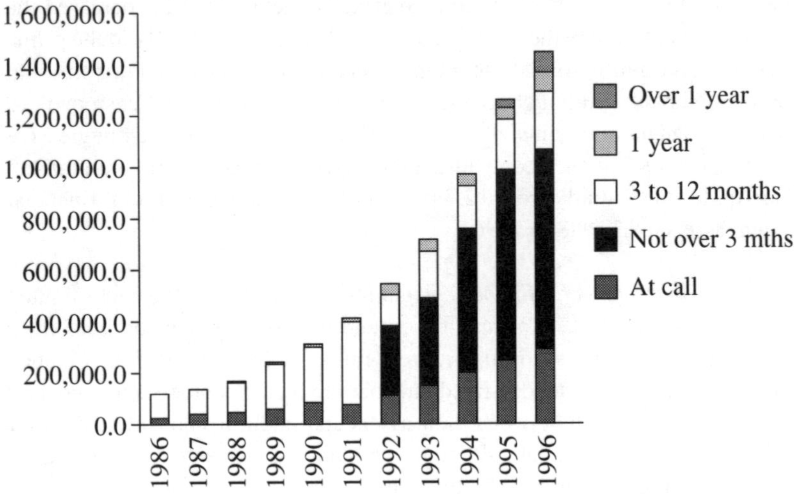

Figure 5.4 (a) *Thailand: Finance companies' borrowing by maturity (million baht)*

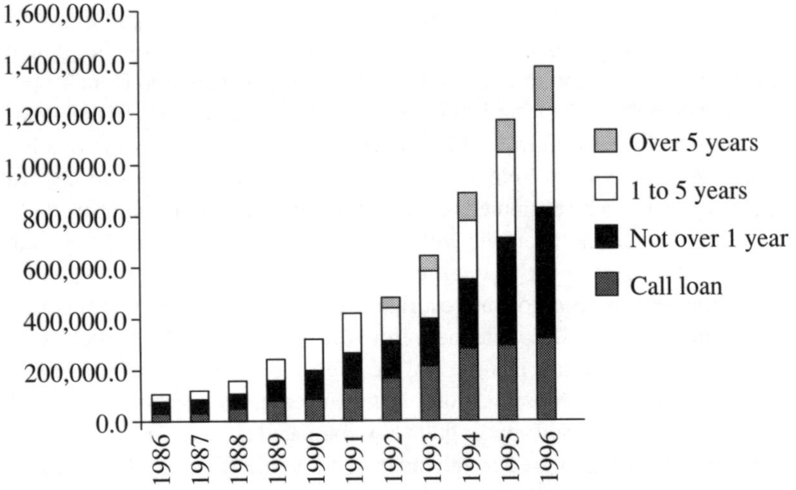

Figure 5.4 (b) *Thailand: Finance companies' lending by maturity (million baht)*

Source: Bank of Thailand.

(ROAE) was 30.6 per cent, but this declined sharply to 21 per cent in 1996. Furthermore, banks never managed to reduce non-performing loans (NPLs). As a ratio of total loans, NPLs remained around 7 per cent, despite the rapid loan growth during the same period, indicating that portfolio problems continued to persist. From 1994 on, accrued interest receivables, often a leading indicator of problem loans, started to rise considerably to 25 per cent in 1994 and 27 per cent in 1995. This increase also suggests that the rapid credit growth did indeed strain assessment and monitoring skills at banks and made them vulnerable to an economic downturn.[30] Due to weak loan provisioning guidelines, banks also inadequately provisioned against specific and general loan losses.[31]

Finance companies' profitability also improved during the early 1990s.[32] The high profitability was due to (1) an increase in net interest rate margins, (2) a higher share of risk assets, and (3) an increase in income from trading and brokerage activities. From 1993 to 1996, however, profitability of finance companies decreased quite markedly. For instance, in 1995 financial companies (Fincos) had a ROAE of 20.9 per cent, but this dropped to 16.7 per cent in 1996. Most of this decline was due to a fall in non-interest income from securities trading (which fell 77 per cent during 1993–96) and brokerage fees (which decreased by 47 per cent over the same period).

While finance companies showed strong profits in the early 1990s, the quality of their loan book continued to be problematic (Figure 5.5). The portfolio deteriorated sharply in 1995 with rising NPLs and a significant increase in interest accrued. This deterioration can be attributed to three main factors: (1) the collapse of the property market with, its repercussion on the construction sector

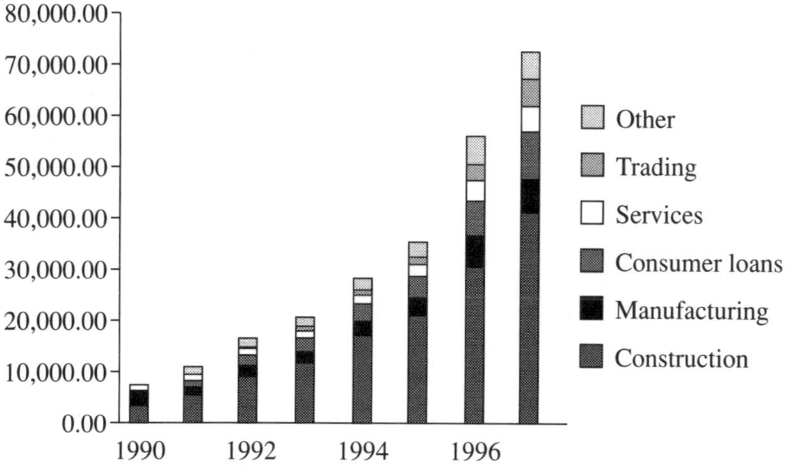

Figure 5.5 Thailand: Finance companies' non-performing loans (million baht)

and the slump in the stock market; (2) a slowdown in the economy and high and rising interest rates that adversely affected both the consumer portfolio and interest rates margins since finance companies were highly exposed to interest rate risk (see above); and (3) deficient risk and liquidity management practices coupled with poor prudential regulation, deficient supervision and weak enforcement.

In sum, the high growth in credit strained banks and finance companies in their capacity to screen and assess credit risk, and led to weaker portfolios. In addition, banks and finance companies increased their exposure to riskier (i.e., more volatile) sectors of the economy. Hence, as a result of the lending boom and coupled with the practice of collateral based lending, banks and finance companies became more vulnerable to economic shocks in the 1990s, mainly because of two factors: (1) by lending excessively to sectors or firms whose debt service capacity was particularly susceptible to shocks; and (2) by reducing their own capacity to absorb negative shocks, especially by exacerbating currency and maturity mismatches, by mis-pricing loans, and by under-provisioning for future potential losses.

4. THE POLICY RESPONSE

This section analyses the policy measures implemented by the government in the macroeconomic and financial sector areas to: (1) control overheating pressures in the face of massive capital inflows, (2) create an incentive compatible environment for market participants to minimize excessive risk taking, and (3) strengthen the regulatory and supervisory framework of financial institutions and corporates. With the benefit of hindsight, it is now obvious that these policies were insufficient. However, they did to some extent contain the most extreme manifestations of overheating, such as rapid inflation and the appreciation of the exchange rate, particularly during the early years of the boom in capital inflows and credit. But overheating pressures built up quickly again, starting in 1993 and, as discussed in the previous section, the economy at both the micro and macro levels became increasingly vulnerable to external shocks. This section, hence, will analyse why the macro and financial sector policies failed to contain overheating and vulnerability, and indeed why they may have even contributed to the build-up of macrofinancial vulnerabilities and fragility in the banking and corporate sectors.

A. Macroeconomic Policies

Capital flows can be procyclical for several reasons. First, private capital flows can accommodate excess demand pressures as domestic residents borrow overseas to fund their expansion plans. Second, capital flows, attracted by high potential returns, can generate domestic cycles by contributing to domestic investment. Finally, capital flows may exacerbate asset price inflation and indirectly contribute to consumption and investment booms. In all three cases, excess demand will be manifested by increases in the current account if there is excess demand in tradables, and in rising inflation if there is excess demand in non-tradables. Excess demand for non-tradables will also lead to a deterioration in the current account as the real exchange appreciates.

In Thailand, the demand pressures were manifested primarily in a widening of the current account deficit, although there was also an increase in inflation. As measured by both the current account and inflation, both 1990–91 and 1994–96 are the periods when overheating is most evident (see Figure 5.6) coinciding also with the two peak capital inflow periods. During most of the capital inflow period domestic demand, in particular investment, was the major contributor to GDP growth. The contribution of the external sector to GDP growth was negative in Thailand during 1990–96, except for 1991 and 1992 when the current account deficit improved.

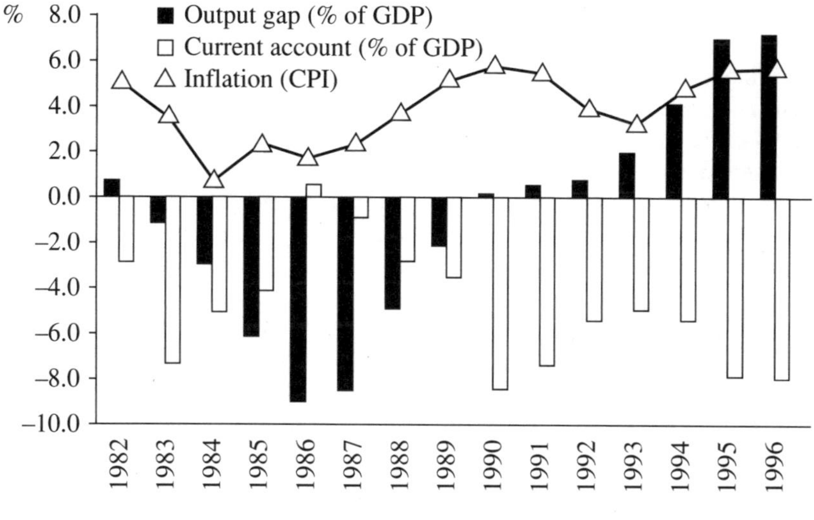

Figure 5.6 Thailand: Overheating symptoms

There are important differences between the two periods when overheating pressures were most evident. First, while during the period 1988–92 output recovered quickly and grew at about 11 per cent per year on average, it remained below or close to its potential level. This implies that the growth in investment was driving GDP, and also that the increase in the current account deficit was creating productive capacity. During the latter period, 1993–96, output growth quickly surpassed capacity, reflecting the increasing importance of consumption as a source of growth as well as the decline in investment efficiency. For example, while the average incremental capital–output ratio during the period 1988–92 was 3.5, it increased to 5.4 for the period 1993–96. As mentioned before, recent studies on growth performance in Thailand also suggest that Total Factor Productivity (TFP) growth was declining during this period (see Tinakorn and Sussangorn 1998). Second, as shown above, short-term debt intermediated by domestic banks dominated the composition of capital inflows during the second overheating period, compared to a more balanced composition of equity (including FDI) and debt during the initial period. We believe that the macroeconomic policy mix is an important albeit partial explanation of these differences. This hypothesis is explored further below after analysing the determinants of capital inflows.

B. Economic Policies and the Determinants of Capital Flows

Both *push* and *pull* factors have played a role in determining private capital flows to Thailand. Our analysis focuses on the determinants of shorter-term flows (net of FDI), since these inflows are more volatile and the primary cause of vulnerability.[33] As described in more detail in Appendix 1, bank and non-bank flows are analysed separately since they may respond differently both in terms of magnitude and speed to changes in push and pull factors. Following the literature, the factors included in the empirical analysis are the differential between foreign and domestic interest rates, a measure of country creditworthiness, a variable measuring domestic output that serves to capture the demand for financing (as well as prospects for the economy), and four dummy variables to capture changes in tax-adjusted rates of return and administrative controls.

Our empirical analysis presented in Appendix 1 illustrates that high domestic interest rates were a major factor in attracting short-term capital in Thailand during 1988 to 1992, and that non-bank flows were slower in reacting to the interest rate differential. The faster adjustment of bank flows to changes in interest rates may reflect easier access of financial institutions to short-term lines of credit overseas which in turn allows them to quickly take advantage of opportunities for interest arbitrage. Similarly, both bank and non-bank flows are sensitive to country risk. As country risk declined over the 1990s, the same interest rate differential would lead to larger inflows of private capital.

Administrative measures regarding capital account transactions were also important in Thailand, but seemingly more in changing the composition of flows rather than their total magnitude. The empirical analysis confirms that the establishment of the BIBF led to a large increase in bank flows. It also confirms that the 7 per cent reserve requirement imposed by the BoT on foreign short-term borrowings by banks and finance companies had a large negative impact on short-term bank inflows. Given that bank and non-bank flows are strong substitutes, however, the impact on total flows of such measures is significantly reduced although not totally offset. For example, while the establishment of the BIBF strongly encouraged the intermediation of foreign capital by banks, it also led to a decline in inflows intermediated through other channels. These results have strong implications for the effectiveness of monetary policy.

C. Monetary Policy

Starting in 1988, the Bank of Thailand began sterilizing the surge in capital inflows by accumulating foreign assets and receiving deposits from the public sector. Despite very substantial increases in net foreign assets – net foreign assets grew on average by about 54 per cent per annum, and in some periods skyrocketed to as high as 89 per cent – the BoT succeeded in containing reserve money growth to an average of 17 per cent during the entire period (1988:Q4–1996:Q3) (Figure 5.7).

Thailand relied primarily on monetary tightening and the sterilization of capital inflows to deal with overheating pressures resulting from an upturn in domestic demand and capital inflows (see Appendix 2). Nevertheless, in raising

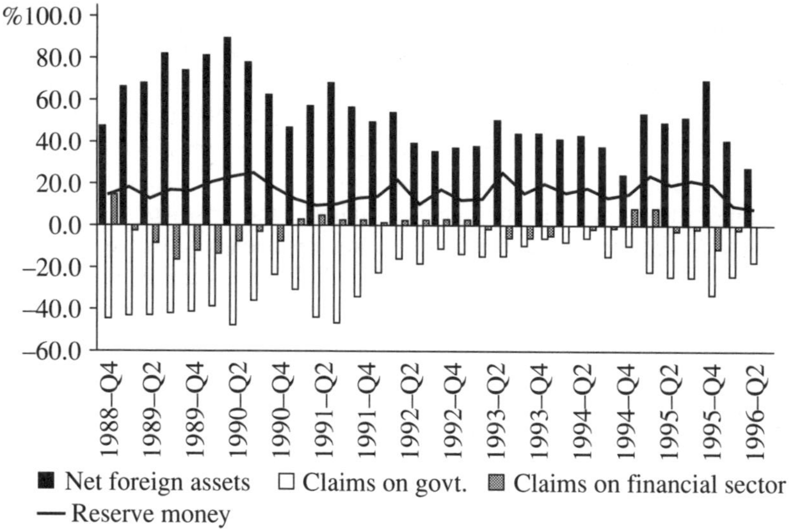

Note: Annual growth measured as the percentage change from the same quarter one year before.

Figure 5.7 Thailand: Growth in reserve money and its components

interest rates, Thailand was simply providing an impetus for further capital inflows, since the latter were very responsive to interest arbitrage opportunities. Indeed, as investor perceptions regarding Thailand strengthened during this period, capital inflows became more sensitive to the measured interest rate differential. Structural factors, such as the progressive liberalization of the capital account during this period and the increasing familiarity of investors with emerging markets, also worked in the same direction. Hence, monetary policy during 1993–96 was becoming less effective as an instrument to deal with overheating and capital inflows (for example, the offset coefficient was increasing; see Appendix 2), and was in fact encouraging further inflows and the accumulation of external short-term liabilities.

D. Fiscal Policy

Despite the decreasing effectiveness of monetary policy, fiscal policy was not used to contain overheating during the period 1993–96, and indeed may have added to demand pressures. As discussed above, Thailand had succeeded in eliminating fiscal deficits following the fiscal consolidation of the mid-1980s. The underlying fiscal policy position remained strong in Thailand during 1988–1996, and Thailand recorded surpluses every year except 1996/97. Although fiscal surpluses declined during the period 1992–96 – as the focus of fiscal policy shifted towards addressing infrastructure bottlenecks – they remained around 2 per cent of GDP during 1992–94. In 1995, the fiscal surplus rose to 2.5 per cent of GDP. However, the fiscal stance which had been expansionary in 1994 (and hence had been counter-cyclical given that the economy was not experiencing overheating pressures) turned slightly more expansionary in 1995 (so that the fiscal impulse was expansionary) when excess demand pressures emerged. In 1996, the fiscal surplus declined to 1.6 per cent of GDP, entailing a strong expansionary impulse – although the growth of the economy had only slowed slightly and demand pressures remained very high as measured by the output gap and the current account deficit. In both years, therefore, fiscal policy was procyclical. The procyclical nature of fiscal policy during this period is also reflected in the correlation between the fiscal impulse and excess demand pressures in Thailand, which turned positive over 1993 to 1996. In sum, while the fiscal stance remained conservative over 1988–96, fiscal policy imparted a positive impulse to the domestic pressures in the critical 1993–96 period, thereby aggravating the pressure on interest rates.

E. Exchange Rate Policy

From 1985 to mid-1997, the nominal exchange rate in Thailand remained fairly constant. Indeed, after a 10 per cent devaluation in mid-1981, and another 18 per cent devaluation in late 1984, the baht stabilized at about Bt25 per dollar, showing only small changes around this value – the average monthly variation during this period was an appreciation of 0.82 cents of a baht per month, while the coefficient of variation of the exchange rate was only 0.02[34] (see Box 5.2).

BOX 5.2 TARGETING A NOMINAL BAND FOR THE BAHT

A closer examination to the evolution of the nominal exchange rate in Thailand gives some additional light regarding the policy followed by the authorities during 1985–97. Although still showing little variation for the whole 1985–97 period, an even narrower band appears to have been targeted by the authorities starting in 1987. Indeed, as shown in the figure below, after an appreciation of about 8 per cent between early 1985 and late 1986, the baht fluctuated within a very narrow band of ±3 per cent around its mean – of B/US$25.4 – for the entire period 1987 – mid-97 (in absolute value, the Baht fluctuated by ± 0.08 around its mean, with a minimum and a maximum of 24.6 and 26.1, respectively).

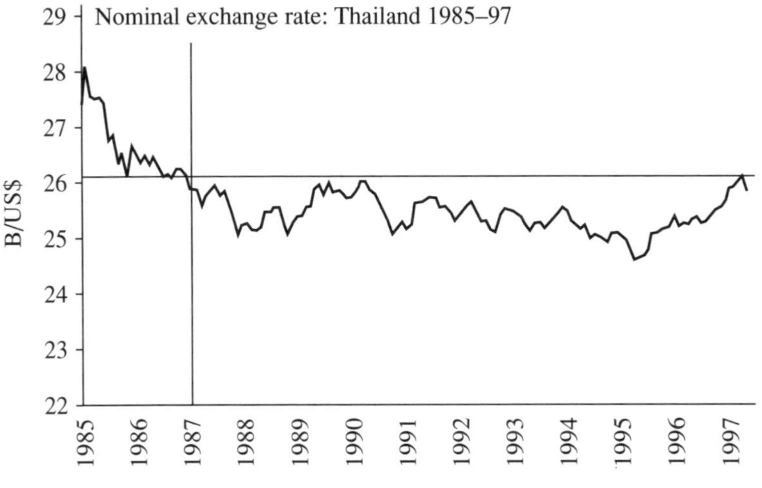

The inflation rate in Thailand during this period also remained stable at about 0.38 per cent per month, on average, with a standard deviation of about 0.45 per cent. In this domestic environment, with an average international inflation rate at about 0.18 per cent per month – measured by the US Wholesale Price Index (WPI) – and a depreciating dollar *vis-à-vis* other major currencies, the real effective exchange rate in Thailand declined steadily until the first quarter of 1995. The trend reversed when the US dollar began appreciating *vis-à-vis* the yen and other major currencies in international markets in the second quarter of 1995 (see Figure 5.8).

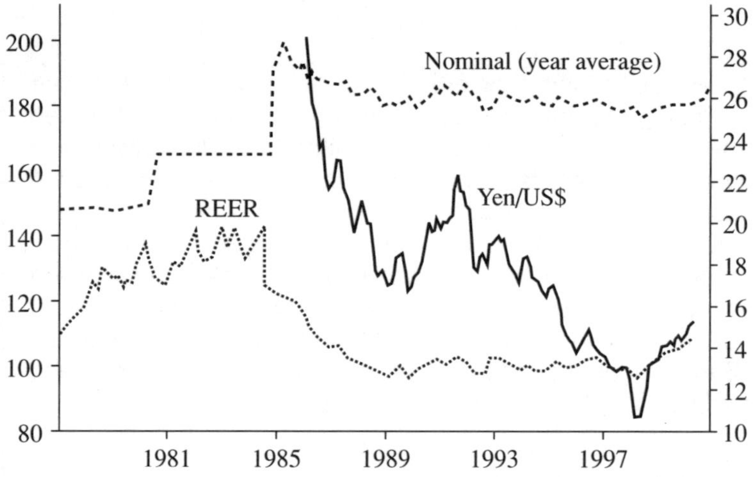

Figure 5.8 Thailand: real effective and nominal exchange rate

International market conditions during 1985–95 facilitated achieving high economic growth in Thailand – based on a sustained development of exports – by maintaining a stable nominal exchange rate, despite domestic inflation being higher than the relevant international (US) one. Indeed, the strategy adopted by the monetary authorities in Thailand until the devaluation of the baht in July 1997, was to maintain a stable nominal exchange rate, although they systematically implemented small changes to its value whenever there were signals that the differential between the domestic and foreign inflation rates was widening and that the real sector was growing too fast – which could lead to potential overheating. These results are obtained by estimating the BoT exchange rate reaction function: i.e., by regressing the change in the exchange rate parity (dependent variable) on the domestic inflation rate, the external (US) inflation rate, and a proxy variable measuring the gap between actual output and its long-term trend (independent variables). The estimation results using monthly data under alternative specifications of the model are reported in Appendix 3. The important result drawn from this exercise, as discussed in Appendix 3, is that, starting in early 1992, the authorities partly abandoned the policy of correcting the exchange rate for changes in inflation differentials and excessive output growth. In other words, during 1992–96 the policy of keeping an almost constant nominal exchange rate was strengthened, further decreasing the perceived exchange risk and therefore giving more incentives to borrow short-term from abroad.

In sum, the Thai authorities, concerned with preventing an appreciation of the real exchange rate to retain Thailand's export competitiveness, maintained a pegged exchange rate system and intervened in the foreign exchange market to maintain the peg in the face of the large capital inflows. By preventing the nominal exchange rate from departing significantly from the central peg (in particular, by preventing the exchange rate from appreciating), the policy resulted in a fairly predictable nominal exchange rate, which reduced foreign exchange risk faced by investors and increased the incentives of domestic residents to incur unhedged, short-term foreign debt. Hence, a more flexible exchange rate policy could have reduced capital inflows and thus overheating pressures, obviating the need to tighten monetary policy in the first place and avoiding the perverse cycle of tight monetary policy, resulting in an increase in interest rates, attracting additional inflows, which result in further tightening of monetary policy.[35]

F. Policy Response in the Financial System

Policy measures that the government implemented in the financial system can be grouped into two different categories: (1) (delayed) measures that were aimed at deterring short-term capital flows through the banking system; and (2) measures aimed at strengthening the broader incentive framework of financial institutions.

Measures aimed at deterring short-term foreign capital flows

As outlined above, the government promoted BIBF operations by granting bank tax incentives on their BIBF operations and excluding them from reserve requirements, which effectively lowered funding costs (of foreign instruments) even further. Starting in 1995, the BoT implemented measures aimed at curbing (short-term) capital flows mostly by aligning the treatment of BIBF transactions with other bank transactions and thus reducing banks' incentives to engage in BIBF transactions. The measures included the following:

- Increasing the minimum credit level for credit extended through BIBF from $500,000 to $2 million (to ensure that loans were granted to larger-size businesses).
- Raising the reserve requirement for non-resident baht accounts from 2 to 7 per cent in late 1995.

- Implementing a 7 per cent cash reserve requirement on short-term monetary instruments under 12 months for both banking and finance companies effective, on 23 June 1996.
- Lowering the credit tax for BIBF business from 30 to 10 per cent.

As described above, while these measures were successful in reducing incentives for BIBF operations (see Appendix 1), they were of limited effectiveness in curtailing total short-term foreign borrowing. As BIBF operations became more expensive, domestic firms increased their direct foreign borrowings since they continued to remain attracted to the differential between domestic and international interest rates. Banks and corporations, assuming that the currency peg was credible, piled on more short-term foreign debt as it represented (a supposedly) low-cost and low-risk financing option. And importantly, the measures were too late in that banks and corporates had, by end 1995–mid-1996 when these measures were implemented, highly vulnerable balance sheets.

Changes to the regulatory regime in the aftermath of liberalization

Financial liberalization and the opening of the capital account changed the business of banking in Thailand. For example, before the reforms risky projects were usually priced out of the market, since lending rates were subject to ceilings and banks could not charge appropriate risk premia. When ceilings were lifted during 1992, and lending requirements to priority sectors were relaxed, it became possible for financial institutions to finance riskier ventures. Moreover, the removal of currency controls and the setting up of BIBF operations allowed financial institutions to take on foreign exchange risk by raising foreign currency funds on international markets and lending them to local borrowers – in other words, transforming currency risk into credit risk by lending foreign currency to unhedged domestic borrowers.

While liberalization increased the opportunities for financial institutions to take on risk, financial institutions' incentives to evaluate and manage the downside risks of their activities were not strengthened – for instance, by increasing the capital to asset ratio and imposing stricter loan classification and loan loss provisioning guidelines – and the relatively weak regulatory and supervisory framework was not improved upon. This was compounded by the fact that the resolution of the crisis in the 1980s appeared to have signaled to depositors that deposits were implicitly guaranteed, thus reducing incentives for market monitoring and increasing the scope for moral hazard. Moreover, as emphasized by Caprio and Summers (1993) and Hellman et al. (1994), another factor that may have contributed to moral hazard was the reduction in franchise value as competition increased and ceilings on interest rates were eliminated.

During the mid-1990s, attempts were made to strengthen the prudential regulatory framework. Starting in 1993, the BoT took a number of measures to reform the regulatory and supervisory system, albeit as Table 5.6 illustrates, the BoT failed to bring it closer in line with global best practices (especially in the area of loan classification and loan loss provision guidelines, concentration and exposure ratios and limits on connected lending). Moreover, the finance company sector remained more lightly regulated than commercial banks despite the fact that these companies engaged in similar activities (but in riskier market segments) to banks.

Table 5.6 Thailand: Changes to the regulatory and supervisory framework

	Measures
1993/January	• Imposing BIS capital adequacy standards on commercial banks. Initially, minimum capital-to-risk-asset ratio at 7 per cent for domestic banks and 6 per cent for foreign banks.
1993/December	• Increasing minimum capital-to-risk ratio to 7.5 per cent for domestic banks and to 6.5 per cent for foreign banks.
1994/June	• Imposing net foreign exchange position limits on finance companies (25 per cent on overbought side and 20 per cent of tier 1 capital on oversold side).
	• Increasing minimum reserve for doubtful debts of commercial banks from 50 to 75 per cent.
1995/March	• Commercial banks have to submit details of their risk management to BoT.
1995/December	• Increasing minimum reserve for doubtful debts of commercial banks from 75 to 100 per cent.
1996/May	• Imposition of 100 per cent provisioning requirement against doubtful loans for finance companies, finance and securities companies, and credit foncier companies.
1996/October	• Increasing the first tier capital fund to risk asset ratio of commercial banks from 5.5 per cent to 6 per cent.
	• Increasing the overall capital-to-risk asset ratio of finance companies to 7.5 per cent (equivalent to commercial banks).
1997/March	• Further strengthening of the loan loss provisioning requirements,

Source: Bank of Thailand, Financial Institutions and Markets in Thailand, 1998.

Domestic policies and economic vulnerability: a summary

Private capital flows validated and exacerbated the domestic macro cycle in Thailand, and despite efforts to the contrary, led in several instances to overheating pressures as manifested by the growing current account deficit and rising inflation. More importantly with regard to vulnerability, however, was that the policy mix created incentives for large current account deficits to be financed through the rapid build-up of short-term, unhedged, external liabilities. The macro policies that jointly contributed to vulnerability in Thailand were:

- *Monetary policy stance* Monetary policy during 1993–96 was becoming less effective as an instrument to deal with overheating and capital inflows, and was encouraging further inflows, by raising domestic interest rates, and stimulating the accumulation of short-term liabilities.
- *Exchange rate policy* By allowing the nominal exchange rate to only fluctuate in a narrow band and by not permitting it to appreciate, Thailand's exchange rate policy contributed to vulnerability, most importantly by encouraging both short-term and unhedged borrowing by reducing the perceived exchange rate risk. If authorities had been more flexible and had permitted the nominal exchange rate to appreciate, incentives to borrow abroad would have declined as the rise in the value of the baht would have led to expectations of a depreciation. A more flexible exchange rate could have reduced capital inflows and overheating pressures, obviating the need to tighten monetary policy and thus avoiding the perverse cycle of tight monetary policy, additional capital inflows and further tightening of monetary policy.
- *Fiscal policy* Despite the fact that the underlying fiscal policy remained conservative throughout 1987–96, fiscal policy became procyclical during 1993–96 and imparted a positive impulse to domestic demand pressures, thereby aggravating pressures on interest rates.

In the financial sector, administrative measures to curb capital inflows and dismantle tax and other advantages were too little, too late. Moreover, the incentive and regulatory as well as supervisory framework, which were weak at the onset of the liberalization, were not strengthened sufficiently to align incentives of bank owners, managers and supervisors with prudent banking. Finally, market discipline continued to remain severely curtailed as disclosure and accounting were not improved substantially and the government failed to curtail the safety net (or implicit deposit insurance), which was implanted during the resolution of the 1983–87 crisis.

5. CONCLUSIONS

Our analysis suggests that the interaction between macroeconomic policies and the institutional framework under which Thai financial institutions operated created many vulnerabilities, which came home to roost in July 1997. The main elements of our conclusions are that: (a) the build-up in vulnerability was rooted in private behavior, in particular, regarding the magnitude of investment, its composition and how it was financed, rather than in the public sector; (b) financial sector weaknesses – including the inadequate regulatory and supervisory system, (implicit) deposit insurance, concentrated ownership structures, poor accounting and disclosures – combined with financial and capital account liberalization, which contributed to the build-up of vulnerabilities by creating incentives for excessive risk-taking among financial institutions; (c) weaknesses in the governance of corporations, including close links with the banking sector, induced risky investments and over-diversification in the corporate sector; (d) while many aspects of the macro fundamentals were strong, the macro policy mix that combined a tight monetary policy with an inflexible exchange rate created strong incentives for residents to expose themselves to excessive foreign exchange and liquidity risks.

Inadequate macro-economic policies increased vulnerabilities Regime shifts in macrofinancial regulation (liberalization of the capital account and financial sector in the late 1980s and early 1990s), without an adequate upgrading of the regulatory and supervisory framework led to rapid credit growth. In parallel, attracted by Thailand's rapid growth rate and improving creditworthiness, starting in 1988 there was a large surge in net private capital inflows. Both, in turn, fueled over-investment in unprofitable industrial capacity and in the real estate sector, creating an asset price boom-and-bust cycle and macroeconomic overheating pressures. Loans were committed on inflated collateral values and often funded through (mostly short-term) foreign currency liabilities without appropriate hedging strategies. Monetary and exchange rate policy encouraged off-shore short-term funding. The macro policy mix maintained domestic interest rates above international comparable levels, while foreign currency risk appeared minimal against the background of stable nominal exchange rates. Rapid accumulation of domestic and foreign currency credit rendered the corporate sector increasingly leveraged and vulnerable to financial shocks.

And micro-deficiencies led to poor resource allocation and added risks The institutional framework affecting financial institutions was not conducive to prudent behavior. The resolution of the crisis in 1983–84 did not lead to a renewal and upgrade of managerial capabilities in Thai financial institutions. Moreover, deregulation had increased competition, resulting in a decrease in franchise value of financial institutions, which further reduced their incentives for prudent behavior. This was compounded by lax supervision and ineffective regulators, which had weak problem recognition capacity and engaged in forbearance. Market oversight was limited due to the poor disclosure and quality of financial information, a concentrated ownership structure and cross-ownership links between financial and non-financial entities. Moreover, incentives for market oversight were possibly reduced by the highly visable bailout of depositors following the mid-1980s crisis.

Weak governance of financial institutions – due to a lack of market for corporate control and nontransparent, cross-ownership – allowed for bank lending to, and investment in, unviable projects. Financial institutions relied more on collateral rather than on evaluation of project viability, or borrower creditworthiness, or cash flows, which encouraged the build-up of real estate and equity market exposure and increased vulnerabilities. In addition, the lending boom strained the credit assessment and monitoring capacity of financial institutions and, coupled with insufficient internal risk control mechanisms and risk management practices, rendered financial institutions vulnerable. Similarly, weaknesses in the governance of corporations induced risky investments and over-diversification, with low returns on investment.

While some of these policy distortions and institutional weaknesses had been festering for some time, the vulnerability build-up was particularly quick and severe during 1994–96. On the macro side, fiscal policy on a cyclically adjusted basis was expansionary during this time period and monetary policy bore most of the burden in managing the large overheating pressures. Combined with nominal exchange rate stability, the macro policy mix, by increasing the risk-adjusted interest rate differential, is an important factor explaining the surge in short-term private capital inflows that peaked in 1995. On the financial sector policy side, the establishment of the BIBF in late-1993 is another significant factor in explaining the rapid accumulation of short-term foreign exchange liabilities. The tax and reserve treatment of BIBF institutions acted like the Chilean capital controls used in the 1990s but in reverse, increasing instead of deterring short-term debt inflows.

Thailand is not the first country to experience a financial sector crisis after financial sector liberalization. Indeed, many financial liberalization episodes in the past have led to a lending boom, increased financial fragility, and a crisis. Examples of this are the USA in the mid-1980s, Sweden, Finland and Norway in the late 1980s and early 1990s, and Mexico in 1994–95. Nevertheless, Thailand's crisis illustrates – like Chile's in the early 1980s – that opening the capital account and integrating with global financial markets while liberalizing the domestic financial sector, should be contingent on adequate domestic institutional development. The benefits of an open system have to be weighted against the risk of financial crisis, especially in countries with not only fragile financial systems but also weak regulatory and supervisory frameworks and (implicit) government guarantees on deposits. Moreover, the liberalization of the financial sector needs to be carefully managed as it increases competition and thus lowers the franchise value of (existing) financial institutions, creating incentives for unsound banking practices.

APPENDIX 1 DETERMINANTS OF SHORT-TERM PRIVATE CAPITAL FLOWS

Following the literature, factors that may affect both bank (*FBNKS*) and non-bank flows (*FNBNK*), net of FDI, are the following:

- *Interest Rate Differential (IDIF)*: the differential between domestic (the interbank rate) and foreign interest rates (dollar overnight LIBOR). This captures both push and pull factors. Given the stability of the baht/dollar rate and the credibility of the exchange rate policy during the period of analysis and the lack of a complete data set on exchange rate expectations, the rate differential is not adjusted for the depreciation premium. The data that are available on exchange rate expectations of selected institutional investors and banks supports this unorthodox approach.[36] If 1995–96 is a representative period, investors expected the baht/dollar rate to hover around 25, as implied by Figure A5.1, and the exchange rate plays only a minor role as a determinant of expected returns and risks.
- *The Institutional Investor Country Rating (IIRAT)*: a measure of creditworthiness. Since this country rating measures country risk, it complements the interest rate differential variable to the extent that the latter does not fully capture changes in country risk. (It was not possible to directly account for country risk for lack of good data on spreads demanded by the market for holding Thai sovereign dollar bonds.)
- *A Proxy for GDP (GE)*: the 12 months' growth in electricity consumption.
- Since bank and non-bank flows are strong substitutes, as discussed above, it seems plausible to include the contemporaneous value of their counterparts in the respective equations.
- Four dummy variables to capture changes in tax adjusted rates of return and administrative controls on capital inflows:

  - *A dummy (DUMBIBF)* to capture the impact of the BIBF start in March 1993.
  - *A dummy (DUMNRBCON1)* to capture the impact of the change in how commercial banks hold the 7 per cent reserve requirements on

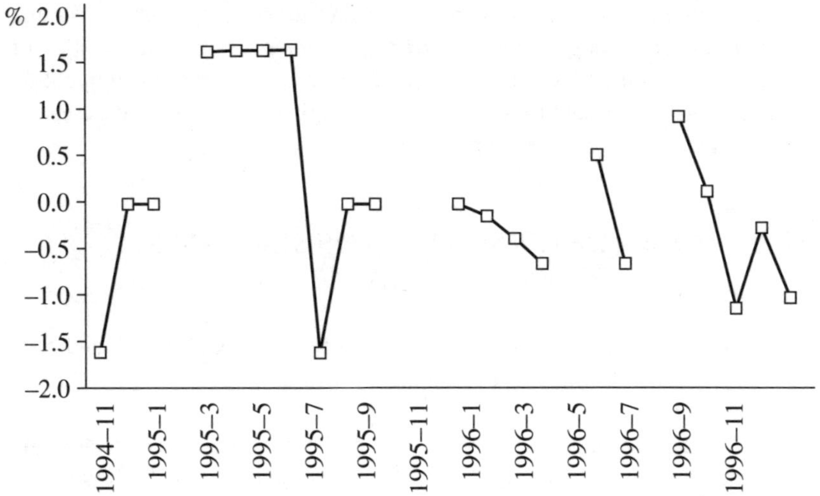

Figure A5.1 Investor expectations (annualized expected change in the dollar/baht rate two months forward)

NR baht deposits. Effective 8 August 1995, banks were required to hold all 7 per cent reserve requirements at the BoT (with no interest) rather than the previous minimum 2 per cent.

- *A dummy (DUMNRBCON2)* to capture the impact of the BoT requirement, effective 4 April 1996, for fincos to deposit at the BoT 7 per cent of their short-term (< 1 year) baht currency borrowings from nonresidents. This measure would indirectly discourage NR deposits since these accounts serve several purposes, including the purchase of short-term finco paper.
- *A dummy (DUMBBORCON)* to capture the impact of the BoT measure, effective 23 June 1996, that extended the 7 per cent reserve requirement to all new short-term foreign borrowings of commercial banks, BIBFs and fincos. This measure is designed to discourage capital inflows, especially short-term.

Table A5.1 shows the surprisingly strong result. To avoid simultaneity biases, the equations have been estimated by two-stage least squares using all the exogenous variables of both equations and lagged endogenous variables as instruments in both equations. Both equations were estimated in levels with monthly data starting in January 1992 as both capital inflow variables were found to be stationary. As expected, the two types of flows are strong substitutes during the sample period. In both equations, the coefficients for the values of the other types of flows are large in absolute terms but negative, and very significant. These results show further that private capital flows, however, are not sensitive to growth performance, at least as measured by electricity consumption.

Table A5.1 Determinants of capital flows

(US$ millions, monthly, 1992–96)

Variable	Coefficient	t-statistic
Bank intermediated net		
Constant	–12329.71	–3.65
GE(–1)	1635.82	0.84
IDIF	108.98	3.60
DUMBIBF	678.31	5.07
DUMBBORCON	–976.63	–2.91
IIRAT	196.83	3.51
FNBNK	–0.75	–5.67
R-square	0.75	
S.E of regression	415.45	
No. of observations	55	
Non-bank intermediated net		
Constant	–9278.90	–2.19
IDIF(–1)	100.31	2.58
FBNKS	–0.32	–1.87
IIRAT	151.73	2.18
FNBNK(–1)	0.38	2.81
DUMNRBCON2	57.38	0.21
R-square	0.61	
S.E of regression	559.56	
No. of observations	55	
Excludes FDI		

Source: Financial Times Currency Forecaster.

The empirical analysis illustrates that high interest rates were a major factor in attracting short-term capital in Thailand during 1988–92. Moreover, the significance of the lagged endogenous variable in the non-bank equation suggests that non-bank flows were slower in reacting to the interest rate differential. The faster adjustment of bank flows to changes in interest rates may reflect easier access of financial institutions to short-term lines of credit overseas which, in turn, allows them to quickly take advantage of opportunities for interest arbitrage. Similarly, both bank and non-bank flows are sensitive to country risk (the coefficients are positive and significant), with a one-point increase (improvement) in the institutional investor rating leading to an increase in non-bank flows of US$150 million, and in bank flows of US$200 million. In other words, as country risk declined over the 1990s, the same interest rate differential would lead to larger inflows of private capital.

Administrative measures regarding capital account transactions were also important in Thailand, but seemingly more in changing the composition of flows rather than their total magnitude. That such measures had an impact is indicated by the large and highly significant coefficients for two of the dummy variables. That is, the establishment of the BIBF led to a large increase in bank flows, while the imposition of the 7 per cent reserve requirement on foreign short-term borrowings by banks and finance companies had a large negative impact on bank inflows. Given that bank and non-bank flows are strong substitutes, however, the impact on total flows of such measures is significantly reduced, although not totally offset. For example, while the establishment of the BIBF strongly encouraged the intermediation of foreign capital by banks, it also led to a decline in inflows intermediated through other channels.

APPENDIX 2 STERILIZING PRIVATE CAPITAL FLOWS

To confirm that the BoT attempted to sterilize the surge in capital inflows, this appendix estimates the monetary policy reaction function of the central bank. The policy variable determined by the authorities is the stock of domestic assets – claims on government plus claims on the financial sector – which is assumed to be affected by the stock of foreign assets held by the central bank, the real exchange rate, and output growth. The equation to be estimated is specified as follows:

$$\Delta MP_t = \alpha + \beta \Delta FA_t + \chi p_{t-1} + \delta \ln(Y_{t-1}/Y_{t-2}) + \mu_t,$$

where ΔMP is the change in central bank's net domestic assets, ΔFA is the change in central bank's net foreign assets, and p and Y stand for the real exchange rate and aggregate output, respectively. The first two policy-related coefficients, β and χ, are expected to be negative, while the third, δ, is expected to be positive. In other words, the authorities are expected to tighten monetary policy to compensate for larger capital inflows (and current account surpluses) and an appreciating real exchange rate, while they are expected to accommodate the increases in money demand that are due to increases in aggregate output. The results of estimating equation using monthly data during 1986–96 are reported in Table A5.2.

Table A5.2 Regression results

	Sample period		
	1986:1 1996:11	1986:1 1991:12	1992:9 1996:11
β	– 1.09**	– 0.55*	– 1.04**
χ	– 166.2	– 0.01	+ 0.01
δ	– 941.6	– 459.7	– 3038

Notes: Due to simultaneous equations bias the estimation results are obtained using instrumental variables techniques. Instruments used were lagged ΔMP, lagged ΔFA, foreign interest rates, and monthly dummies.
* significant at 10%, ** significant at 5%.

The empirical findings confirm that the Thai monetary authorities attempted to sterilize the inflows of capital, and that they intensified their efforts starting in late 1992 (β was the only coefficient that turned out to be significantly different from zero). This finding is consistent with the fact that in 1993 the BIBF was launched and the inflows accelerated. It is also consistent with the fact that sterilization became less effective as the Thai economy became financially more integrated with the rest of the world. In other words, to achieve a pre-specified target for monetary growth, during 1993–96 the authorities had to intervene by sterilizing larger volumes of funds. Indeed, estimations based on a structural model of the offset coefficient for the Thai economy – the degree in which a reduction in domestic credit by the central bank is offset by an additional inflow of foreign capital – shows that during 1993–96 a decrease in domestic credit by the central bank of US$100 was offset within the same month by an additional inflow of US$54. For the entire sample period, 1986–96, the offset coefficient was only 0.38, implying an additional inflow of US$38 for each US$100 reduction in domestic credit.

APPENDIX 3 THE EXCHANGE RATE REACTION FUNCTION

The results on exchange rate policy discussed earlier in this chapter are based on a regression between the change in the exchange rate parity (dependent variable), and the domestic inflation rate, the external (US) inflation rate, and a proxy variable measuring the gap between actual output and its long-term trend (independent variables). The estimated model is specified in this equation:

$$\Delta FX_t = \beta_0 + \beta_1 \pi^d_{t-1} + \beta_2 \pi^{us}_{t-1} + \beta_3 \gamma^{gap}_{t-1} + \varepsilon_t,$$

where ΔFX stands for the absolute change in the exchange rate, π^d stands for domestic inflation, π^{us} stands for the international (US) inflation rate, γ^{gap} is the proxy used for overheating,[37] and ε is an error term. The estimation results using monthly data under alternative specifications of the model are reported in Table A5.3.

Table A5.3 Exchange rate reaction function

	1986–96	1986–96	1986–91	1992–96
Dependent variable	Monthly ΔFX	Three-month moving average ΔFX	Three-month moving average ΔFX	Three-month moving average ΔFX
β_0	– 0.012	– 0.008	– 0.017	0.003
β_1	0.041 *	0.011 *	0.019 **	0.002
β_2	– 0.047 **	– 0.015 ***	– 0.013 **	– 0.020
β_3	– 4.91 E-07 ***	– 1.10 E-07 **	– 2.49 E-07 ***	– 5.27 E-09
AR(1)	0.379 ***	1.224 ***	1.292 ***	1.165 ***
AR(2)	– 0.189 **	– 0.613 ***	– 0.663 ***	– 0.602 ***
N	128	126	60	60
R^2	0.183	0.746	0.789	0.714
Adj. R^2	0.149	0.735	0.769	0.687

Note: * significant at 10 per cent; ** significant at 5 per cent; *** significant at 1 per cent.

The results in the first column of the table show that an increase in domestic inflation of one percentage point (monthly) led to a depreciation of about Bt0.04 per dollar the next month, while an increase in external (US) inflation of one percentage point led the authorities to appreciate the currency by a slightly higher magnitude. In the long run, the same changes in domestic and foreign inflation led the authorities to depreciate the baht by about Bt0.05 and to appreciate it by about Bt0.06 *vis-à-vis* the dollar, respectively. Also, excessive growth in output led the authorities to appreciate the currency by about Bt0.5 *vis-à-vis* the dollar, for each MM 1 megawatts of electricity consumed above its trend and seasonal components. This is consistent with the view that economic growth during this period was export-driven and, therefore, an appreciation was needed to slowdown the economy.[38] The same excess increase in output led the authorities to induce an appreciation of the baht in the long run of about 60 cents per dollar.

Changes in the exchange rate during this period were highly volatile, however, which leads to poor overall results (measured by the adjusted R-square). The second column in the table tries to minimize this problem by taking a three-month moving average of the dependent variable (see Figure A5.2).[39] The results are qualitatively identical to the ones reported in the first column of the table, although the coefficients are smaller in absolute value. Indeed, according to these estimates, an increase in domestic inflation of one per cent per month led to a depreciation by the authorities of only Bt0.01 in the short-run (about Bt0.03 in the long-run), while an increase in external inflation of one per cent led to an appreciation of the baht of about Bt0.015 in the short-run (about Bt0.04 in the long-run). Similarly, increases in output beyond its trend led to an appreciation of the baht of about 11 cents per dollar in the short-run and about 28 cents in the long-run.

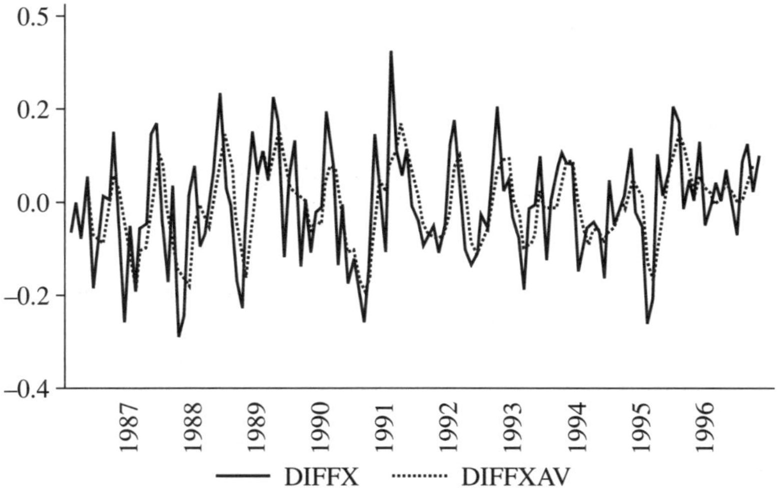

Note: DIFFX = absolute change in the exchange rate; DIFFXAV = three-month moving average of DIFFX.

Figure A5.2 Exchange rate movements

More importantly, the evidence suggests that starting in early 1992 the authorities partly abandoned the policy of correcting the exchange rate for changes in inflation differentials and excessive output growth. Indeed, the third and fourth columns in the table show the results of breaking down the sample into two sub-periods, 1986–91 and 1992–96. In general, the results show smaller and insignificant coefficients during the second half of the sample, which suggests that the results for the overall 1986–96 period are driven by those during the first half of the sample.[40] This change in policy may have been partly motivated by the steeper depreciation of the dollar *vis-à-vis* the yen during 1991–95, which probably made less important correcting for differences between domestic and foreign inflation. This finding is robust to using the change in the exchange rate (instead of the three-month moving average) as the dependent variable.[41]

NOTES

1. Valuable comments were received from Gerard Caprio, Simeon Djankov, Swati R. Ghosh and Giovanni Majnoni. The findings, interpretations and conclusions expressed in this chapter are those of the authors and do not necessarily represent the views of the World Bank.
2. According to the poverty index compiled by the NESDB.
3. By trade we mean the sum of imports and exports of goods and non-factor services as a ratio to GDP.
4. The magnitude and duration of the crisis in Thailand is unprecedented in recent Thai economic history. GDP is estimated to have declined by 0.5 per cent in 1997, and is estimated to have declined by another 8 per cent in 1998, with a recovery beginning only in 1999.
5. It is difficult, however, to disentangle the extent to which the decline in credit growth reflects tight supply conditions or a decline in the demand for credit, in turn, reflecting the downturn in aggregate demand.
6. World Bank 1990. However, savers in Thailand had traditionally few alternatives to investments in bank or finco accounts and direct investment in the equity market. More recently, the deregulation of the mutual funds industry has opened up alternative avenues for investments, e.g., in 1992, licenses were granted to seven fund management companies.
7. Excluding insurance companies and credit foncier institutions.
8. As the specialized banks are of minor importance for the analysis performed in the chapter, the following sections will only focus on commercial banks and finance companies.
9. Bank of Thailand, *Monthly Bulletin*, and World Bank 1990.
10. Foreign banks faced the following three main restrictions: (1) foreign banks were hampered in their deposit mobilization activities as they suffered from a prohibition of branches (only two grandfathered sub-branches exist); (2) they faced a 35 per cent income tax which is higher than the tax rate domestic banks are subject to (as they can be listed on the SET, their income tax rate is 30 per cent); and (3) they paid a 16.5 per cent witholding tax on dividends transferred overseas. Thus, foreign banks mainly focused on financing of international trade transactions; while they are active in the foreign exchange market, most of their business relates to trade transactions of their own clients (see World Bank 1990).
11. Figures according to Bank of Asia cited in World Bank 1990. The Herfindahl index, a measure commonly used to measure concentration in an industry, also suggests that the Thai banking system was highly concentrated. If the index is adjusted for market size, among 15 developing countries Thailand's banking system had the third highest concentration in the late 1980s (World Bank 1990).
12. While a single shareholder of a finance company cannot hold more than 10 per cent of total shares legally, in practice, banks have complete control over their affiliated companies. The legal restriction on the extent of ownership by one financial institution in another have only resulted in a complex network of multiple and cross-ownership between commercial banks

and securities and finance companies, and the ownership structures have become highly opaque (World Bank 1990).

13. Where these notes are payable in small denomination, they have the liquidity characteristics of demand deposits. At the end of 1987 this type of promissory notes were of relatively little importance as their share of total promissory notes was only 10 per cent.
14. While finance companies as banks came under the supervisory authority of the BoT, just as banks, they were subject to a separate legal framework and were prohibited from foreign exchange transactions, from offering checking accounts, and from opening branches.
15. Figures provided by the Bank of Thailand. These figures are, however, likely to be understated because of loopholes in the classification of loans, which are categorized according to the business of the borrower not by purpose.
16. Moreover, the tax treatment of provisions acted as a disincentive to adequate provisioning since an institution had to have exhausted nearly all legal remedies before the tax authorities would consider the loss as a deductible expense (World Bank 1990).
17. Figures cited after Claessens et al. 1999.
18. For a detailed account of the 1983 crisis, see: Johnston 1991 and Caprio and Klingebiel 1996a, 1996b.
19. Existing shareholders had a buyback option at a predetermined price and under a five-year time horizon.
20. While the comparability of cross-country data is limited because of differences in accounting conventions regarding the valuation of assets and loan loss provisioning, and interest rate accrual norms and tax regimes differ across countries, with an average of 1.9 per cent operating expenses over average assets over 1990–97, Thai banks' operating ratios were lower than those of other East Asian economies (Philippines 4.2 per cent, Indonesia 2.9 per cent, Korea 2.8 per cent) (see World Bank 1999).
21. For an extended discussion, see Alba et al. 1998b.
22. It solves the agency problem since large shareholders are able to more easily assert control over a firm and limit management inefficiency and abuse.
23. At the microlevel, rapid credit growth strained financial institutions credit assessments' and monitoring capacity. See Section 4.2b.
24. The data also illustrate that measures taken in 1995–96 by the government to curb short-term capital inflows (via BIBFs) seem to have had some effects (See Section 5.2). In 1996, short-term, in particular bank, debt declined both in absolute terms and in relative terms, and as noted above, firms increased their direct external borrowing. However, according to World Bank DRS data, the average maturity of private debt continued to decline in 1996.
25. Figures cited from Claessens et al. 1998.
26. As much as 7 per cent of the Financial Restructuring Agency's assets consisted of loans to real estate and construction business, which absorbed the loan portfolio of defunct finance companies.
27. Loans are categorized according to business of the borrower, not the purpose.
28. ROE in the 1990s are most probably overstated as financial institutions were subject to lenient interest accrual and loan loss provisioning guidelines. By the same token, their capital is most likely overstated.
29. Compared to banks operating in more stable economies such as the UK and Germany (where banks recorded average net interest margins of 2.9 and 3.1 per cent respectively over 1990–97), Thai net interest rate margins (2.8 per cent) appear out of line in terms of risk profile (data source: Worldscope).
30. However, the quality of the loan portfolio differed across banking institutions. Big banks still showed moderate levels of non-performing loans and a smaller increase in accrued interest while smaller banks were more adversely affected by the slowdown in the economy and the collapse of the real estate sector.
31. The tax treatment of provisions also did not provide adequate incentives for commercial banks to provision. Thailand does not allow deductions from taxes that are greater than the lower of 0.25 per cent of loans each year or 20 per cent of interest income.
32. Data for finance companies reported refer to 30 largest companies in the market. Data cited after World Bank, 1998.

33. As a general observation, longer-term FDI flows should be analysed as a separate category since they respond to a different set of push and pull factors than the more shorter term (portfolio) flows (Hernández and Rudolph, 1997). Given a longer gestation and implementation period, FDI should be sensitive to longer term trends rather than short-term variations.
34. Average values are calculated between January 1985 and May 1997.
35. A wider band would have reduced the incentives for short-term borrowing since these flows are more sensitive than longer-term flows to fluctuations around the central parity. Long-term flows are determined by perceptions regarding the medium- to long-term sustainability of the central parity.
36. The data are from a repeated survey of investors for the period 1995–96 on their expectations for the level of the baht/dollar exchange rate.
37. The proxy variable for overheating is based on the consumption of electricity in the Bangkok metropolitan area, and is measured as the seasonally adjusted deviation from its long-term trend. The long-term trend is estimated using a simple regression of consumption of electricity on time and time square. The results of this estimation are as follows: $elect = c + 10553\, time + 32.34\, time^2$, where both estimated coefficients resulted significant at 1 per cent levels and both R^2 and adj-R^2 were about 96 per cent.
38. An increase in the use of electricity signals an acceleration in output growth when electricity is seen as an input in the production function.
39. The correlation of the original series with its moving average is 0.64.
40. Simple descriptive statistics show that the exchange rate was slightly more volatile during the first half of the sample than during the second half: during 1986–91 the difference between the maximum and minimum values was bt1.42 and the standard deviation 0.36, while during 1992–96 the same measures were only 1.06 and 0.23, respectively.
41. When using the change in the exchange rate instead of the three-month moving average, the coefficient for domestic inflation, β_1, not only becomes insignificant (like all the other coefficients) but also turns out to have the wrong sign.

REFERENCES

Alba, P., Amar Bhattacharya, Stijn Claessens, Swati Ghosh and Leonardo Hernandez (1998a), 'The Role of Macro-economic and Financial Sector Linkages in East Asia's Financial Crisis,' mimeo, World Bank, Washington, DC.

Alba, P., Stijn Claessens, Simeon Djankov and L.H.P. Lang (1998b), 'Thailand's Corporate Financing and Governance Structures,' Policy Research Working Paper 2003, World Bank, Washington, DC.

Bank of Thailand (1998), 'Financial Institutions and Markets in Thailand,' mimeo, Economics Research Department, Bangkok.

Bank of Thailand (1998), 'Focus on the Thai Crisis,' *Economic Focus: A Quarterly Review of Thailand's Economic Issues* 2, (2): April.

Bank of Thailand (1996), 'Private Saving in Thailand,' *Economic Focus: A Quarterly Review of Thailand's Economics Issues* 1, (2): April.

Bank of Thailand (1996), 'Analyzing Thailand's Short-term Debt,' *Economic Focus: A Quarterly Review of Thailand's Economics Issues* 1, (3): July–September.

Bhattacharya, Amar and Johanes F. Linn (1998), 'Trade and Industrial Policies in the Developing Countries of East Asia,' World Bank Discussion Paper No. 27, Washington, DC: World Bank.

Caprio, G. and Daniela Klingebiel (1996a), 'Bank Insolvency: Bad Luck, Bad Policy, or Bad Banking?' in Michel Bruno and Boris Pleskovic (eds), *Annual World Bank Conference on Development Economics*, Washington, DC: World Bank, pp. 79–104.

Caprio, G. and Daniela Klingebiel (1996b), 'Bank Insolvencies, Cross-Country Experience,' Policy Research Working Paper 1620, World Bank, Washington, DC.

Caprio, G. and L. Summers (1993), 'Finance and its Reform: Beyond Laissez-Faire,' Policy Research Working Paper 1171, World Bank, Washington, DC.

Claessens, S., Simeon Djankov, Joseph P.H. Fan and Larry H.P. Lang (1998), 'Diversification and Efficiency of Investment by East Asian Corporations,' Policy Research Working Paper 2033, World Bank, Washington, DC.

Claessens, S., Simeon Djankov and Larry H.P. Lang (1999), 'Who controls East Asian Corporations?', Policy Research Working Paper 2054, Washington, DC: World Bank.

Hellmann, T., K. Murdock and J.E. Stiglitz (1994), 'Addressing Moral Hazard in Banking: Deposit Rate Controls vs. Capital Requirements,' mimeo, Washington, DC: World Bank.

Hernandez, Leonardo and Vittorio Corbo (1998), 'Private Capital Inflows and the Role of Economic Fundamentals,' Working Paper No. 45, Central Bank of Chile, December.

Hernandez, Leonardo and H. Rudoph (1997), 'Sustainability of Private Capital Flows to Developing Countries: Is a Generalized Reversal Likely?', *Cuadernos de Economia*, No. 102, August: 237–66.

Johnston, Barry R. (1983), 'Distressed Financial Institutions in Thailand: Structural Weaknesses, Support Operations, and Economic Consequences,' mimeo, International Monetary Fund, Washington, DC.

Johnston, Barry R. (1991), 'Distressed Financial Institutions in Thailand: Structural Weakness, Support Operations, and Economic Consequences,' in V. Sundararajan and T.J. Baliño, *Banking Crisis: Cases and Issues*, Washington, DC: International Monetary Fund, pp. 234–75.

Johnston, Barry R., Salim M. Darbar and Claudia Echeverria (1997), 'Sequencing Capital Account Liberalization: Lessons from the Experiences in Chile, Indonesia, Korea, and Thailand,' IMF Working Paper WP/97/157, International Monetary Fund, Washington, DC.

Kawai, Masahiro and Kentaro Iwatsubo (1998), 'The Thai Financial System and the Baht Crisis: Process, Causes and Lessons,' mimeo, Institute of Social Science, University of Tokyo.

Kolchar, Kaplana, Lois Dicks-Mireaux, Balazs Horvarth, Mauro Mecagni, Erik Offerdal and Jianping Zhou (1996), 'Thailand – The Road to Sustained Growth,' IMF Occasional Paper 146, Washington, DC.

La Porta, Fafael, Florencio Lopez-de-Silanes, Andrei Shleifer and Robert W. Vishny (1998), 'Law and Finance,' *Journal of Political Economy*, **106**: 113–55.

Nijathaworn, Bandid (1995), 'Capital Flows, Policy Response, and the Role of Fiscal Adjustment: The Thai Experience,' *Quarterly Bulletin Bank of Thailand*, **35**: 12–34.

Radelet, Steven and Jeffrey Sachs (1998), 'The East Asian Financial Crisis: Diagnosis, Remedies, Prospects,' *Brookings Papers on Economic Activity*, **1**: 1–90.

Renaude, Bertrand, Ming Zhang and Stegan Koeberle (1998), 'How the Thai Real Estate Boom Undid Financial Institutions – What Can be done Now,' paper presented at the Conference on Thailand's Dynamic Economic Recovery and Competitiveness, Bangkok: Office of the National Economic and Social Development Board of the World Bank.

Robinson, D., Yangho Byeon and Ranjit Teja with Wanda Tseng (1991), 'Thailand: Adjusting to Success – Current Policy Issues,' IMF Occasional Paper, Washington, DC, August.

Tinakorn, Pranee and Chalongphob Sussangorn (1998), 'Total Factor Productivity Growth in Thailand: 1980–95,' mimeo, Bangkok: Thailand Development Research Institute.

Wibulswadi, Chaiyawat (1995), 'Strengthening the Domestic Financial System,' mimeo, Bangkok: Bank of Thailand.

World Bank (1990), 'Thailand Financial Sector Policy,' mimeo, Washington, DC: World Bank.

World Bank (1995), 'The Emerging Asian Bond Market: Thailand,' June, Washington, DC.

World Bank (1997a), *Private Capital Flows to Developing Countries*, Washington, DC: World Bank.

World Bank (1997b), 'Thailand: Shadow Financial Sector Report,' mimeo, Washington, DC: World Bank.

World Bank (1998), 'The Thai Finance Company Sector,' mimeo, Washington, DC: World Bank.

World Bank (1999), *Global Economic Prospects and the Developing Countries*, Washington, DC: World Bank.

6. Revisiting the East Asian crisis and its aftermath: A political economy approach

Luis A. Rivera-Batiz and Maria-Angels Oliva

1. INTRODUCTION

In July 1997, Thailand entered into an economic crisis that gave rise to a web of contagion effects throughout East Asia and subsequently spread outside the region, particularly to Russia and Latin America. The crisis put an end to the spectacular period of miracle growth in East Asia. The social consequences were serious. By the end of 1999, 20 million workers had lost their jobs in Indonesia, Thailand, Malaysia, Korea and the Philippines alone.

Observers did not heed the warning signs anteceding the crisis. In 1996, Thailand's current account deficits had reached a critical level of 8 per cent of GDP and the stock market collapsed. Malaysia had gigantic investment rates that amounted to over 40 per cent of GDP both in 1996 and 1997. The country had gone into a feast of fast growth financed by over-extension of credit and was running current account deficits exceeding 5 per cent of GDP. Korea ran current account deficits exceeding 4 per cent of GDP, financed by short-term capital flows. The country featured a bankrupt banking system at the end of 1996. Indonesia, a country with good basic macroeconomic fundamentals, was considered the riskiest country in the region following political unrest and massive anti-government demonstrations in 1996. Indonesia was the country that got hit hardest by the crisis and its contagion effects. All of these economies had weak financial markets that had been liberalized while remaining subject to lax regulation and supervision.

Troubling indicators of economic and policy weaknesses were said not to apply to East Asian countries. Their superior growth experiences were used by economists to 'show' that the IMF approach stressing sustainable current account and fiscal deficits, sound financial policies, transparency, and adequate supervisory institutions, did not apply in this type of growing environment. On the contrary, the over-extension of credit to finance risky investment projects was viewed as a sign of healthy economic prospects. The sustainability of rapid growth was taken for granted except for a few observers such as Paul Krugman. The possibility of strong financial and real contagion effects was overlooked, even though these effects were detected in the previous currency crises in Europe (1992–93) and Mexico (1994–95).

This chapter focuses on the interaction between economic, political and institutional elements surrounding the crises experienced by East Asian economies. We argue that the crises were due to short-term shocks and contagion effects that were accentuated by conjunctural political factors, weak financial systems, and institutional factors such as inadequate supervision by authorities. The crisis got transmitted through real and financial contagion effects but, contrary to the common predictions of long-lasting stagnation, the crises had the usual duration of one to two years. In fact, except for Indonesia, rapid growth prevailed in 1999 and 2000.

A major drawback of many analyses is that political and institutional elements are bypassed. Yet these elements played a critical role in the origin and dynamics of the East Asian crisis. Our analysis points to the role of conjunctural political elements and weak political systems and institutions rather than to a particular form of political regime. Korea's economic vulnerabilities were accentuated by a decision-making process that became paralysed by election year political uncertainty in a young democracy. Extreme political fragmentation delayed and impeded action in Thailand. Long-lasting one-man rules led to willful and unchallenged approaches in Malaysia and Indonesia. Interest group lobbying, lying behind institutional and economic weaknesses, contributed to generate the crisis and supported inaction or inadequate responses to it. Still, because these institutional elements had existed for a long time and had been improving, even though slowly, rather than deteriorating, it is difficult to attribute the crisis solely to corruption, political fragmentation and other long-term institutional factors. Therefore, the East Asian crisis and its aftermath are better explained by a mixture of economic shocks, conjunctural political factors, contagion and policy responses, combined with institutional features accentuating the vulnerability to shocks.

The chapter is organized as follows. The next section presents a set of puzzling facts to be explained. Section 3 examines the political basis of the crisis in the country where it first started: Thailand. Sections 4 through 7 discuss the role of political uncertainty, political fragmentation, corruption, exchange rate regimes, and poorly managed or weak financial systems. Section 8 addresses the controversial issues relating to the nature and consequences of IMF programs in the region and current approaches to establish a well-functioning international financial system. Section 9 offers explanations of the puzzling facts presented in section 2.

2. THE PUZZLING FACTS

The East Asian crisis displays a number of puzzling facts that should be addressed by any attempt to provide a coherent explanation of the complex phenomenon. Notable among these puzzles is that the major economic fundamentals were good or superior. The puzzles are (see Tables 6.1 and 6.2):

1. East Asian countries were growing rapidly before the crisis. In fact, Thailand, Indonesia, Malaysia and Korea, the hardest hit countries, were among the fastest growing countries worldwide since the mid-1980s and all of them were growing fast until the eve of the crisis in 1996.
2. Fiscal accounts were in balance before the crisis. Specifically, countries had fiscal surpluses or small deficits.
3. The balance of payments accounts were in equilibrium in the sense that there were no large losses of international reserves and current account deficits were not excessively large except in the case of Thailand.
4. The countries had ample foreign exchange reserves and did not exhaust them through foreign exchange intervention.
5. The financial collapses in Thailand, Indonesia and Malaysia were attributed to corruption, lack of reform, imperfect liberalization and institutional weaknesses. However, these factors had been present throughout decades of rapid growth in these countries and continued to be present in the post-crisis recovery. Furthermore, it is difficult to associate differences in indexes of corruption and economic freedom to performance during the crisis. Hong Kong fell into recession even though existing indexes show low levels of corruption and very high levels of economic freedom by world standards. The Philippines avoided a full recession but indexes of corruption exceeded those of all other countries in the region except Indonesia.
6. The crisis was a short-term phenomenon that did not result in medium-term stagnation. In fact, all East Asian countries except Indonesia recovered in 1999. Korea's real Gross Domestic Product grew at more than 10 per cent in 1999 and is expected to grow at a similar rate in the year 2000. The recovery went on despite the fact that the Japanese economy stagnated in 1999 and remains so in the year 2000.
7. Most of the East Asian economies in crises had pegged exchange rate regimes (Singapore is an exception).
8. The crisis did not extend to China, despite the decision to keep the dollar value of the Chinese currency fixed, strong regional recession, negative growth in Japan during 1998–99, and large currency devaluations and depreciations throughout the region. China's real growth rates were around 6–8 per cent in 1998–99.

Table 6.1 Economic indicators, selected countries

	Real GDP growth (%)				Inflation (%)				Current account balance as % of GDP			
	1996	1997	1998	1999	1996	1997	1998	1999	1996	1997	1998	1999
Singapore	7.5	9.0	0.3	4.5	1.4	2.0	–0.3	0.2	15.9	15.7	20.9	21.1
Hong Kong SAR	4.5	5.3	–5.1	1.2	6.0	5.7	2.6	–3.1	–1.0	–3.2	0.7	1.5
Taiwan, China	5.7	6.8	4.9	5.0	3.7	0.9	1.7	1.0	4.0	2.7	1.3	2.6
Malaysia	8.6	7.7	–6.7	5.4	3.5	2.7	5.3	3.0	–5.2	–5.1	12.9	11.7
Rep. of Korea	6.8	–5.0	–5.8	6.5	4.9	4.4	7.5	0.8	–4.4	–1.7	12.5	5.9
The Philippines	5.8	5.2	–0.5	2.2	8.4	6.0	9.7	8.5	–4.9	–5.3	2.0	2.2
Thailand	5.5	–1.3	–9.4	4.0	5.9	5.6	8.1	0.5	–7.9	–2.0	12.2	8.8
Indonesia	8.0	4.7	–13.7	–0.8	7.9	6.6	59.6	22.7	–3.5	–1.8	4.0	2.4
New Zealand	3.1	2.1	–0.3	2.6	2.3	1.7	1.5	1.3	–4.1	–7.1	–6.1	–6.7
Australia	4.0	3.9	5.1	4.0	2.7	1.7	1.6	1.8	–3.9	–3.1	–4.8	–6.0
Japan	5.0	1.4	–2.8	1.0	0.1	1.7	0.6	–0.4	1.4	2.2	3.2	3.4
China	9.6	8.8	7.8	6.6	8.4	2.8	–0.8	–1.5	0.5	3.8	3.5	1.3
Russia	–3.4	0.9	–4.6	0.0	47.8	14.7	27.7	88.4	0.5	–0.7	0.8	7.8
Vietnam	9.3	8.2	3.5	3.5	5.8	3.2	7.7	7.6	na	na	na	na

Source: International Monetary Fund, International Financial Statistics, various issues.

9. The East Asian crisis was associated with the onset of recession in other regions such as Latin America even if trade and financial relations with East Asia were (and remain) relatively small.

In order to address all these puzzles, we will go back to the origins of the crisis in Thailand and examine its diffusion in the region. The analysis will suggest the economic distinctions and political elements needed to explain the puzzles raised.

Table 6.2 Fiscal deficit as percentage of GDP, selected countries

	1996	1997	1998	1999
Singapore	11.9	9.6	14.0	7.7
Hong Kong SAR	2.2	6.1	–1.8	–4.0
Taiwan, China	–3.2	–2.1	–1.2	–2.1
Malaysia	4.0	5.5	–1.0	–4.9
Rep. of Korea	0.3	–1.6	–4.2	–4.5
The Philippines	–0.3	–0.9	–3.2	–3.4
Thailand	2.7	–2.1	–2.9	–6.0
Indonesia	0.6	–1.0	–2.8	–4.5
China	–1.5	–1.6	–5.1	–6.7
Russia	–7.9	–7.1	–5.0	–2.4

Source: Goldman Sachs, *Emerging Markets Economics Quarterly*, Vol. 3, No. 4, November 1999.

3. THE GENESIS AND AFTERMATH OF A CRISIS: THAILAND

Thailand's collapse highlights the role of political uncertainty, fragmentation, deadlock and corruption in igniting and keeping a crisis alive. It also calls attention to the deleterious effects of a weak financial system subject to inadequate supervision. Finally, it shows the importance of prospective fiscal deficits, which appear to have had negative effects even before they actually materialized.

On 2 July 1997, the Bank of Thailand was forced to abandon the exchange rate peg it was maintaining with respect to the US dollar. The move followed a series of speculative attacks against the currency and a series of failed actions aimed at stopping the drain in reserves. The devaluation touched off a major financial crisis. In the midst of the crisis, Thailand authorities reached an agreement with the IMF on an official financial package exceeding US$17 billion accompanied by an economic adjustment program.

At first sight, Thailand's fundamentals in the period preceding the crisis looked strong. The country's remarkable economic performance was widely hailed before the July 1997 crisis. Real GDP had been growing fast for a decade. In 1996, the real growth and inflation rates were 5.5 per cent and 5.9 per cent, respectively (see Table 6.1). Before the crisis erupted, Thailand benefited from a fiscal surplus. It only fell into fiscal deficits after the crisis. Even then, deficits remained under control. As a percentage of GDP, fiscal balances were –0.3 per cent, –2.8 per cent and –3.3 per cent during 1997–99 (see Table 6.2).

Despite the strong fundamentals, the loss of confidence and eventual collapse of the Thai economy was not a sudden event. Weaknesses were seen earlier in the external sector, financial institutions, and the political regime. In 1996, the current account deficit was critically high at 7.9 per cent of GDP and was being financed by a build-up of short-term debt.

Political disarray and the presence of bad lending practices generated an environment plagued by uncertainty. Confidence was shaken by a weakened banking system and corruption in an unstable electoral environment. In May 1996, the Democrat members of parliament revealed that the Bangkok Bank of Commerce (BBC) was in deep trouble and would collapse. They also revealed the concession of loans to cabinet ministers allegedly used in bad investments and manipulation of shares. Shortly after, the allegation was made that there had been an 80 billion baht fraud involving banks, ministers and international investors. Estimated rescue costs mounted to 178 billion baht. As a result, the BBC suffered a damaging run on deposits.

In the face of uncertainty about the banking system and allegations about share manipulations, the stock market index collapsed from a level of 1200 in 1996 (the stock market had peaked at 1500 shortly before this) to near 500 in 1997. The 1996–97 stock market collapse reduced asset values, and thus the value of borrowers' collateral, and signaled further financial difficulties ahead. At end-1996, there were 91 finance companies, which accounted for 25 per cent of total credit. These finance companies fell into deep trouble in 1997 following the end of a real estate boom in 1996 that reduced the value of collateral, amid surging interest rates.

The collapse of the stock market and the financial sector was accompanied by the loss of confidence in the exchange rate peg that led to repeated speculative attacks and the onset of the crisis in July 1997. Furthermore, the 1996 political environment was highly uncertain. Observers feared a coup, following the vicious circle of democracy and dictatorship that had characterized politics since the 1940s and up to the 1980s.

Real GDP growth fell from 5.5 per cent in 1996 to –1.3 in 1997 and –9.4 in 1998. The fiscal accounts deteriorated dramatically. The fiscal deficit as a percentage of GDP went from 0.9 per cent in 1996 to –0.3 per cent, –2.8 per cent, and –3.9 per cent in 1997–99. The cost of financial sector assistance as a percentage of GDP increased from 0 per cent in 1996 to 2.5 per cent and 1.7 per cent in 1997 and 1999 (preliminary). These figures show the materialization of prospective deficits arising from the need to bail out a collapsed financial system. Well-informed rational agents should be able to anticipate these developments and protect themselves financially (Burnside et al. 1999).

Lack of financial transparency, inadequate financial supervision and alleged corruption played a key role both in igniting the financial crisis and in its aftermath. In the face of recession and high interest rates, the debt-to-GDP ratio jumped from 49.8 per cent to 76.5 per cent from 1996 to 1998 and the debt service ratio as a percentage of total exports increased from 12 per cent in 1996 to 20.7 per cent in 1998.

Following the implementation of an IMF program (discussed below), the economy recovered in 1999, led by a rapid 20 per cent increase in manufacturing output and a 6 per cent export growth. The current account balance in 1998 and 1999 produced huge 12 per cent and 9 per cent surpluses. These figures contrast sharply with the –7.9 per cent current account deficit in 1996. Because exports had been relatively stable during 1996–99 the improvement in the current account balance is accounted for by a collapse of imports from US$70.8 billion to US$40.6 in 1998 and US$46.4 billion in 1999.

The overnight repurchase rate, the Bank of Thailand's main policy interest rate, was lowered from 25 per cent in late 1997 to 1 per cent in mid-1999. The Bank of Thailand has maintained the flexible exchange rate regime that suddenly came into being in July 1997 and has announced that it will introduce an inflation-targeting framework.

Despite substantial progress, the IMF Article IV consultation with the government of Thailand, made public in February 2000, expressed concerns about several aspects. These included the continuing high levels of non-performing loans, the importance of reprivatizing intervened banks, corporate debt restructuring, the reform of bankruptcy and foreclosure procedures to ensure credit discipline, and the strengthening of the capital position of banks.

4. POLITICAL STRUCTURE, CRISIS AND POLITICAL REFORM

This section examines the relationship between political regimes, institutions and crisis. Political uncertainty (Korea), fragmentation (Thailand) or one-man rules (Indonesia, Malaysia) prevailed in the four countries hit hardest by the crisis. On one side, political uncertainty and fragmentation led to stalled policy initiatives. Governments were blocked from carrying out reform and following consistent policies. This element was important in touching off the crisis and framing a hesitant response to it. On the other side, one-man rules that had previously responded firmly to crisis displayed inconsistent behavior this time around (Pempel 1999). As a result, confidence in the political regime came into question and economic policy lost credibility. In all cases, the nature of the political regime was critical in framing the response to bad economic news.

We provide first a general overview of the East Asian countries' political regimes in terms of democratic institutions. Table 6.3 presents data for East Asia on an index of democracy constructed by Robert Barro (Barro 1997). The index ranges from 0 to 1, with 0 corresponding to the fewest political rights and 1 denoting the most political rights. The index is based on data assembled from the Freedom House Survey of Political Rights and Civil Liberties. The definition of political rights used in the survey follows these guidelines: 'political rights enable people to participate freely in the political process. By the political process we mean the system by which the polity chooses the authoritative policymakers and attempts to make binding decisions affecting the national, regional, or local community' (Karatnycky 1997, p. 572).

Table 6.3 Democracy index, selected countries

	1975	1994
Singapore	0.33	0.33
Hong Kong SAR	0.67	0.33
Taiwan, China	0.17	0.67
Malaysia	0.67	0.50
Rep. of Korea	0.33	0.83
The Philippines	0.33	0.67
Thailand	0.83	0.67
Indonesia	0.33	0.00

Source: Barro 1997.

According to the data in Table 6.3, authoritarianism streaks prevail in several countries. Indonesia has a value of 0.0 in the index in 1994, down from 0.33 in 1975. This reflects the authoritarian rule of Suharto, who was president of Indonesia for 32 years before leaving office in May 1998. In Malaysia, the index has a value of 0.5 in 1994, down from 0.67 in 1975. Malaysia's Prime Minister Mahathir Mohamad's one-party rule extends from 1981 to the present. Singapore also has a low value for the democracy index. This country features a one-party (People's Action Party) political regime that faces periodic electoral tests but traditionally holds 90 per cent of parliamentary seats and gets an electoral support of over 60 per cent of the total vote. Hong Kong has a value of 0.33 in the democracy index, reflecting its political situation under both British and Chinese tutelage.

The Republic of Korea displays a substantial increase in the democracy index between 1975 and 1994. This country made the transition from a traditional authoritarian government to a civilian government in 1992. A hotly contested change in government took place in 1997, precisely when the crisis came into being. Democratic regimes have achieved relative stability in the Philippines and Taiwan. In 1992, newly elected President Ramos initiated a technocratic regime that introduced reforms reducing government regulation and opening the Philippine economy. Similar policies were followed by his successor President Estrada. Reform and strong economic fundamentals precluded the string of recessions felt by neighboring countries. Taiwan has a democratic regime that faces a permanent legitimacy challenge from the Chinese government. Finally, Thailand displays a comparatively high democracy index. Political institutions in Thailand are discussed next.

Thailand

Thailand has a well-established democratic regime suffering from serious problems of political and electoral fragmentation reflected at various levels. These include the proliferation of multiple parties, the inability of political parties to achieve anything close to an electoral majority, the associated recourse to unstable party alliances, and parliamentary fragmentation. In this environment, governments have often been blocked from carrying out reforms and following consistent policies. This element was especially important in framing a hesitant response to the crisis and revealed deep, institution-based vulnerabilities.

Table 6.4 shows the fraction of the total vote obtained by the Thai parties with the most electoral votes. In none of the elections held during the period 1975–96 did a single party obtain a majority of the votes. The two major parties in the 1996 election obtained 31.8 per cent and 31.3 per cent of the total vote. This problem of fragmentation is compounded by the fact that politicians often change party in each election. Some provincial politicians supported Chat Thai in 1988, Samakkhitham in 1992, Chat Thai in 1995 and changed over to New Aspiration in 1996 (Phongpaichit and Baker 1998). The result of this unstable political membership and lack of clear and stable majority is that reform initiatives are prevented from being implemented. Furthermore, frequent challenges in parliament led to frequent changes of premier, the average tenure of whom has been 18 months in recent years.

Table 6.4 Thailand: Political fragmentation (percentage of total vote)

	1975	1976	1970	1983	1986	1988	1992a	1992b	1995	1996
Democrat	26.8	40.9	10.6	17.3	28.8	13.4	12.2	22.4	22.0	31.3
Chat Thai	10.4	20.1	12.6	22.5	18.2	24.4	20.2	21.4	23.6	9.9
Social Action	6.7	16.0	27.6	28.4	14.7	15.1	9.0	6.0	5.7	5.1
New Aspiration							20.0	14.2	19.6	31.8
Chat Phatthana								16.7	13.6	13.2
Samakkhitham							22.4			
Others	56.1	23.0	49.2	31.8	38.3	47.1	16.2	19.3	15.5	8.7
Total	100.0	100.0	100.0	100.0	100.0	100.0	100.0	100.0	100.0	100.0

Source: Computed by authors from Phongpaichit and Baker (1998), p. 247.

The problem of political fragmentation and short-lived administrations was as alive as ever both before and after the crisis. During the pre-crisis period in 1995–96, the Thai government was constituted by seven parties and 11 factions (the so-called 7–11 government). The reliance on a shaky coalition to keep power led to inaction in key public policy spheres, except government spending, before and after the onset of the crisis. While major financial regulatory and supervision reforms were delayed, the government boosted spending on construction and other ambitious developing projects.

The government of Prime Minister Chavalit Yongchaiyudh was unable to get financial and fiscal sector reform going. In November 1997, the coalition of political parties supporting Prime Minister Chavalit unraveled. A new coalition government was formed bringing the opposition Democrat Party, and its leader Chuan Leekpai, into power. General Chavalit led the new opposition.

The new Leekpai government implemented an IMF program as a condition for the 1998 financial package discussed below. The outlook for the economy is mixed: real GDP grew at a 4 per cent rate in 1999 and the current account surplus represented almost 9 per cent of GDP. However, the fiscal deficit was 3.3 per cent of GDP.

Indonesia

The Indonesian plight is a case of contagion aggravated by political uncertainty after the fact. Even if the political elements were not important in initiating the crisis, the policy response to the crisis was critical in transforming the financial crisis into the worst recession among East Asian countries.

In July 1997, the Indonesian economy did not seem to be ready to collapse. Up to June 1997, the economy was growing at an annual rate of 7.4 per cent. Export growth had slowed down but was positive. International reserves were rising. The Jakarta Stock Exchange (JSE) market index increased from 533 in July 1996 to a peak of 720 in July 1997. Foreign debt, at around 55 per cent of GDP, was not excessively high. Inflation was less than 8 per cent in both 1996 and 1997. The 1996 current account balance deficit of 3.5 per cent of GDP was not high for an economy that grew in real terms at 8 per cent and 4.7 per cent rates in 1996 and 1997. The government fiscal balance was at a surplus in 1996 and experienced a small deficit in 1997.

Indonesia suffered from a serious case of contagion related to the speculative attack on the Thai baht in July 1997. The rupiah depreciated from 2 400 per dollar in 1996 to 4 650 per dollar in December 1997, 8 325 per dollar at the end of the first quarter of 1998, collapsing to 14 900 per dollar before appreciating back to 8 025 per dollar at the end of the year. In March 2000 the rupiah was trading at 7 692 per dollar.

When the rupiah came under attack, interest rates were increased to defend the currency, which brought about a liquidity squeeze. The financial sector collapsed, throwing the economy into a deep recession. In October 1997, the IMF announced an assistance package requiring the closing of 16 private banks. The government response and the IMF program are discussed in a later section.

Political uncertainty loomed large after the crisis became a reality. President Suharto's thirty-year government displayed inconsistent and, at times, chaotic policy behavior during and after the crisis erupted. The uncertainty was compounded by internal conflict between Suharto and central bank officials regarding the best policy course. An IMF bailout was initially arranged in late October 1997, but the severity of the crisis and the chaotic policy reactions by the government led to a revision of the agreement in early 1998. In February 1998, Suharto dismissed the central bank governor and considered replacing the central bank with a currency board, a move which was radically opposed by the IMF, the World Bank and most Indonesian economists handling the crisis. The currency board proposal was later abandoned. Throughout this period, uncertainly regarding Suharto's regime itself was substantial, as the aging leader faced a deepening social and economic debacle. The government was perceived to be stalling key policy measures in order to protect the wealthy business dealings of Suharto's family and associates.

After an extended period of social and political unrest, Suharto stepped down in May 1998, giving way to B.J. Habibie, who was Vice-President at the time. President Habibie's administration, which operated under the influence of Suharto and his political party Golkar, did not reduce uncertainty significantly. The economic crisis raged on in the second half of 1998, with an acute food shortage and fears of widespread starvation. Moreover, a sensitive situation regarding East Timor independence from Indonesia dominated the headlines throughout 1999. When the country's military entered the island in 1999 and the government refused to allow United Nations peacekeeping troops to go in, both the World Bank and the IMF suspended discussions regarding an expansion of loans over those provided under the 1997–98 bailout. Political scandals continued throughout 1999, with accusations that funds intended to salvage Indonesian banks were being diverted to government officials and political parties. In June 1999, democratic parliamentary elections were held but in October 1999, rioting erupted after the People's Consultative Assembly (MPR) selected Abdurrahman Wahid as president, even if his party had finished fourth in the June election, the first free election in four decades. None the less, in November the parliament confirmed the new president.

Indonesia continued in recession in 1999, with two-digit inflation, and a fiscal deficit in excess of 4 per cent of GDP. However, GDP grew by almost 6 per cent in the fourth quarter compared with a year earlier. Political risks remain high. Regional unrest surrounding East Timor, and the demands for autonomy, or independence by provinces such as Aceh and Riau (which produces over half of Indonesia's oil), remain alive and raises questions about the future stability of the country.

Malaysia

The Malaysian crisis came after five years of high-growth policies characterized by increased government spending and financial deepening. In the mid-1990s, Prime Minister Mahathir's ambitious program to transform Malaysia into a developed country by 2020 (Vision 2020) resulted in increased public investment expenditures that led to investment rates of over 40 per cent of GDP in 1996 and 1997. This gigantic investment rate is among the largest historically on a worldwide basis and greatly exceeded the still very high investment rates previously achieved by Malaysia in the early 1990s, which hovered around 30 per cent. This boom, however, was associated with an over-extension of credit, the stock of which had reached 170 per cent of GDP at the time of the crisis. This level represents one of the highest worldwide.

The ringgit came into strong speculative attack in May 1997. The currency was not immediately devalued but was allowed to float in July following strong speculative attacks. Continued currency and stock market speculation prompted Dr Mahathir to launch widely reported verbal attacks against speculators in public forums, ban the short-selling of 100 blue chip stocks in August, and introduce capital controls. The widely reported criticisms of speculators went on unabated. The heated exchanges between Mahathir and George Soros, the well-known speculator, made it into the headlines worldwide.

Throughout this period, the government declared a stoic optimism, ignoring the burgeoning crisis. Indeed, in late October 1997, Malaysia offered to contribute $1 billion to Thailand and $1 billion to Indonesia to help them beat their financial collapse. The policy problems were compounded by a bitter clash between government technocrats and Prime Minister Mahathir on how to respond to the crisis.

In contrast to the Prime Minister's denial of the crisis, the technocrats wanted to respond by presenting an adjustment program that would introduce austerity measures and raise interest rates. These would have put an end to the high-growth programs sponsored by Mahathir and clashed with the Prime Minister's intent to keep his pet programs alive and protect the elites benefiting from them. The policy measures were not implemented. Still, the Finance Ministry's policymakers pressed for change. The ringgit continued to depreciate, they argued, partly because interest rates were not increased to defend the currency. The failure to increase interest rates has been viewed by many observers as a policy mistake in the sense that it prevented the re-establishment of confidence in the ringgit. The large depreciation hurt domestic companies that had borrowed in terms of US dollars offshore. In mid-1997, the private sector accounted for half of the country's foreign debt, a large amount of which was denominated in US dollars. Malaysian firms borrowed in dollars through the offshore subsidiaries of Malaysian financial institutions, including the offshore centers in Hong Kong and Labuan in East Malaysia. These funds were invested in countries whose currencies fell. The currency mismatch of assets and liabilities resulted in large financial losses.

The problems with policymaking institutions in the country were not circumscribed to the battles between the Finance Ministry and the Prime Minister. Bank Negara Malaysia, the country's central bank, was considered one of the most effective central banks in East Asia. For instance, Malaysia has a modern system for provisioning and recognition of non-performing and bad loans. Contrary to other countries in the region, banks are required to take losses and the central bank publishes the amount of non-performing loans. However, reports that Bank Negara Malaysia was an active speculator in international financial markets and had incurred large financial losses on speculative transactions hurt central bank credibility. Credibility was also hurt by new information indicating that reported levels of international reserves were misleading due to a web of transactions in derivatives markets (e.g., forward contracts). This revealed previously unknown central bank transparency problems.

The onset of strong recession and the reappearance of rioting, combined with openly violent ethnic conflict, threw the country into a social and economic maelstrom. The delicate equilibrium between competing class and ethnic interests that had supported decades of rapid industrialization and poverty reduction was temporarily broken.

In December 1997, an economic program of fiscal austerity was introduced. However, the program was not able to stop the recession, the depreciation of the ringgit, and the fall of stock market prices, which had gone down from over 1 200 in December 1996 to 600 in December 1997 (reaching 450 in June 1998). The fall of the stock market had strong repercussions due to the high stock market capitalization in Malaysia (much higher than in Korea or Indonesia), which fell from 320 per cent of GDP in December 1996 to below 140 per cent in December 1997.

Intense pressure by Mahathir on the finance ministry led to a gradual policy turnaround between July and September 1998 that reduced interest rates, restored public sector spending on infrastructure projects, and reimposed fixed exchange rates, with wide-ranging controls on currency trading and international financial transactions. The fate of this Ministers' policy package and political leadership was sealed shortly thereafter. He began to criticize Mahathir's political and business associates, declaring that cronyism and corruption should stop. The continuing recession, widespread discontent and the rise of a political rival posed a threat to Mahathir's leadership. The Minister was dismissed on 2 September 1998 and accused of financial and sexual misconduct. He was later convicted and jailed.

The credit boom of the 1990s ended in a banking crisis following the mid-1997 currency crisis. Banks were not directly hurt by the depreciation of the ringgit because they did not lend much in terms of foreign currency. The 1997 stock market collapse did not deeply hurt banks either because, in contrast to Japan, Malaysian banks do not hold equity investment except in their own financial subsidiaries. Financial companies were exposed to the stock market, though, through the loans extended to security houses and because stock holding represented an important part of borrowers' collateral. The recession contributed to increase the extent of non-performing loans. In March 1998, the ratio of non-performing loans to total lending was around 10 per cent.

As the banking crisis developed, a bailout policy was formulated. The central bank guaranteed all bank, merchant bank, and finance company deposits. The Malaysia Asset Management Corporation, created in 1998, acquired bank loans at what it deemed to be the market value and bought distressed assets at a discount. The cash received provided liquidity, allowing the banks to continue lending. The bailout policy aimed to avoid a systemic collapse without recurring to bank nationalization.

The Malaysian economy experienced a recovery in 1999. Real GDP grew by about 9 per cent in the last two quarters of 1999 and the Malaysian government reported 5.4 per cent growth for the whole year. The Kuala Lumpur Stock Exchange Composite Index surged from around 300 in August 1998 to over 800 in December 1999. International credit rating agencies upgraded sovereign ratings in late 1999 or early 2000.

The financial crisis induced households to increase savings. The private savings rate went up from 27.6 per cent in 1997 to 33 per cent in 1998. The combination of higher private savings and the fall of private investment improved the current account in 1998 and 1999. As a result, the current account showed a surplus in 1999. The currency was considered to be undervalued. Exports grew by 20 per cent in 1999 while the trade balance displayed a surplus. Net international reserves had increased to over $30 billion in February 2000 and were enough to finance over six months of imports. The exchange control rule on one-year holding of portfolio investments was liberalized.

Interest rates also dropped. The three-month interbank rate declined to 3.2 per cent while the commercial average lending rate declined from double digits to less than 8 per cent at end-1999. Because local interest rates were below the interest rates that Bank Negara Malaysia could earn on international reserves, it issued debt to sterilize the balance of payment surplus. The sterilization operation produced gains for the central bank.

Korea

The Korean crisis was initiated by the deterioration of corporate and bank balance sheets. Hahm and Mishkin (2000) present evidence of deteriorating corporate balance sheets before the crisis. They raise the possibility of increasingly inefficient corporate investment (see also Mishkin 1999). However, political factors played a key role in setting the stage for the eruption of the crisis.

First of all, the parliament failed to pass a key financial bill that represented the major policy initiative to deal with the crisis before the December 1997 election. In fact, the end of the parliamentary season was a turning point in financial markets. The heatedly contested 18 December 1997 election helped to create a period characterized by government paralysis. As a result, the government was not capable of addressing the corporate bankrupcies, rising non-performing loans and bad debts plaguing the economy. The situation was not helped by the declarations by political candidate Kim Dae-Jung and others stating their intention to renegotiate, if elected, the terms of an IMF agreement being implemented. This caused the won to sink by 10 per cent in two days. The $57 billion IMF rescue package was the largest ever in IMF history. The election of Kim Dae-Jung pushed the won exchange rate to an historic low of 1962 won per dollar on 23 December while the stock market continued to fall. On the other hand, with the election over, the parliament did manage to pass the legislation needed to deal with the crisis. Markets did not begin to react positively until the National Assembly passed the major financial reform bills at the end of December 1997 and newly elected president Kim Dae-Jung expressed his support for the IMF package.

Another source of economic policy delay was the presence of major disagreements on monetary policy and financial institution supervision between the Ministry of Finance and Economy and the Bank of Korea. The Ministry, which had the upper hand in policymaking before the crisis, eventually lost much of its power as a result of the debacle, for which it was blamed in local circles. Monetary policy was taken away from the Ministry and is now in the hands of the central bank. Financial regulation was transferred to the Financial Supervisory Commission. And budgeting, which was under the control of the Ministry, was transferred to the Ministry of Budget and Planning.

As in Malaysia, political leaders in Korea blamed foreign investors for the fall of the equity market. Dornbusch and Park (1995) have argued that foreign investors pursue positive feedback strategies that cause stock prices to overreact to changes in fundamentals. However, Choe, Kho and Stulz (1998) do not find any evidence supporting the claim that foreign investors destabilized Korean stock markets during the period 30 November 1996 to the end of 1997.

The Korean economy experienced the strongest recovery in East Asia. It grew at 8 per cent in real terms and it is expected to grow at over 6 per cent in 2000. Rapid growth has led to fears of overheating. The currency depreciated to 1 200 won per dollar in September 1999 but recovered to 1 107 won per dollar on 31 March 2000. Despite rapid growth, the chaebol restructuring continues to face problems. For instance, the Daewoo group was facing a debt crisis in early 2000. This created fears that investment trust companies holding Daewoo and other troubled chaebol bonds may be in trouble.

Short-term interest rates are between 6.5–7.5 per cent. The monetary authorities have issued monetary stabilization bills to restrain liquidity. In other words, continued sterilized intervention is pursued through the issuance of monetary stabilization bills.

5. DID THE CRISIS LEAD TO POLITICAL CHANGE?

A full answer to the question of induced political change must wait. Up to now, the extent of political change varies substantially across countries. Available evidence does not support a clear-cut conclusion.

Political fragmentation in Thailand remains in year 2000. Both political fragmentation and allegations of vote-buying marred the country's first senate election on 4 March 2000. In Bangkok alone there were 265 candidates vying for 18 seats. Confusion due to this outstanding level of political fragmentation was compounded by limits on campaign activities that did not allow candidates to discuss policies and affiliate themselves with a political party. Any form of campaigning or advertising except through the distribution of pamphlets was prohibited (*Washington Post*, 5 March 2000, p. A26).

The Indonesian one-man rule fell under heavy rioting and President Habibie succeeded General Suharto in 1998, well before Suharto's term would have ended in 2003. The political dominance of General Suharto was replaced by a unique electoral process. The June 1999 elections for national, provincial and municipal assemblies took place with 48 parties bidding for 120 million voters spread over 17 000 islands and over 320 000 polling stations. Over 600 000 national monitors and 600 international observers aimed to ensure fraud-free proper procedures in the emerging democracy.

In Korea, the democratic government of reform-minded Kim Dae-Jung was elected in the December 1997 election that took place after the Korean economy fell into financial crisis and entered into recession. The new government had enough support to implement an adjustment program agreed with the IMF and gathered enough confidence to put the economy back to a rapid growth path in 1999.

In Malaysia, the political opening has been minimal. The country fell into political turmoil during the 1998 crisis but effective political change was blocked. Prime Minister Mahathir, the 74-year-old leader who has ruled since 1981, was re-elected in the 1999 general election. The victory hinged on the support of the Chinese and Indian minorities that had been subject to attack by a rioting Malay ethnic majority during the crisis. Subsequently, Mahathir indicated that this would be his last term.

6. CORRUPTION

Is corruption associated with the crisis in East Asia? Following recent work showing that corruption is negatively associated with growth (Mauro 1995), and allegations of widespread corruption in the region, observers have attributed the financial collapse in Thailand, Indonesia and Malaysia to high levels of corruption. In order to assess this hypothesis, we must consider the historical behavior of corruption across countries.

Let us measure the extent of the crisis by the fall in GDP and the length of the recession. According to this measure, the crisis hit harder in Indonesia, followed by Thailand, Malaysia, Korea, Hong Kong and the Philippines. China was the most rapidly growing country of the group, followed by Taiwan and Singapore which did not fall into recession but experienced a slowdown.

Table 6.5 shows a global index of corruption since the 1980s. The index, the Corruption Perceptions Index, is calculated by Transparency International on the basis of local surveys of households and businesses. Table 6.5 shows the ranking of East Asian economies as well as other countries. We include New Zealand, Australia, Japan and Russia as reference points. Note that corruption levels are not associated with the strength of the crisis. For example, Hong

Kong fell into recession in 1997 even if the index shows low corruption levels and very high levels of economic freedom by world standards. On the other hand, the Philippines avoided a strong recession but indexes of corruption for that country exceed those of all others in the region except Indonesia.

Table 6.5 Corruption Index, selected countries

	1980–85	1988–92	1996	1997	1998	1999	Change index 1996–99	World ranking 1999
New Zealand	8.4	9.3	9.4	9.2	9.4	9.4	0.0	3
Singapore	8.4	9.2	8.8	8.7	9.1	9.1	0.3	7
Australia	8.4	8.2	8.6	8.9	8.7	8.7	0.1	12
Hong Kong	7.4	6.9	7.0	7.3	7.8	7.7	0.7	15
Japan	7.8	7.3	7.1	6.6	5.8	6.0	–1.0	25
Taiwan, China	6.0	5.1	5.0	5.0	5.3	5.6	0.6	28
Malaysia	6.3	5.1	5.3	5.0	5.3	5.1	–0.2	32
Rep. of Korea	3.9	3.5	5.0	4.3	4.2	3.8	–1.2	50
The Philippines	1.0	2.0	2.7	3.1	3.3	3.6	0.9	54
China	5.1	4.7	2.4	2.8	3.5	3.4	1.0	58
Thailand	2.4	1.9	3.3	3.1	3.0	3.2	–0.1	68
Indonesia	0.2	0.6	2.7	2.7	2.0	1.7	–1.0	96
Russia	5.1	3.3	2.6	2.3	2.4	2.4	–0.2	82

Source: Transparency International, Corruption Perceptions Index (CPI), 1999: 99 countries; 1998: 85 countries; 1997: 52 countries;1996, 1988–92, and 1980–85: 54 countries.

Has the crisis and the responses to it induced a reduction in corruption levels? Table 6.5 shows that corruption continues during the post-crisis recovery. Moreover, the countries that were hit hardest by recession, such as Korea, Thailand and Indonesia, experienced increased corruption levels. The same applies to other stagnant countries in the reference group, such as Japan and Russia. This pattern of behavior suggests that, if there is a relation between growth performance and corruption, it is one in which deteriorated performance leads to subsequent increase in corruption. We must therefore be wary of attributing a causal relation going from corruption to growth or of mechanically attributing this relationship to particular countries undergoing distress.

Table 6.5 also shows that high corruption has been present in East Asia for many years now, including the period of rapid growth. Given that this growth was one of the highest in the world, it is unlikely that one can simply attach the crisis to the presence of cronysm and corruption. This does not minimize the effects of corruption, which distort markets and may become a major cost of doing business. However, it suggests that further analysis must be conducted before one could reasonably attribute the crisis to high corruption. The data do not show any obvious connection going from corruption to performance before, during or after the East Asian crisis.

7. CURRENCY AND MATURITY MISMATCHES UNDER FINANCIAL OPENNESS

Table 6.6 shows a classification of countries according to their financial openness, as measured by the ratio of capital inflows to GDP. This measure of financial openness displays wide divergence across countries. On one side, there are economies that display relative financial segmentation. For instance, the People's Republic of China has strict regulations on foreign investments and maintains restrictions on capital flows, trade flows and currency convertibility. On the other side, Singapore is among the most open economies in the world from a financial perspective. Indonesia, Malaysia, the Philippines and Thailand lie in the middle.

Table 6.6 Stock of capital inflows in East Asia, as percentage of GDP

	Commercial capital inflows		Total capital inflows	
	1996	1997	1996	1997
Australia	71.3	69.5	71.3	69.5
Singapore	126.3	65.5	126.3	65.5
Malaysia	60.1	65.8	64.4	69.9
Rep. of Korea	26.0	28.1	26.9	30.0
The Philippines	28.3	34.1	52.7	56.6
China	23.7	25.8	28.4	30.2
Thailand	49.4	60.8	55.2	71.2
Indonesia	37.3	40.6	57.7	60.4

Note: Commercial capital inflows refers to the total stock of capital inflow liabilities, net of government debt, divided by GDP.

Source: International Monetary Fund and Inter-American Development Bank.

Was financial openness associated with the East Asian financial crisis? Financial openness can lead to currency and maturity mismatches that create havoc in emerging markets. Currency mismatches take place when agents borrow in one currency and invest in a different currency. A typical case is a developing country bank that borrows externally in dollars and lends in local currency. Another example is a local corporation that borrows in US dollars to finance its domestic operations. A third example is a sovereign government that cannot issue external debt in its own currency and must thus denominate its external borrowing in foreign currency. In all of these cases, the depreciation of the local currency will create difficulties in paying external debts. The problem associated with currency mismatches cannot be solved in emerging countries that lack adequate instruments for currency hedging.

Currency mismatches characterized the situation in East Asia following financial opening in the late 1980s and early 1990s. Table 6.7 shows the percentage of the external debt denominated in domestic currency for a number of countries. All East Asian countries in the sample except Hong Kong do not issue external debt in their own currency. These countries are thus highly vulnerable to currency depreciation.

Table 6.7 External debt denominated in domestic currency, selected countries (as a percentage of total external debt)

	1995	1996	1997	1998	1999
Australia	0.28	0.27	0.24	0.20	0.19
Singapore	0.08	0.01	0.01	0.01	0.00*
Hong Kong	0.18	0.42	0.39	0.33	0.39
Taiwan, China	0.00	0.00	0.00	0.00	0.00
Malaysia	0.00	0.00	0.00	0.00	0.00
Rep. of Korea	0.00	0.00	0.00	0.00	0.00
The Philippines	0.02	0.01	0.01	0.01	0.01
China	0.00	0.00	0.00	0.00	0.00
Thailand	0.01	0.01	0.01	0.04	0.06
Indonesia	0.00	0.02	0.02	0.01	0.00*

Notes:
* The figures 0.004 for Singapore and 0.002 for Indonesia are rounded to zero.
External debt or money market debt denominated in a country's currency divided by the external debt or money market issued by the country in all currencies.

Source: Bank for International Settlements.

A second financial problem faced by developing countries concerns maturity mismatches. For the most part, East Asian countries lack long-term financial markets. Most bank loans are short-term or medium-term and bonds rarely have maturities beyond seven years. For instance, the average maturity of Korea's bonds was less than three years at the onset of the East Asian crisis. This meant that Korean corporations were financing long-term projects with short- and medium-term loans and were thus highly vulnerable to interest rate increases.

The combination of currency and maturity mismatches accentuate the difficulties facing countries that have national currencies lacking credibility. Countries in Latin America and East Asia lack significant long-term capital markets and are not able to issue external debt in their own currencies. In these countries, exchange rate volatility causes financial fragility. The 'original sin' hypothesis (Eichengreen and Hausmann 1999) emphasizes that incompleteness in developing countries' financial markets prevents the domestic currency from being used to borrow abroad or to borrow long-term even domestically.

The mismatching problem faced by Korea was compounded by its entry as a member of the OECD in 1996. This step relaxed supervision on loans to Korea. The reason is that the risk weight assigned to an OECD country under Basle rules is zero. In addition, high interest rates on loans to Korea created incentives for OECD countries to lend to that emerging market. In fact, short-term lending to Korea surged in 1997 and ended in a potential default that was avoided at the eleventh hour by an IMF package.

8. IMF PROGRAMS: WERE THEY ON TARGET?

What was the response of the IMF to the East Asian crisis? The major response was to introduce stabilization programs that varied from country to country. A second element of the IMF response was to encourage the restructuring of the financial sector, including closing down institutions considered non-viable. The IMF also required the compliance with internationally accepted best practices including the Basle capital adequacy standards, adopting internationally accepted accounting practices, and implementing disclosure rules. These IMF programs in East Asia faced tough criticism. This section examines the Fund's performance during the East Asian crisis.

Are IMF Policies Recessionary?

Radelet and Sachs (1998a, b) have argued that the IMF has prescribed recessionary policies that in many countries have transformed a liquidity crisis into a full-fledged financial panic, pushing the real economy toward collapse. Sachs and others argue that the IMF needs to reformulate its standard formula for macroeconomic stabilization and economic reform. The IMF answer is that tightened fiscal policies are needed to balance the fiscal accounts and re-establish balance of payments equilibrium (i.e., lead to a sustainable current account deficit).

Other critics have argued that IMF programs create a moral hazard problem that encourages excessive lending to developing countries. But the IMF responds that the moral hazard problem is partially solved because the possibility of losing access to capital markets, facing higher interest rates, suffering from output losses, and having to negotiate a conditional agreement with the IMF, represent major incentives for repaying international debt. Dooley (2000) argues that in this environment private debtors and creditors have strong incentives to design international contracts with costly renegotiations. The trade-off involved is that debt contracts without renegotiations generate deadweight losses but current proposals to introduce renegotiations in debt contracts weaken the incentives to repay private debt.

What was the actual performance of IMF programs in East Asia? Korea and Thailand stayed within their IMF program's monetary growth rate target and reserve money growth expectations (Lane et al. 1999). The performance criteria of the Thai and Korean programs were (1) a ceiling on net domestic assets of the central bank and (2) a floor on net international reserves. The ceiling on net domestic assets was intended to limit money growth. The floor in international reserves was intended to allow the use of depreciation as an adjustment variable.

The case of Indonesia shows a dramatic deviation from IMF targets. The program's performance criterion was a ceiling on base money rather than net domestic assets. Because net domestic assets are consistent with many different levels of base money, there was no nominal anchor consistent with a floating rate regime. The program also set a low international reserves floor on the assumption that Indonesia's problem was based on contagion and that there was no need to devalue heavily. The near collapse of the banking system in the period of November 1997 to January 1998 led policymakers to increase liquidity, despite the IMF program restrictions. In the first half of 1998, for instance, the country deviated substantially from the prescription of the IMF program. The growth rate of reserve money approached 100 per cent on an annual basis while the IMF target was around 20 per cent.

The Indonesian actions were aimed to provide liquidity support to the banking system. The effects were not as intended. The liquidity support, combined with limited sterilization, resulted in large increases in the net domestic assets of the central bank, which in turn translated into international reserve losses but to a lesser extent than the increase in net domestic assets. During the first quarter of 1998, the rupiah depreciated heavily from 4 650 rupiah per dollar to 8 325 rupiah per dollar. The depreciation in turn accentuated corporations' difficulties in paying dollar-denominated debts.

In April 1998, the IMF replaced base money as a key performance criterion of its monetary program in Indonesia. Control over net domestic assets of the central bank became the new performance criterion of the program. The program, however, was not implemented and broad money and the monetary base grew far more than envisioned.

In mid-1998, a new monetary program was established and the goals were fulfilled. The currency appreciated sharply from 14 900 rupiah per dollar in the second quarter to 8 025 rupiah per dollar at the end of the year. In March 2000 the currency was trading at 7 692 rupiah per dollar.

Capital Controls

A number of scholars have proposed the use of capital controls as a policy mechanism that can assist in preventing or alleviating the effects of a crisis. Jagdish Bhagwati, for example, has argued that capital flows are unstable and has defended capital controls to deal with this instability. Paul Krugman has argued that exchange controls can be useful as a response to crisis and has criticized IMF programs (Krugman 1999). Joseph Stiglitz has also argued against free short-term capital flows.

The answer to these arguments has two key elements. First, the fact is that the IMF Articles of Agreement explicitly allow controls on capital flows, following the idea that Keynes and other IMF founders had that capital flows, especially short-term capital flows, can be destabilizing. Free capital flows are not required as a goal that IMF members should attain and in fact capital controls have been in use in many developing countries during the 1990s, including East Asia. There were recent talks at the IMF of officially establishing the goal of free capital flows, at the same level as the goal of free trade. However, up to now this has not been pursued. Therefore, this tough 'criticism' of the Fund is already incorporated in the Articles of Agreement of the organization. The IMF cannot attempt to free capital flows as part of its conditionality doctrine, as this would be inconsistent with its own Articles of Agreement. Furthermore, the effectiveness of capital controls is undermined by the East Asian experience itself since they were in place in East Asia and were unable to avoid the crisis.

9. BACK TO THE PUZZLING FACTS

Let us go back to the puzzling facts and attempt an explanation based on our analysis:

1. The experience of fast growth in East Asia indicates strong fundamentals but it was not necessarily sustainable, especially since it was financed by unusually high credit.

2. Fiscal accounts were in relative balance before the crisis. However, the potential crises of the financial sector in these countries entailed large prospective deficits that were discounted by the market before they actually took place.
3. The balance of payments can be in equilibrium but its composition creates problems such as when there are large short-term flows denominated in external currencies.
4. The countries did have ample foreign exchange reserves and, in general, did not exhaust them through foreign exchange intervention. A crisis, however, can occur even if international reserves are not totally exhausted, as in the speculative payment model of Obstfeld (1996).
5. Corruption is consistent with growth at boom times but can distort the response to a crisis and exacerbate its effects. The causal relationship that goes from growth to corruption levels appears to be as valid as the opposite causality.
6. Various East Asian countries trade more with Europe and the USA than with Japan. For instance Thailand trades more with the USA, Europe and other ASEAN (Association of South-East Asian Nations) countries than with Japan.
7. The pegged exchange rate regime puzzle is really based on a technical mistake. It is usually argued that the East Asian countries in crises had pegged exchange rate regimes with the exception of Singapore, and that the crisis was precipitated by the maintenance of the pegged currency regime. Technically, this is not a correct statement. Most of the countries in the region were under a floating regime, specifically, managed floating regimes. The Philippines peso was floating but there was little variation in the exchange rate and this type of managed floating was perceived by some market participants to be similar to a standard peg. Singapore was also a managed floater. The Korean won fluctuated within a band.
8. The fast growth in China, with a fixed exchange rate, can be explained by the presence of exchange controls, increasing trade with a booming USA, and the fact that China underwent a large devaluation previous to the crisis.
9. The East Asian crisis was transmitted within and outside the region, even when trade with these regions was small, through various channels. First, currency devaluations and depreciations of floating currencies had competitiveness effects, causing trading partners to lose competitive power, which harmed their trade sectors. These effects happened even when the devaluations were not intended to be competitive, beggar-thy-neighbor devaluations, but were rather caused by speculative attacks. Second, the stock market nose-dive caused other stock markets to decline and increased stock price volatility. Third, East Asian countries fell into recession, reducing their spending on oil, wheat and other commodities. As commodity

prices declined, the recessions were transmitted to commodities' exporters throughout the world. This affected Chile and many developing countries while also impacting resource-based economies like Canada.

10. CONCLUSIONS

We do not find a single explanation of the East Asian crisis but rather a combination of factors that vary with the country considered. Our analysis points toward the important role played by conjunctural political elements and weak political systems on the policy process in the aftermath of the East Asian crisis. The interactions of fundamental economic shocks with political and institutional factors account for the severity of the crisis. Authoritarianism, electoral paralysis, the proliferation of political parties, parliamentary fragmentation, unstable party alliances and internal strife between various parts of the government led to policy deadlocks in the various countries, which blocked the formulation of consistent policies and the implementation of needed reforms after the crisis occurred.

This political economy perspective complements, but does not substitute for, the presence of fundamental economic forces behind the crisis. We have stressed that a government-supported over-extension of credit had greatly increased systemic risk in East Asia. At the time of the crisis, the ratio of the stock of credit to GDP ranged dangerously high, between 130 per cent and 170 per cent of GDP in Thailand and Malaysia. The crisis can also be linked to spillovers from neighbors, weaknesses in domestic financial intermediation, poor corporate governance, and deficient government policies, including inadequate macroeconomic responses to large capital inflows.

In terms of the role of the IMF in the aftermath of the crisis, we believe that it is difficult to argue that the role of the IMF was deleterious to the countries involved. The multiple observers that predicted a prolonged state of recession due to IMF programs were off the mark. All countries that followed IMF programs in a timely way recovered within a year of the initiation of the adjustment programs. Perhaps the best comparison is with Japan. Free from the constraints imposed by the IMF, the Japanese delayed intervention and stagnated for a whole decade. An example of success without the IMF is Malaysia, which did not seek IMF assistance. However, rhetoric apart, we have seen that Malaysia has an effective central bank and the government implemented a successful reform and bailout program.

The rapid recovery observed in 1999 and 2000 suggests that the East Asian crisis can be better explained by conjunctural economic and political elements than by structural factors. The adjustment pattern of East Asian economies differs widely from the decade-long stagnation of the Japanese economy, which is afflicted with structural problems. If it were true that structural problems plague East Asia, as it is often argued, the structural crisis has not taken place yet.

REFERENCES

Alba, Pedro, Amar Bhattacharya, Stijn Claessens, Swati Ghosh and Leonardo Hernandez (1998), 'Volatility and Contagion in a Financially-Integrated World: Lessons from East Asia's Recent Experience,' Policy Research Working Paper Series 2008, Washington, DC: World Bank.

Barro, Robert (1997), *Determinants of Economic Growth. A Cross-Country Empirical Study*, Cambridge, MA: MIT Press.

Burnside, Craig, Martin Eichenbaum and Sergio Rebelo (1999), 'Hedging and Financial Fragility in Fixed Exchange Rate Regimes,' mimeo, World Bank, April.

Choe, Hyuk, Bong-Chan Kho and René M. Stulz (1998), 'Do Foreign Investors Destabilize Stock Markets? The Korean Experience in 1997,' National Bureau of Economic Research Working Paper No. 6661, July.

Dooley, Michael P. (2000), 'Can Output Losses Following International Financial Crisis Be Avoided?', National Bureau of Economic Research Working Paper No. 7531, February.

Dornbusch, Rudiger and Y.C. Park (1995), 'Financial Integration in a Second-Best World: Are We Still Sure about Our Classical Prejudices?' in Rudiger Dornbusch and Y.C. Park (eds), *Financial Opening: Policy Lessons for Korea*, Seoul: Korea Institute of Finance.

Eichengreen, Barry and Ricardo Hausmann (1999), 'Exchange Rates and Financial Fragility,' National Bureau of Economic Research Working Paper No. 7418, November.

Hahm Joon-Ho and Frederic S. Mishkin (2000), 'Causes of the Korean Financial Crisis: Lessons for Policy,' National Bureau of Economic Research Working Paper No. 7483, January.

International Monetary Fund (1998), *World Economic Outlook and International Capital Markets: Interim Assessment*, Washington DC: IMF, December.

International Monetary Fund (1999), *World Economic Outlook*, Washington DC: IMF, October.

Karatnycky, Adrian (1997), *Freedom in the World: The Annual Survey of Political Rights and Civil Liberties*, New Brunswick, NJ: Transaction Publishers.

Krugman, Paul (1994), 'The Myth of Asia's Miracle,' *Foreign Affairs*, 73(6), November/December: 62–78.

Krugman, Paul (1999), 'The Return of Depression Economics,' *Foreign Affairs*, 78(1) January/February: 56–74.

Lane, Timothy, Atish Ghosh, Javier Hamann, Steven Phillips, Marianne Schulze-Ghattas and Tsidi Tsikata (1999), *IMF-Supported Programs in Indonesia, Korea, and Thailand: A Preliminary Assessment*, Ocasional Paper No. 178. Washington DC: International Monetary Fund.

Mauro, Paolo (1995), 'Corruption and Growth,' *Quarterly Journal of Economics* (110): 681–712.

Mishkin, Frederick S. (1999), 'Lessons from the Asian Crisis,' National Bureau of Economic Research Working Paper 7102, April.

Obstfeld, Maurice (1996), 'Models of Currency Crisis with Self-Fulfilling Features,' *European Economic Review* (40): 1037–48.
Pempel, T.J. (ed.) (1999), *The Politics of the Asian Economic Crisis*, Ithaca, NY and London: Cornell University Press.
Phongpaichit, Pasuk and Chris Baker (1998), *Thailand's Boom and Bust*, Chiang Mai, Bangkok: Silkworm Books.
Radelet, Steven and Jeffrey Sachs (1998), 'The Onset of the East Asian Financial Crisis,' National Bureau of Economic Research Working Paper No. 6680, August.
Sachs, Jeffrey and Steven Radelet (1998), 'The East Asian Financial Crisis: Diagnosis, Remedies, Prospects,' *Brookings Papers on Economic Activity*, No. 1, 1–74.

PART III

The International Political Economy of the Crisis

7. The US role in the long Asian crisis of 1990–2000

Robert Wade

1. INTRODUCTION

The world has been experiencing a 'boom in busts' – a much higher frequency of financial instability in the 1980s and 1990s than in the post-World War II period up to the end of the Bretton Woods regime in the early 1970s.[1] During the decade of the 1990s a major financial crisis erupted every two or three years.[2] During the longer period from the late 1970s to 1996 at least 69 countries had at least one major banking crisis, when the net worth of the banking system sank to zero or less.[3] Between 1975 and 1995 at least 87 countries had at least one major currency crisis, when the currency depreciated by more than 25 per cent in one year.[4]

Both banking and currency crises are typically very expensive in terms of both the amount of GDP lost (the fall in growth rates) and of the portion of the remaining GDP that has to be diverted to resolving the crisis. The US banking and real estate ('savings and loan') crisis of the 1980s cost over 3.5 per cent of GDP to restore the banks to viability – but does not make it into the list of the world's 25 most expensive banking crises since the early 1980s.[5] When banking and currency crises occur together the results are much worse – not just crisis but collapse. From the mid 1970s to the mid 1990s at least 10 countries, *not* including the Asian ones of 1997–99, experienced simultaneous banking and currency crises causing GDP falls of 5 to 12 per cent in the first year and negative or only slightly positive growth for several years thereafter.

There is little doubt that the higher frequency of banking and currency crises since the 1980s is causally related to the much greater cross-border capital flows relative to GDP compared to the 1950s and 1960s, at least for the developed countries and the 20 or so developing countries of interest to international investors (the economies with emerging financial markets, named the 'emerging market economies'). Large capital inflows and outflows place enormous strains on economies. However, the exact relationship between financial *opening* and the probability of banking or currency crises does not seem to have been investigated with cross-sectional data. On the other hand, 'the evidence that financial *liberalization* [as indicated by the relaxation of controls on interest rates, for example] increases the vulnerability of countries to crises is overwhelming'.[6] And domestic financial liberalization is often associated with financial opening. All in all, the cross-sectional and historical evidence suggests that quick financial opening, especially when it goes with domestic financial liberalization, substantially raises the probability of a major crisis within the next several years.

This chapter takes for granted that the (non-Japan) East Asian crisis, whose onset is conventionally dated as July 1997, was due, *proximately*, in large part to the fast build up of foreign capital stocks over the 1990s and then the precipitous flight of both foreign capital and domestic capital. Much of the literature about the crisis, by both economists and political scientists, focuses on the domestic economic and political factors – the 'homegrown' factors, in the IMF's term – that explain the fast build-up of foreign capital stocks and then the precipitous capital flight. In political scientist Linda Weiss's formulation, for example, the key variable is 'state capacity.' 'The relative weakness of state capacity (in Southeast Asia), and its marked if incomplete decomposition (in Korea), made these economies more prone to speculative investment (in the Korea case, over-investment), asset bubbles and current account deficits, and consequently more vulnerable to financial upheaval.'[7] Her argument is that weak or decomposing state capacity resulted in failure to regulate in finance and failure to upgrade or coordinate in industry, which were then associated with the crisis.

The problem with internally-focused explanations is that they take the external context as given. But if many middle-income developing countries and some highly developed countries have had major financial crises during the period from 1980 to 2000, many more than in 1950–70,[8] this suggests that something might have changed in the external context to raise the probability of *any* country of interest to international investors experiencing a financial crisis.

The external factors, or some of them, are the subject of this essay. I describe, first, the 'structural' role of the US economy and US state in generating excess Asian liquidity; and second, the 'instrumental' role of the US state in effecting a quick financial opening and liberalization (FOLI) in Asia, making it easier for foreign capital and foreign financial services firms – specifically, US capital and US financial services firms – to enter Asia and reap higher Asian returns. The focus is on the creation of the bubbles. This again distinguishes the argument from the most of the rest of the literature, where the USA appears, if at all, only at the stage of managing the crisis. In Weiss's formulation, for example, weak or decomposing state capacity made the economies vulnerable to bubbles and over-investment, which then became a 'normal' crisis; then the US intervention in the handling of this normal crisis turned it into an 'abnormal' crisis. I stress the US role in blowing out the bubbles in the first place, because once bubble dynamics took hold a crash became likely. The discussion is limited to the Asian crisis for the most part, or more exactly, to the 'long Asian crisis' beginning in Japan in 1990; but the argument implies that much the same causality should be found in other financial crises. At the end I say something about policy lessons.

2. BLOWING UP THE BUBBLE

Discussion of the Asian crisis has been hobbled by treating it separately from the Japanese crisis. In fact, much the same mechanism that produced the Asian crisis also produced the earlier Japanese crisis. They should be considered as a single 'long Asian crisis' of 1990 to 2000, the Japanese crisis feeding into the Asian crisis. ('Asia' is shorthand for non-Japan East and Southeast Asia.)

The Invisible Strings

The key to the long Asian crisis is the foreign capital inflows into Japanese and Asian banks during the 1980s and 1990s. These foreign capital inflows permitted an explosion of domestic credit. Without the foreign capital inflows (as in a closed economy), credit creation would have been constrained by the rate of domestic saving; and growth would have been slower and less variable. The difference between the rate of credit creation based on domestic savings and the actual rate of credit creation reflects the impact of the foreign capital inflows.

The credit was used to debt-finance a surge of (a) industrial capacity and (b) purchases of land and stocks. At some point the amount of foreign capital entering the economy began to exceed the amount that could accelerate economic growth without creating a bubble. Bubble dynamics based on euphoric expectations took hold. Lenders ratcheted up their lending on the basis of increasingly inflated collateral asset values.

Land and share prices rose by many times from the mid-1980s to the early 1990s, helping to support a several-times expansion of industrial capacity in both tradable goods industries and non-tradable goods industries (those related to property, for example).

Eventually industrial capacity reached the point of overcapacity – relative to domestic demand, regional demand, and demand for Asian exports in the US market – where utilization rates fell to relatively low levels and corporate revenues and profit rates became insufficient to service the debt incurred in expanding the capacity. Asset values also eventually inflated to a similar point.

As this point approached, creditors tried to pull back their loans, investors tried to sell their stocks, and creditors and investors tried to convert out of the domestic currency. The result was a stock market crash combined with overcapacity in industry and in property, that yielded sharp devaluation, deflation, economic contraction, rising unemployment, increased poverty, and erosion of the middle class.

Japan led the way with its financial sector crisis and general recession starting in 1990. In response, desperate Japanese banks intensified their lending into Asia. Asia in the 1990s experienced an even larger foreign capital surge than it had experienced earlier, coming from all three components of the core of the world economy – Japan, Europe, and the USA. This inflow blew up the bubble which broke across the region in 1997, causing the financial cum currency collapse.

Conversely, and contrary to the great bulk of the crisis literature, even 'best practice' corporate governance and bank regulation in Asia would have been unlikely to stop the bubble and crash if the foreign capital surge had not been prevented (limited to, say, half of what it actually was). Also, again contrary to much of the literature, the crisis was at its core a crisis of overcapacity in industry and of inflated values in asset markets. The banking and currency crises were by-products. Certainly the explosion of credit drove the overcapacity and inflated asset values; but resolving the financial sector crisis is only a necessary, not sufficient, condition for restoring growth. Even if a set of healthy new banks were established, the economies would remain very vulnerable because the overhang of excess capacity, debt and inflated asset prices will weigh down them down for long into the future – unless additional sources of demand are found.

The Japanese Bubble and Crash

Japan began to run large current account surpluses in 1983, when the surplus rose to almost three times the previous year's, and rose again by one and two thirds times the following year. For a time, however, the impact of these surpluses on central bank reserves was neutralized by massive Japanese capital exports to the USA and to Asia. In 1986, the jump in surpluses was so large, from $49 billion to $86 billion, that the current account surpluses spilled over into central bank reserves, producing an almost 60 per cent jump in reserves. The following year, 1987, reserves rose by 90 per cent over the previous year's, and rose again by 20 per cent in 1988. This explosive growth in Japan's central bank reserves set off a surge in credit in 1986–90, that financed a surge in property values, share prices, and fixed capital formation (plus continuing very high rates of Japanese capital formation in Asia). Industrial production rose 25 per cent between 1986 and 1990.[9]

The bursting of the bubble began with the plunge in the Nikkei Index in early 1990. Industrial production rose slightly in 1990 and then fell by 10 per cent between 1991 and 1993. The wholesale price index, which had fallen earlier in the 1980s because of falling prices of oil imports, then began to drop because of the fall in demand, indicating excess capacity. Credit growth fell sharply despite a sharp decline in interest rates. Japan fell into a Keynesian 'liquidity trap' where demand for credit is unresponsive to very low interest rates. The stock market and property prices also fell persistently.

The 1990s was a two-stage story. The first stage lasted to 1995–96. By this time share and land prices stopped falling and the banks were well on the way to dealing with the overhang of non-performing loans. Massive lending into fast-growing Asia helped to bolster bank balance sheets. Output, profits and inventories started increasing again and fiscal 1996 had 5 per cent GNP growth. Assuming that the recession was past, the government started to put public finances on a sound footing again and increased taxes and social security charges – most notoriously with a 2 per cent increase in sales tax. It expected that these tax increases would choke off consumption for about 6 months and then growth would resume in a sounder fiscal environment. At the point when recovery should have begun, two 'exogenous' shocks aborted it. First, the Asian crisis began, damaging exports and giving the banks more bad loans. Second, the 'stern austerity' faction in the Ministry of Finance prevailed, and the Finance Ministry got tough with banks that had been just about keeping their heads above water ('trading through'). A big bank and a big securities firm were allowed to go bust. The combination of these two shocks made fearful consumers save rather than spend and made gloomy industrialists hold back investment, prompting general alarm about a banking crisis and another downward spiral from which – thanks to massive deficit spending – Japan is sputteringly recovering in 2000.

The Thai Bubble and Crash

Thailand illustrates the Asian sequence. Unlike Japan, Thailand and the other southeast Asian countries were running current account deficits through the 1990s. They were nevertheless accumulating central bank reserves because of an inflow of foreign capital far larger than that needed to finance the current account deficit. The foreign capital poured in from Japan, the USA and Europe as the owners and managers of capital in the core economies sought to package domestic savings, central bank reserves and financial capital attracted from the rest of the world and invest them in fast-growing Asia, all the more so because their own economies were in recession.

Thailand's central bank reserves spurted from 1986, growing at 20 per cent or more in almost every year up to 1995. Between 1987 and 1990 they grew at 40 per cent or more a year. Domestic credit spurted too – it being impossible for the monetary authorities to sterilize an appreciable part of such fast growing reserves. Domestic credit grew at 20 per cent or more in every year up to 1995. Gross fixed capital formation grew at 15 per cent or more a year in most years between 1987 and 1995.

Or in terms of averages, over 1988 to 1995 central bank reserves grew at an annual rate of 30 per cent, domestic credit grew at just under 30 per cent a year, and GDP grew at about 9 per cent a year – despite serious social and political unrest in 1991 and 1992. The stock market index rose 75 per cent in the last quarter of 1993 alone, driven by a surge of hedge fund foreign investment. Industrial overcapacity became pervasive. Office space in Bangkok rose by four times between 1986 and 1995. Building cranes so filled the skyline of Bangkok as to prompt the quip that the building crane had become Thailand's national bird.

This was the Thai miracle, one of the fastest sustained growth records that the world has ever seen. But by the early 1990s a fast rising part of the growth increment was bubble growth rather than real growth. Most of the incoming capital, much of it from Japanese banks, took the form of short-term, hot money deposited in Thai financial institutions to benefit from rates of interest much higher than in the core economies – and apparently secured against exchange rate risk by the commitment of the Thai authorities to a fixed exchange rate with the US dollar.

Once the pullout began in response to fears that debtors could not possibly service their debts the exchange rate fell 33 per cent between June 1997 and the end of 1998; GDP fell about 10 per cent in 1998; imports (in US dollars) fell 34 per cent, exports (in US dollars) fell 7 per cent in 1998.

3. THE USA's STRUCTURAL ROLE: PUMPING OUT LIQUIDITY

All this is only half the story. The other half concerns where the foreign capital came from and why there was so much of it. This takes us to the USA's 'structural' role in the long Asian crisis.[10]

The End of Bretton Woods

The first point is the end of the Bretton Woods regime and the US role in ending it. The Bretton Woods regime contained a self-adjusting mechanism through the link between the US dollar (the main international currency) and gold. When the USA ran current account deficits dollars accumulated abroad. The USA's ability to continue to run the deficits was limited by its gold supplies. As other countries' central banks asked the USA to pay for its deficits in gold, the fall in US gold reserves would squeeze bank lending in the USA (lending being a function of reserves) and eventually also aggregate demand. The US demand for imports would fall, producers would have more incentive to find export markets, and the US deficit would shrink. In the surplus countries, on the other hand, the rise in central bank reserves would boost domestic money supply, raise aggregate demand, and thereby raise demand for imports and encourage diversion of exports to domestic market sale; the surpluses would shrink. The rules of the Bretton Woods international financial system therefore applied a discipline on both deficit and surplus countries that operated to cut their deficits and surpluses.

As the USA continued through the second half of the 1960s to fight the Vietnam War and the War on Poverty simultaneously its budget and current account deficits reached the point where it could not continue both to run the deficits and maintain the link between the dollar and gold; it simply did not have enough gold. The Nixon administration in 1971 broke the link with gold. Henceforth the US dollar would be a fiduciary currency only. The USA could finance US current account deficits by printing dollars or selling treasury bills, with much less of a limit than had existed earlier.

Under Bretton Woods, as one (surplus) country gained central bank reserves another (deficit) country lost, so world central bank reserves increased only slowly. The new system had no such constraint. Persistent US current account deficits raised central bank reserves in the surplus countries without causing a fall in the USA's. The result was a surge in world central bank reserves, which increased by over seven times between 1969 and 1981 and another two times between 1982 and 1996. The expansion of reserves permitted a multiplied expansion of credit. An increase of reserves of, say, $100 million permitted a first round credit expansion of, say, $90 million (with $10 million put aside for reserves), the $90 million permitted a second round expansion of $81 million ($9 million put aside for reserves), and so on. This set the stage for investment, property and stock market booms, overcapacity and asset bubbles, panic, and collapse.

US Budgetary and Current Account Deficits

The US role in changing the rules of the international financial system in a way that greatly weakened the self-adjusting mechanism is one part of its structural role in the long Asian crisis. The second part is the USA's budgetary and current account deficits that began to grow fast after 1982. US budgetary deficits financed by government debt stimulated consumer demand, which stimulated demand for imports. The US income elasticity of demand for imports was higher than the rest of the world's income elasticity of demand for US exports. Except when US income growth was very low and aggregate demand depressed relative to foreign demand, the result was a US current account deficit. Persistent US deficits and persistent depreciation of the US dollar have been a source of imbalance and instability in the world economy.

The US current account deficit was financed for the most part by foreign capital inflows, much of it in the form of foreign purchases of US government debt denominated in US dollars. This accumulating US government debt then became part of the central bank reserves of the source countries, which allowed for multiplied domestic credit creation – at the same time as the USA continued to enjoy increasing central bank reserves, domestic credit expansion, and sustained excesses of imports over exports.

For much of the 1980s and the 1990s up to 1995, relatively slow US growth kept the US current account deficit from becoming a major generator of global excess liquidity. The mid-1980s, however, was an exception, when the USA enjoyed a spurt of growth above the OECD average and experienced a dramatic worsening of its current account deficit – the other side of which was the fast increase in central bank reserves in Japan and the onset of the Japanese bubble. In 1995 the USA moved into a period of significantly faster growth than in the rest of the OECD and experienced a rapid deterioration of the current account – the other side of which was the fast increase in central bank reserves in Asia and the onset of bubble dynamics there.

In short, US current account deficits, and the change in the rules of the international payments regime in a way that enabled US deficits to continue more or less indefinitely (when US incomes were growing at or above the rest of the OECD), together caused a surge of world liquidity. The surge manifested itself first in the major current account surplus country, Japan, in the form of the Japanese bubble of 1985 to 1990, and then in the fast growing Asian countries in the form of the bubble of 1992 to 1997. Japan contributed to blowing up the Asian bubble both before its crash and especially afterwards; but its bubble and crash were themselves rooted in the earlier US deficits.

4. THE US's INSTRUMENTAL ROLE: PUSHING FOR CAPITAL OPENING

I take for granted that quick financial opening and liberalization (FOLI) in Asia was an important enabling condition of the crisis, more important than the factors emphasized in the bulk of the literature, such as cronyistic or 'relationship-based' economic structure, moral hazard, and opacity of corporate and governmental accounts. FOLI enabled the huge inrush of foreign capital, setting in motion the dynamics just described. I also take for granted that Asian governments undertook FOLI not only for 'domestic' reasons: not only because they believed that the technology of moving money made controls unworkable; or because they believed that to finance the current account deficits they had no choice but to lift controls; or because they believed that their economies would experience large net benefits from unrestricted capital mobility; or because they believed that they and their citizens would simply miss out on the train of history if they did not integrate domestic financial markets into the world financial market as quickly as possible; or because they were pushed to do so by a rapidly growing domestic constituency of owners of highly mobile assets, such as financial services firms and wealthy individuals, who succeeded through the late 1980s and 1990s in tipping the balance of influence away from 'nationalists,' including labor unions, local banks, and locally-oriented firms.

All these things may have been operating. But to understand them as 'domestic' causes is to misunderstand the nature of US hegemony. Antonio Gramsci suggested that 'the supremacy of a social group manifests itself in two ways, as "domination" and as "intellectual and moral leadership".' Gramsci went on to argue that, 'A social group dominates antagonistic groups, which it tends to "liquidate," or subjugate perhaps even by armed force; it leads kindred or allied groups.' The US in Asia, however, has applied *both* domination-coercion and intellectual and moral leadership strategies to the same group – the same Asian states – in order to secure Asian FOLI. It has not only raised the penalties against not undertaking rapid financial opening and liberalization; it has also sought to persuade Asians that FOLI is in their own best national interest. This is close to Gramsci's notion of hegemony as the additional power, beyond domination, that accrues to a dominant group by it convincing subordinate groups that its rule serves not only its own interests but also those of the subordinate groups.[11] The US role in Asian FOLI therefore has to include the US role in fostering Asian and world beliefs about the rightness of free capital mobility, as well as more direct US pressure on Asian and other governments to open up.

The push in Asia was just one part of a larger push to institutionalize free capital markets worldwide, prosecuted both bilaterally and through multilateral organizations including the World Bank, the IMF, the OECD, and the GATT/WTO, as well as by US consultancy firms with close ties to the Treasury and USAID, like the Harvard Institute for International Development (HIID). The campaign involved specific pressures of rewards and penalties on both the governments of emerging market economies and on the international financial institutions; also the diffusion of more ideological 'definitions of reality' that identified open capital markets as a key part of the new realities that countries everywhere had to embrace if they wished not to be left behind; as well as the more capillary actions of promoting proponents of unrestricted free markets into positions of power in emerging market countries and in international organizations, and training large numbers of students from emerging market countries, especially Asians, in neoclassical economics at US universities. The following sections describe the various 'track-laying' vehicles, and then the case of Korea.

The US Government's Campaign from Reagan to Clinton

The US Treasury was concerned to improve the access of US financial firms to foreign markets long before Asia mattered – from at least as far back as the early 1970s, when the Eurodollar market began to be important. More than its predecessors the Reagan Administration that began in 1981 pressed for free movement of capital worldwide. '*Our task is to knock down barriers to trade and foreign investment and the free movement of capital*,' Reagan declared imperially.[12] Only a few years after the end of the mammoth Tokyo Round (in 1979), the US spearheaded the start of the Uruguay Round of trade negotiations in 1982, with the express purpose of liberalizing two domains that had been left off the agenda of the Tokyo Round, agriculture and services, especially financial services.

Meanwhile Europe was committing itself to open its capital markets. The Single European Act, signed in February 1986, called for the elimination of capital controls between European Community states and – more qualifiedly – for 'the highest possible' degree of capital liberalization between member states and the rest of the world.

The Bush Administration (1988 to 1992) continued. President Bush described his Latin American initiative as a commitment to 'free markets and to the free flow of capital, central to achieving economic growth and lasting prosperity.' (Note that in these and other such statements, free trade and free capital mobility are treated as merely different aspects of the same good thing, free markets.)

By the late 1980s 'financial deregulation' and 'free flow of capital' had become ideas in good currency in the world's most powerful countries (like the related idea of an 'independent central bank'). They were taken to denote governmental actions that would yield large benefits to all, and they thereby legitimized maximum pressure by the more powerful states on the less powerful not to 'defect' from the possibilities of large *mutual* benefits.

In the North American Free Trade Agreement (NAFTA) negotiations of 1991–93 the USA pressed Mexico hard to undertake domestic financial liberalization and financial opening. The Mexican banks were protected by quantitative restrictions on the share of total deposits that foreign banks could hold. The USA wanted this protection lifted so that American banks could get a larger market share. The Mexican government resisted, insisting that the NAFTA agreement give banks a long phase-out of protection, the longest of any sector. After the Mexican crash of late 1994, when Mexico needed rescue, the government agreed to accelerate the phase-out of banking protection. The Mexican crash brought benefits to American banks, from this point of view.

The Clinton Administration, that started in 1993, intensified the push for financial opening. A senior Clinton Administration official remarked that, 'We pushed full steam ahead on all areas of liberalization, including financial. I never went on a trip when my brief didn't include either advice or congratulations on liberalization.' He went on to observe that, 'Wall Street was delighted that the broad trade agenda now included financial services.'[13] In 1997 Deputy Treasury Secretary Lawrence Summers said, 'Financial liberalization, both domestically and internationally, is a critical part of the US agenda.'[14]

But the Uruguay Round had been unable to reach an agreement on financial services, and the round was concluded in December 1993 with an agreement on agriculture but without a financial services agreement.

The Clinton administration responded with aggressive bilateral and multilateral pressure. Senior Treasury officials in 1995 wanted to force Chile to scrap its capital controls, for example. (Chile had a tax on capital inflows such that the tax was effectively higher the sooner the money was withdrawn.) They insisted on Chile lifting the controls as part of the negotiations over a free-trade agreement. In the end the agreement was not signed because of US congressional opposition, so the issue of forcing Chile to abandon its capital controls did not come to a head.

Of course, the administration paid special attention to Asia's capital controls, because Asia 'was seen as a potential gold mine for American banks and brokerages,' in the words of a *New York Times* report.[15] And the administration paid more attention than its predecessors to advancing the agenda not just through the GATT/WTO but also through other multilateral fora.

The International Monetary Fund and the World Bank

Throughout the late 1980s and 1990s, the IMF and the World Bank reinforced US pressure. This was not a case of independent convergence to the same agenda. As *The Economist* observed, 'In recent years the Fund and the Bank have been hijacked by their major shareholders for overtly political ends. Whether in Mexico in 1994, Asia in 1997 or Russia through the 1990s, the institutions have become a more explicit tool of western, and particularly American, foreign policy.'[16] In the words of *The Financial Times*, 'The future role of the International Monetary Fund in the global financial system is now under debate. At issue is whether Washington will be able to use its 17% shareholding in the IMF to continue (as it often has since its inception more than half a century ago) to use the Fund as an extension of US foreign policy.'[17]

The International Monetary Fund

The Fund and the Bank claim that their decision-making procedures are blind to everything except criteria of 'sound' economics, and especially blind to everything 'political.' The evidence suggests this is mostly untrue. Kendall Stiles examined seven cases of Fund lending, and found that in only one case did the Fund adopt a politically neutral, technocratic approach to lending.[18] Tony Killick found that of his 17 cases of countries with Fund programs, at least one third secured favorable loan terms on their programs because of the intervention of major shareholding countries on their behalf.[19]

The *coup de grace* is the recent study by Strom Thacker. He tested the hypothesis that the Fund's lending to a country – the probability that the Fund will lend to it – is positively related to: (a) the country's political closeness to the USA, as indicated by the extent to which its UN General Assembly (UNGA) representative votes with the USA on votes that the US State Department deems 'key' votes for the USA; and (b) the country's movement towards the US position, as indicated by reductions in the gap between its votes in the UNGA and those of the USA on key votes.[20] Thacker found that in the pre-Cold War period, 1985–89, countries that moved towards the US position were very likely to be rewarded with IMF loans, while the degree of static closeness seemed to have little effect. Since the end of the Cold War both the degree of static closeness and movement towards the US position seem to matter more. 'This suggests that the U.S. is both playing the realignment game as vigorously as ever and is rewarding the allegiance of those who stay close without necessarily moving any closer.'[21]

One might expect that the change in the structure of the international system represented by the end of the Cold War would make genuine multilateralism more likely. Thacker's results suggest, on the contrary, that 'The ability of the U.S. to influence IMF behavior to achieve its own political goals has not eroded.... [M]ultilateralism, while useful for facilitating cooperation among a small number of like-minded states, may not be an effective buffer of U.S. power in the modern global political economy.'[22] Thacker does not examine the mechanisms by which the USA exerts its influence. One is through its large share of voting rights a multiple of the share of the next largest member and sufficient to veto on certain major decisions. Presumably this discourages Japanese or German assertion of leadership which the USA can then present as 'unwillingness' on the part of Japan and Germany to lead. Nor does Thacker examine the invisible strings between UN General Assembly votes and US Treasury decisions about what it wants the Fund to do, an interesting question during the Clinton administrations when relations between the State Department, which handles the UN, and the Treasury, which handles the Fund, have generally been bad.

In short, the studies of Stiles, Killick and Thacker confirm that Fund decisions about which countries get loans are influenced, strongly, by the preferences of the major industrial states, especially the USA.

My argument here is related but different. It says that the Fund and the Bank promote – directly through conditionalities and more indirectly – a limited set of market institutions whose closest empirical referents are those of Anglo-American capitalism, among which open capital markets and linked systems of corporate governance are central. Conversely, they do not promote the institutional structures of, say, the continental European and Scandanavian welfare states, or Japanese capitalism, or Taiwanese or Korean capitalism.[23]

Through the 1990s the IMF contributed to the inclusion of financial liberalization and free capital mobility as a core element of 'sound' policy, and pushed this agenda in its country consultations. But it had less influence in the 'Asian miracle' countries than the Bank, until 1997.

The World Bank

The World Bank, in its Structural Adjustment Programs and in its dialogue with governments through the 1980s and 1990s, pushed the liberalization of foreign exchange and financial systems, the privatization of state-owned enterprises, the development of stock markets and their opening to foreign investors, and the liberalization of foreign direct investment rules.

The Bank's policy guidelines on financial sector operations as they were formulated in the late 1980s and early 1990s called for comprehensive financial liberalization in its borrowing countries, including removal of all interest rate controls and all directed (or targeted) credit programs.[24] Its efforts to promote these guidelines in Asia led it into head-on disagreement with the Japanese government. The Japanese government, through aid and advice, was helping Asian governments strengthen financial systems to function more like Japan's during the catch-up phase, including interest rate controls and directed credit programs. However, the Japanese program largely failed, to the extent that Asian governments went ahead and liberalized along the lines advised by the World Bank, HIID and the US Treasury.

The power of the USA over the Bank varies according to type of issue.[25] On some the US Treasury has a veto. On other issues the USA has to act as leader of a G7 cartel. Decisions about whether to lend or not lend to a country tend to fall into this category. But where the USA sees its vital interests at stake it can virtually always prevail in lending decisions. A case in point is the Bank's refusal to lend to Vietnam in the 1980s, contrary to the Bank's articles of agreement, despite lending to many other countries with worse policies than Vietnam. Other examples include cutting off loans to Chile after Allende, to India after its nuclear test of 1998, and to China after Tianamen Square. And continuing to lend to Russia through the 1990s, despite very poor risk indicators. On other issues, where the USA does not see vital interests at stake (and outside French West Africa, where France has a similarly hegemonic role), the Bank management has more autonomy.

In the 1980s and 1990s the USA defined financial liberalization and free capital mobility as its vital interest, and the Bank, having to be very responsive, raised the priority of these issues in its own operations. The Bank in any case, like the Fund, contained a sizable constituency of neoclassically-trained economists who believed that rapid financial liberalization was the right thing to do.

The Multilateral Agreement on Investment and the Financial Services Agreement

In the 1990s the push to get Asian and other emerging market governments to do more capital liberalization continued in new fora. After the Uruguay Round was signed in 1994 things that it had taken off the table, notably investment and finance, became the subject of separate multilateral negotiations.

The newly formed World Trade Organization (formed out of the GATT in 1994) started to prepare negotiations for a Multilateral Agreement on Investment. The initial drafts of the MAI came from the International Chamber of Commerce and the Business and Investment Advisory Council (the multinational business group affiliated with the OECD). The content of the proposed agreement was all about the rights, the protection of foreign investors, not about their obligations; and contained nothing about the conditions in a signatory developing country that would warrant exceptions to the rights of investors. Moreover, 'investment' was defined to go well beyond foreign direct investment, to include even *short-term speculative flows*. The agreement would also require signatory governments to grant foreign companies treatment no worse than that of national counterparts, leaving open the possibility that they could be granted better treatment. This would allow international firms to be exempt from 'national' treatment when national treatment involved constraints they did not like.

Developing country members of the WTO were not happy with such a lop-sided agreement. In the WTO developing countries have substantial influence in terms of being able to block things they do not like – and the WTO has an appeals procedure where developing countries can challenge rulings made under the agreement. In the circumstances, the USA, leading the effort, thought it best to withdraw the MAI from the WTO and get it negotiated between the smaller number of OECD members alone, where it would be free of developing country obstruction. Developing countries would later be invited to sign on – or risk being by-passed by investors. Negotiations started in the OECD in 1995.

Meanwhile, the World Trade Organization began to negotiate the related Financial Services Agreement, intended to allow free trade in banking, insurance and securities services. This was to include not only free cross-border transactions in these areas but also – which takes it much further – the establishment of wholly foreign-owned or majority foreign-owned foreign financial services firms free to compete equally with domestic financial service firms. The US dominated the negotiations – 'the power of the US was omnipresent,' the USA was 'the de facto power broker in the negotiations,' according to newspaper reports.[26] In June 1995 the USA 'walked away from a potential agreement, thereby scuttling the deal,' an agreement that the Europeans were prepared to sign on to, because the USA wanted developing countries to make greater concessions on market access to foreign banks and insurance companies. Malaysia was a prominent hold-out against US wishes. I come back to this case later.

Revision of the IMF's Articles of Agreement

Also in the mid-1990s the IMF, with strong backing from the USA and UK Treasuries, began the process of renegotiating its Articles of Agreement so as to require member countries both to grant the Fund jurisdiction over the capital account and to commit themselves to liberalize it.[27] This would make a fundamental change in the Fund's formal mandate agreed at the Bretton Woods negotiations, and give it much more power through its fully legitimated ability to use a country's slow progress in opening the capital account to withhold Fund support and thereby also constrain other providers of support too.

The managing director of the Fund, Michel Camdessus, was strongly committed to the revision of the articles. As the top civil servant in the French Treasury and then as governor of the central bank, he had been a member of and chair of the European Monetary Committee (of central bank and finance ministry officials) between 1978 and 1984, and had made capital account opening in Europe the main agenda of the monetary committee.

The US Treasury was equally in favor. In April 1997 US Treasury Secretary Rubin headed a meeting in which finance ministers of the G7 leading industrialized countries issued a statement 'promoting freedom of capital flows' and urging that the International Monetary Fund charter be amended so that it could lead the push for capital account liberalization.[28] In September 1997 at the Hong Kong Annual Meetings of the Fund and the Bank, the Interim Committee of the IMF encouraged the Fund to move aggressively to encourage countries to institute full capital convertibility.

In short, the US Treasury (with sherpa help from the UK Treasury) has been leading the Big Push to change the rules of the world economy so as to hardwire in free capital mobility and remove an array of capital controls from the legitimate instruments for national economic management. Multilateral agencies – the World Bank, the IMF, the OECD, the WTO – have become important vehicles for this purpose. The pressure on Asian countries was part of the wider push.

Complementary Improvements in Bank Regulation?

Any of the American and British officials involved in the Big Push would have agreed that FOLI had to be supported by 'strong' prudential regulation and oversight, and hence that liberalization had to be 'sequenced,' had to be 'orderly.' But they gave little attention to assessing the adequacy of Asian arrangements. Their attention was on getting the Asians to open up.

Joseph Stiglitz, chair of the White House's Council of Economic Advisors through the early and mid-1990s, was an exception. *The New York Times* cites a former senior Treasury official 'ruefully' recalling arguments between Stiglitz and the Treasury, with Stiglitz warning about the need for slower 'pacing' of financial liberalization abroad.[29] 'Nobody listened,' recalled the Treasury official. The official went on to say, 'I viewed "pace" as an excuse by countries to keep their markets closed.' Or in the phrase of the supportive New Zealand Deputy Treasury Secretary, 'reform delayed is reform denied.'[30] Stiglitz was shortly afterwards invited to become chief economist at the World Bank, where he could be less influential in questioning Treasury's designs, or so Treasury hoped.[31]

In short, *attention to building 'strong' regulatory arrangements and linking capital opening to the strength of those arrangements on the ground was deliberately discouraged lest it provide countries with excuses to delay – contrary to US objectives.*

Furthermore, both before the crisis and even after it, when the USA talked of strengthening bank regulation it meant in the *borrowing* countries. One recalls the question once posed by Senator Proxmire, 'Where were *our* bank regulators? … [T]hey did everything except what they are paid to do, and that is to regulate.' He was speaking in a congressional hearing on the Latin American debt crisis, in 1983.[32]

Just how little attention has been given to the lenders' side is seen from Louis Uchitelle's *New York Times* article on the state of thinking about the causes of the Asian crash, in early 1999.[33] 'The Clinton Administration had mostly blamed the countries, and still does. But its view, like that of the IMF, is starting to reflect a more nuanced appraisal. "We have seen that countries need to pursue sounder policies and avoid lurching for short-term capital, as Mexico and Thailand did," said Lawrence H. Summers, the Deputy Treasury Secretary. But … he also called for "more prudence on the part of the lenders".' The statement about the need for borrowing countries to pursue 'sounder' policies – an elastic phrase – again puts the blame onto the borrowers, in keeping with the Treasury's response throughout the crisis. The statement about the need for more prudence on the part of the lenders shifts a little of the blame onto lenders. But it, and a statement from Summers that 'Where countries have controls that restrict short-term lending we have not in general sought to dismantle them,' constitute the sole evidence of the 'more nuanced appraisal' said to be taking root in the Clinton Administration. This underlines the point that the US Big Push was carried out with little regard for the dangers of freer international capital flows and the need to strengthen regulation of the lenders.

USA–Korea Relations

Korea provides a case study of the wider US campaign.[34] Through the 1980s the US government became increasingly worried that Korea would be another Japan – a major industrial powerhouse using 'mercantilist' policies to outcompete US firms in the USA and abroad while allowing only restricted access to its domestic market. This worry became acute after the Plaza Accord of 1985, when the devaluation of the US dollar against the yen caused the Korean won also to devalue against the yen, raising the competitiveness of Korean exports to the USA. The USA made Korea one of the main scapegoats for the US trade deficits, all the more so as the Cold War became less determining of US foreign policy strategy in the late 1980s and Korea lost some of the economic grace it had enjoyed from US geopolitical interests. Determined not to let Korea get away with its mercantilism, the US government took an increasingly aggressive stance towards many of Korea's exports, including through Super 301 sanctions. (Under Super 301 the US government abrogates to itself the right unilaterally to retaliate with fines and tariffs against foreign countries for wrongs decided upon by competing US industries and the US Trade Representative – which could scarcely be more mercantilist, though in official US eyes mercantilism is something that only others do.)

By the late 1980s US financial firms were becoming seriously exasperated at their restricted access to the Korean financial markets. Earlier in the 1980s the Korean government had liberalized enough to allow a small number of US banks to operate in Korea, and the lucky few – Bank of America and Citibank among them – were making very high returns on capital.[35] Other US financial firms wanted in. But by the late 1980s the government 'stalled' on financial liberalization, and US firms saw their prospects fading. They pressed the US Treasury to help.

The US Treasury proposed to bring the Koreans to the negotiating table in the Financial Policy Talks (FPT). These talks went on from 1990 to 1992 (during the Bush presidency). They focused on complaints of US banks and securities firms about restrictions to the Korean market: restrictions on access to local funding sources, on introducing new products, on access to the securities market (including a 10 per cent ceiling on foreign investment in listed Korean firms); and above all, on 'controls on foreign exchange and capital flows that impede foreign banks from competing in their natural lines of business,' in the words of a US Treasury official.[36]

The same official continued, 'As the [Financial Policy Talks] dialogue progressed, it became apparent that many of the difficulties faced by foreign financial institutions in Korea were connected to structural distortions in the financial sector resulting from the highly regulated nature of the system and government's heavy-handed intervention. *We* therefore shifted our focus in the FPT from individual issues to the need for *basic structural reform* of the Korean financial sector' (emphasis added).

Out of this came the Korean government's 'Blueprint for Financial Liberalization.' The World Bank was brought in to advise and supervise the government on the liberalization. This 'Blueprint' then became the basis for the incoming Kim Young Sam government's Five-Year Plan for Financial Liberalization of 1993.

By 1994 the US Treasury (now in the Clinton Administration) had achieved some of its agenda: higher ceilings on foreign participation in the Korean stock market, guaranteed entry for some foreign financial institutions, and higher ceilings for foreign ownership of Korean companies. And *the Korean government had taken two steps, specifically wanted by the Treasury, that were to lead directly to the crisis: the conglomerates (chaebol) were free to borrow internationally; and new merchant banks were free to set up and borrow abroad*. Twenty-four merchant banks sprang up between 1994 and 1997.

The Treasury was not satisfied, however. It laid out detailed lists of further changes, including expedited interest rate liberalization and ceased reliance on 'window guidance,' reduced documentation requirements for forward exchange transactions, and removal of limits on lending to the 30 largest conglomerates. The last point is worth emphasising. The Korean government of Kim Young Sam sought to free the domestic financial system from the grasp of the conglomerates, and therefore tried to impose restrictions on their access to domestic credit. At the same time it eased their access to foreign credit – and even encouraged them to borrow *short-term* rather than long-term by imposing less onerous documentation requirements.[37] The USA wanted the restrictions on the chaebols' access to domestic credit to be lifted as well (US financial firms already in Korea being in a good position to win this business). The US also pressed for funding and lending limits on US banks in Korea to be linked not to their *local* capital but to their global capital.

At about this time the US Treasury began to take a strong interest in pushing financial liberalization through the Asia Pacific Economic Council (APEC). Till then, from the start of APEC in 1989, the US had participated in APEC but not in a leadership role. Around 1994 it climbed into the driver's seat and began to make region-wide financial liberalization a top priority. It saw the regional forum as a way to make financial liberalization gains at lower cost than through multiple bilateral negotiations.

Korea and other Asian countries also wanted to promote APEC as a forum for financial liberalization discussions, in order to give them more protection from unilateral US pressure – and especially in order to allow the financial liberalization to be presented for the domestic audience as the result of mutual agreement rather than US arm-twisting. For the earlier financial policy talks between the Korean Ministry of Finance and the US Treasury, from 1990 to 1992, had stirred up strong anti-American sentiment in Korea.

In the spirit of APEC's 'open regionalism,' the APEC countries agreed (in what was called the Osaka Action Agenda of 1995) that each would propose their own, self-initiated financial liberalization plan. The plan that Korea brought forward committed itself to full financial liberalization by 2010.

This looked like back-tracking to the US Treasury, and the USA became unhappy with the APEC process. It resumed its arm-twisting of the Korean government to remove capital controls faster than the Korean government had planned, dangling the bait of US support for Korea's entry into the OECD – an all-important objective of the Korean government, the very symbol of its arrival in the ranks of the 'developed nations.'

The New York Times quotes an internal Treasury memorandum, dated 20 June 1996, setting out the Treasury's negotiating position with the Koreans. The Treasury required as a condition of US support that the Korean government let foreigners buy Korean bonds; also that the Korean government let Korean companies borrow abroad; and let foreigners buy Korean stocks more easily. These changes would make for a major change in the close relations between Korean companies and Korean banks – away from an 'organizational' relationship towards an arms-length 'market' relationship – and hence further dismantling of the basic structure of the developmental state.

The three-page document says nothing about the need for Korea to strengthen its bank regulation and legal institutions. 'The goal,' comments *The New York Times*, 'is clearly to use the O.E.C.D. as a way of prying open Korean markets – in part to win business for American banks and brokerages.'

US congressional leaders were also active in generating pressure on the Treasury and on the Korean government directly. Doug Bereuter, US House of Representatives member for Nebraska and chair of the Committee on International Relations Subcommittee on Asia and the Pacific, did not mince words in setting out a congressional agenda for improving US–Korea relations, in early 1995. 'I intend to be very aggressive in doing what I can to expose the tariff quotas and the plethora of nontariff barriers that continue to frustrate US exporters in Asia.... America has been tolerant about Korea's nontariff trade barriers for far too long. Now that the Cold War is over, we can and should demand an end to the *unfair treatment for the American side* in this bilateral relationship.'[38]

This account of the US–Korea relation suggests how the US government pressured Korea to open its financial markets. It does not, however, pin down the importance of this external pressure relative to the wishes of segments of the Korean policy-making elite; nor does it say where the Korean government gets its policy 'preferences' from. To what extent do its policies come from Washington ideas about a liberal economy, refracted through calculations of what determines 'confidence' in international capital markets? To what extent did the Korean government move less fast than the USA wanted? Does the fact that the Korean government moved much faster to let Korean firms borrow abroad than to let foreign financial firms operate in the domestic market suggest that the government retained some degree of autonomy? Does the aggressiveness of US language suggest the force of US pressure?

5. WHY THE USA WANTS FREE CAPITAL MOBILITY

In short, Asian governments came under pressure to open the financial system from US-based organizations, including the US Treasury, HIID, the World Bank and the IMF. This pressure became especially strong during the early to mid-1990s. A content analysis of the advice given to East Asian governments by the US government, the World Bank, and the IMF would show, I expect, that much more of it was about FOLI in 1990–95 than in the preceding five years.

The next question is why the US government gave much higher priority to FOLI in emerging market countries *in the 1990s*, especially in East Asia?

US Assertion of a Neoliberal World Order, with Finance as the Last Frontier

Since the Second World War the USA has acted fairly consistently to expand the scope of a world social order based on Lockean individualism and democracy; as part of which it has acted to expand the opportunities and profitability of all US business abroad. This included finance. The United States helped establish a stable international monetary system that made it easy to transfer capital from one country to another.[39] And the US financial industry received various kinds of state support in its overseas ventures once US financial firms began to operate abroad in the 1960s and 1970s (with the development of Eurodollar market, the recession in the USA, and the recycling of OPEC oil money). The state certainly helped US banks to lend to Latin America in the 1970s, and helped to assure their repayment after the debt crisis began in 1982.

Through the 1980s the Treasury orchestrated an aggressive 'export activism' on behalf of US manufacturing and agricultural interests, seeking to curb the rising US current account deficits (of which the unilateral Super 301 was only one of several weapons). Over time the campaign broadened into 'market access activism,' the principle of which was that US firms, including financial services firms, must have the same freedom of access to foreign markets as foreign firms have to the US market. Anything else is 'unfair' to the USA.

The much higher priority given to FOLI in US foreign economic policy in the late 1980s and 1990s might then be explained in terms of changes in two things; the international distribution of power among states, with the USA becoming even more dominant than it had been before; and finance becoming the 'last frontier,' as emerging market countries opened goods markets while delaying opening financial markets.

All victors want to remake the world in their own image. The USA after the end of the Cold War in Europe in 1989 was every bit as tempted to do so as other victors, its confidence caught in Clinton's second Secretary of State Madeline Albright's self-flattering description of the USA as 'the indispensable nation.' Or in Federal Reserve Chairman Alan Greenspan's words, 'It is safe to say that we are witnessing this decade, in the United States, history's most compelling demonstration of the productive capacity of free peoples operating in free markets.' The collapse of the Berlin Wall a decade ago, he went on to say, revealed not only the political success of civilised democracy, but also its economic achievement.[40]

As the USA became the only great power in the late 1980s, its leaders became more focused on imposing their vision of what the global *economic* order should be like, less restrained by geopolitical considerations and less restrained by specific economic interests.

The content of that vision became even more single-mindedly neoliberal than in the past. Neoliberalism seemed to have an obvious 'evidentiary' justification in the failure of all the alternatives: the failure of 'communism,' the failure of 'the Soviet Union,' the failure of 'import-substituting industrialization' in Latin America and India, the failure of 'Japan Inc' as the Japanese recession persisted through the 1990s. Wall Street, the City of London, and Anglo-American economics departments gave neoliberalism a firm institutional base. The deep institutionalization of the neoliberal outlook means that its translation into public policy is partly independent of particular people or particular blocs of interests.

In this vision, freedom to move one's money freely across borders is tied to ultimate values. As the *Financial Times* columnist Samuel Brittan put it, 'The most basic argument against exchange control ... is that it is one of the most potent weapons of tyranny which can be used to imprison citizens in their own country.' (To which Benjamin Cohen replied, 'That capital mobility might exercise its own form of tyranny ... seems, in such thinking, to count for little.')[41]

So the change in the international distribution of power, with the USA becoming even more dominant as the Cold War came to an end in the late 1980s, helps to explain why the USA asserted even more energetically a neoliberal economic agenda in its dealings with other countries; and in that agenda finance had a central place partly for normative reasons.

Moreover, by the 1990s most other sectors had been covered by trade liberalization agreements under the Uruguay Round. Finance, investment and agriculture had, as noted, been taken off the table in the Uruguay Round so that disagreements over them would not jeopardize agreements for other sectors. These sectors therefore became 'the last frontiers,' and as the Uruguay Round neared its end in the early 1990s, they began to receive higher priority in US foreign economic policy. The idea of finance as the last frontier helps to explain why the US government makes no distinction between free trade in goods and free trade in dollars; it presents the latter as merely one more step in the former.

Financialization and the Wall Street–Treasury Complex

But this explanation of why the US government gave high priority to FOLI in emerging market countries during the 1990s – the broader assertion of a neoliberal foreign economic policy and finance as the last frontier in the neoliberal agenda – is too blunt. It overlooks the fact that the financial services industry in the USA (and the UK) has not only grown rapidly to become a major sector of economic activity during the 1980s and 1990s, as it was not before, but also that it has come to dominate the economy over this period. 'Financial encephalitization,' the process might be called, or the 'financialization of the economy' (FOE). Financialization has direct implications for capital flows to emerging markets and for the US foreign economic policy agenda.

Financialization has several sub-trends. One is the rapidly rising ratios of financial assets and flows to real assets and flows. For example, in the US total credit outstanding as a percentage of GDP rose from 148 per cent in 1960, to 168 per cent in 1980, then jumped to 245 per cent in 1990 and up to 275 per cent in 1999. The figures for the 1990s are the highest in US history.

A second sub-trend is the rapidly rising share of the financial sector in total credit, from 25 per cent of the total in 1989 to 55 per cent in 1999. This implies that the rapidly rising volume of financial transactions in the US economy is being supported by even more rapidly rising volumes of *borrowings*. Never before in US history have financial institutions borrowed more than they lend to non-financial customers. As analyst Jane D'Arista comments, 'the amount of credit now required to accommodate US financial activity may be stronger evidence of a bubble than asset prices themselves.'[42]

A third sub-trend is the growing importance of institutional investors (pensions funds, insurance companies, mutual funds, trust funds) relative to banks and other depository institutions, as savers have switched from the latter to the former. In the USA, the share of total financial sector assets held by institutional investors rose from a third in 1978 to over a half (54 per cent) in 1998, while the share of depository institutions fell from over a half (57 per cent) to a quarter (27 per cent) over the same period. This could be called the 'portfolioization of savings.'

We see, then, a rapid rise in the size and significance of the financial economy relative to the real economy over the 1980s and 1990s. The trend has gone much further in the US (also the UK) than in Germany and Japan. For example, the assets of institutional investors in Germany and Japan, relative to GDP, are less than half those in the US and the UK (see Table 7.1).

Table 7.1 Assets of institutional investors

	Ratio to GDP (%)			
	1980	1990	1992	1993
USA	59	95	119	126
UK	64	124	137	165
Germany	20	42	43	47
Japan	23	56	54	n.a.

Source: International Monetary Fund, *International Capital Markets*, August 1995 .

But FOE is more than the rising share of finance. It is the growing dominance of the financial industry over the rest of the economy, especially in the USA, which has altered the system-ness of the economy. Financial dominance over the rest of the economy is achieved through mechanisms of institutional interlock and normative congruence, each mechanism reinforcing the other.

As the size of the financial sector has grown the stock market has become the economy's pivotal institution.[43] In the corporate sector, managers' financial incentives and their perceptions of their responsibilities have been transformed. Their remuneration increasingly takes the form of stock options rather than salaries; and at senior levels they are recruited from the external labor market rather than promoted from within. Both things together promote the notion that maximization of shareholder value is their sole legitimate objective. They raise or lower budgets, buy or sell bits of companies, with the objective of raising the share price, not only because they gain directly from stock options but also because the higher share price reduces the chances of hostile take-over – and their being ousted. The same forces affect who becomes CEOs; they come increasingly from a financial background rather than from engineering or marketing. And the substance of 'corporate strategy' is increasingly focused on buying and selling companies, going with the rising incidence of takeovers.

In the household sector, financial markets have become the pacesetters of consumption markets through the wealth effect, amplifying economic cycles. Those in the top 20 per cent or so of the household income distribution now typically have so much of their assets in the form of stocks that they are as concerned about the movements of financial markets as they are about house prices.

A much larger percentage of the population is now directly affected by those movements, even if not directly invested in the stock market, because of the move away from 'pay as you go' pensions (in which today's pensions are paid out of today's taxes on the incomes of those currently in work) towards 'defined contribution' pensions (in which the individual's pension depends on the performance of their pension fund's investments in the stock market). The shift in the financing of pensions tends to consolidate a political common interest across a large part of the electorate in protecting capital income, perhaps even at the expense of labor incomes. Financialization of the economy has the fortunate consequence for the beneficiaries of capital income that finance becomes too important – in the functioning of the economy and the polity – to be allowed to fail. Various public policy ratchets are put in place to socialize private losses while doing little to curb the taking of private profits.

These are examples of institutional interlock, by which other economic institutions – corporations, households, the pension industry – come to organize themselves around financial markets. Norms adjust, too. It is now taken for granted that the norms for judging economic performance should relate mainly to the returns to capital rather than to labor productivity. 'Efficiency' is generally used to mean efficiency in the use of capital. The quality of corporate management is judged by its success in capital markets, not by its success in labor markets or by the employees' dedication to the firm and the firm's ties to its employees. The share price is accepted as the best composite index of company performance.

The recent OECD report, *Corporate Governance: Improving Competitiveness and Access to Capital in Global Markets*, known as the Millstein Report (April 1998), is a telling illustration of how deeply rooted these norms are. It was written by a committee of people who are not all disciples of the American way. It adopted a studied neutrality between what it called the Anglo-Saxon model and the Rheinish model. Countries can and should have different social or employee-favoring objectives, it said; what matters is that the objectives and the ways of achieving them be 'transparent.' But transparent with respect, implicitly, to potential investors, not to potential employees. The subtitle says it all: the problem of corporate governance is defined to be largely about access to capital.

The active agent of this configuration of interlocking institutions and validating norms that produce FOE is the Wall Street–Treasury complex.[44] Wall Street denotes the sectoral interests, and Treasury (shorthand for Treasury, Commerce, State, CIA) denotes the state power. Both combine to promulgate the ideology and to shape the executive and legislative agendas. This complex is the seat of the pressures on the rest of the world – and on the international financial institutions, including the IMF and the World Bank – to open each part of the world's financial system.

The Wall Street-Treasury Complex and Free Capital Mobility

Financialization of the US economy has raised the USA's premium on a world order of free capital mobility, including accomodative policies in emerging markets. First, the USA has a strong national interest in being able to suck in savings from the rest of the world. It has become the world's biggest recipient of foreign capital inflows, which come in partly to fund the large and growing US external deficit. Foreign holdings of US financial assets are two-thirds higher again than US holdings of comparable foreign financial assets (in 1999).

Second, the Treasury sees a strong US 'national interest' in promoting market access for US financial services firms. US financial services firms have great advantages over competitors in everything from securities placement, debt work-outs, privatizations, and mergers and acquisitions. Even in Europe, the surge of merger and acquisition (M&A) activity in 1999 was done largely by US financial service firms. 'In spite of the shift of M&A activity towards Europe, the region's investment banks failed to overcome US banks' dominance of the sector,' reports *The Financial Times*. The leader of the US investment banks was Goldman Sachs, involved in deals amounting to almost half of the total value of M&A activity in Europe in 1999.[45]

The income earned from US foreign direct investment in finance was about equal to the income earned from US foreign direct investment in the whole of manufacturing, and the net income from finance would be very much greater.[46] Hence the US financial services sector earns a substantial current account *surplus* for the USA. As the overall US current account deficits rise, the surpluses earned by the financial services firms become more and more valuable – and the Treasury becomes more and more concerned to open their surplus-earning opportunities still wider.

Third, the portfolioization of savings – the shift from depository institutions to institutional investors – accelerated the trend to cross-border financial transactions. The Wall Street investment houses had for a long time been building up their foreign operations in privatizations, mergers and acquisitions, and pension funds, in addition to buying and selling securities and underwriting bonds. As US savers increasingly placed their savings in private pension plans, life insurance companies, mutual funds, and investment trusts, and as these in turn invested their pools of savings in securities markets rather than depository institutions, the institutional investors needed to diversify their portfolios geographically. In the 1990s the institutional investors and the banks were also 'restructuring' (cost-cutting, consolidating), following on from the restructuring in US manufacturing during the 1980s. As the financial firms merged, they looked for new global markets; and as new global markets beckoned, the financial services industry consolidated on a world level.

Fourth, the weighting of emerging markets in industrial countries' foreign portfolio investment has increased many times during the 1990s. In 1989 emerging markets constituted just 1 per cent of industrial countries' foreign portfolio investment; in 1993 (the most recent year for which figures are readily available), 16 per cent; the figure would certainly be much higher today.[47]

The switch in many emerging market countries from foreign capital inflows in the form of bank loans in the 1970s and 1980s to securities in the 1990s has itself contributed to the increasing weight of emerging markets in industrial countries' portfolios. The flow of foreign funds into emerging market stock markets fuelled sharp stock market booms. The Mexican stock market rose by over 400 per cent in dollar terms during the four-year period 1990–93, before crashing in 1994. And East Asian stock markets rose very fast in the several years after 1993 as capital was diverted from Latin America after the Mexican crash. The stock market booms allowed emerging markets to absorb much larger volumes of inflows relative to GDP than otherwise, because the rise in the domestic stock market tends in itself to pull in more capital as price per share rises.

In short, the financialization of the US economy during the late 1980s and 1990s has raised the relative importance – in the eyes of US foreign economic policy decision-makers – of opening and liberalizing financial markets in emerging market countries. That goal was in any case receiving higher priority as finance became one of the last items on the neoliberal world order agenda.

The great blessing of financial opening for the US foreign economic policy agenda is that it has no domestic costs. Pushing other countries to open up just about any other sector does have domestic costs, because other countries may demand more access to the US market in related products (think of agriculture), and some of those imports may hurt US producers. No emerging market financial services firm is likely to be able to compete in the USA, so the US can truthfully remove all barriers to entry and claim the same for its firms in emerging markets.

6. CONCLUSIONS

This chapter has argued that a surge of foreign capital directly caused the Japanese bubble of 1985–90 and the Asian bubble of 1992–97. While the capital that blew up the Asian bubble came from Japan and Europe as well as from the USA, the root source of burgeoning domestic credit in both Japan and Asia was growing US current account deficits. The USA's structural role in the long Asian crisis of 1990–2000 is therefore (a) its contribution to the change in the rules of the international payments regime, whereby the dollar, the main international currency, became a strictly fiduciary currency, allowing the USA to finance current account deficits without the checks of the Bretton Woods regime, and (b) the USA's growing deficits, the other end of which were Japan's persistent surpluses.

The USA's instrumental role in the long Asian crisis lay in inducing Asian governments to undertake rapid financial opening and liberalization (FOLI), with little attention paid to linking inflows to the strength of regulatory regimes (linking in such a way that the weaker the ability to subject the flows to the constraints of prudential regulation, the more the use of direct controls to keep inflows to below certain danger thresholds – to keep short-term foreign debt to foreign exchange reserves well below 100 per cent, for example).[48] 'Inducing,' as in 'inducing Asian governments to undertake rapid financial opening and liberalization,' occurred through a whole array of mechanisms and organizations, some bilateral, some multilateral. These became the vehicles which laid the track along which large quantities of capital could flow into Asia.

As for why the US government gave such a high priority to FOLI, perhaps the most important was the growing financialization of the US economy. This refers to a rapidly rising share of financial activity in total economic activity; to a change in structure from banks and other depository institutions to institutional investors and securities markets (the portfolioization of savings); and to financial dominance of the economy, as seen in the reconfiguring of the key economic institutions, including corporations and households, around the stock market as pivot. These trends have gone much further in the USA than in the other core countries (apart from Britain).

Financialization of the economy (FOE) promotes FOLI. The institutional investors sought to diversify their portfolios geographically, in such a way that they could move quickly in and out of any particular stock market. And as they consolidated, following the consolidation wave in manufacturing during the 1980s, the now larger firms looked for new global markets to justify their consolidation; and as they found new markets they further consolidated. Meanwhile, the switch in emerging market capital inflows from bank loans in the 1970s and 1980s towards securities in the 1990s allowed a still greater volume of inflows relative to GDP, because the inflows blew up stock market indices and as price per share rose more capital could be absorbed in the stock market.

Wall Street came together with Treasury (shorthand for the US state) in the Wall Street–Treasury complex to promote market opening and liberalization, especially in Asia, where US financial firms could be sure of being prime beneficiaries. More generally, the complex has made the USA into the world's great savings entrepôt, taking in savings from the rest of the world, repackaging them into other financial instruments, and selling them back to the rest of the world in return for fees and claims on foreign income flows.

Hegemonic states, it is said, act to create a set of rules that allow the smaller states to break out of 'the tyranny of small decisions,' in Kenneth Waltz's phrase, to overcome the tendency of separate states to pursue national interest without cooperating with other states to solve problems that require system-level solution.[49] But in this case the hegemonic state, the USA, has acted to subject smaller states to 'the tyranny of the big decision,' namely, the decision of how to maximize US interests as increasingly defined by the sectoral interests of finance.

It is not surprising, then, that current discussion assumes that the key to Asian recovery lies in restoring high volumes of capital inflows, and that these volumes will not be restored until institutional restructuring along the lines of a neoliberal model is undertaken. In the words of the *Financial Times*, 'until bankruptcy procedures are improved, bad corporate debts written off and the banks restructured, capital inflows will be inhibited ... While access to capital is constrained, the Asian economic machine cannot run at full speed'.[50]

This argument is dangerous. It assumes that a lack of capital – a credit crunch – is inhibiting Asian recovery. It assumes that restoration of foreign capital inflows to close to pre-crisis levels is desirable. And it assumes that restoration of economic growth to pre-crisis levels is desirable.

If the problems of bad corporate debts, bank restructuring and inadequate bankruptcy procedures were magically solved, Asia would still face a fragile near-term future, because the problem of excess capacity would remain. In many sectors investment is now constrained not by lack of capital but by the fact that the existing capacity built up during the heady days of miracle growth can produce much more than can be sold domestically or abroad.

The danger is not that foreign capital inflows will not return to pre-crisis levels, but that they will. Given the fact of excess capacity, they would be seeking speculative short-term gains rather than long-term revenues. They might well blow out another speculative bubble. If a second crash occurs, governments, already saddled with high levels of public debt undertaken to bail out domestic banking systems, would be in much worse fiscal shape to respond than they were the first time.

There are two lines of solution. One is for the 'international community' to accept that governments have a responsibility to limit capital inflows to below the levels at which bubble dynamics come to dominate the real economy, and below the levels at which panic withdrawals become likely. This calls for, among other things, the IMF abandoning the attempt to hard-wire a commitment to full – even if 'eventual' – capital account liberalization as a condition of Fund membership (by way of an amendment to the Articles of Agreement).

The second is for Asia and Asian economies to become more reliant on domestic demand and less reliant on export demand, specifically US demand. Sustainable economic growth requires that supply and demand grow in some sort of balance. In Asian supply conditions (as distinct from, say, African supply conditions), the supply of manufactures is highly elastic with respect to the supply of credit. On the other hand, export demand growth is limited by slow growth in Japan and Europe, and by the financial fragility of the US economy. Domestic demand growth is constrained by low wages and high inequality. The line of solution is here, in expanding domestic demand. It can be boosted by such policies as government-mandated increases in minimum wages (perhaps just in export industries, perhaps by $1 a day each year for several years); increases in pensions; in social security; in inheritance taxes; student loan schemes; expansion of unionization, and civil and political rights. All these have been adopted in the West, and have helped to create the condition where millions of workers have the purchasing power to buy the products that they and their colleagues make – a condition not met in much of Asia. To be introduced on a sizable scale and fast enough to make a difference within a decade or two might require concerted adoption by regional groupings of states. Greater pie in the greater sky? Perhaps, but another financial crisis or two might drive serious action along these lines.

NOTES

1. For discussions about subjects covered in this chapter I thank Jagdish Bhagwati, Richard Duncan, Ronald Dore, Devesh Kapur, Giovanni Arrighi, Kenneth Shadlen, Kiren Chaudhry, Stephen Haggard, Jane D'Arista, Nancy Alexander, William Lazonick, Dietrich Rueschemyer, Arvid Lukauskas, Joseph Stiglitz, Thomas Ferguson, Manfred Bienefeld, and Michael Pettis. The paper was written while I was professor of political science, Brown University. I thank the Russell Sage Foundation for financial support. The paper builds on a string of earlier ones, including 'Wheels within wheels: rethinking the Asian crisis and the Asian model,' *Annual Review of Political Science*, 2000, in press; Wade and Frank Veneroso, 'The Asian crisis: the high debt model versus the Wall Street–Treasury–IMF complex,' *New Left Review*, 228, March–April 1998: 3–23; Wade and Frank Veneroso, 'The gathering world slump and the battle over capital controls,' *New Left Review*, 231, September–October 1998: 13–42; 'From "miracle" to "cronyism": explaining the Great Asian Slump,' *Cambridge Journal of Economics* 22, 3, November 1998: 693–706.

2. The 1990s' episodes of financial instability and crisis in industrial countries started with the lingering effects of the US banking and real estate crises that began in the late 1970s and lasted for more than a decade; then came Japan's bursting of the bubble in early 1990, whose effects on financial instability and slow economic growth have lingered for a decade to date; then the Scandinavian crisis of 1991–92; the European Exchange Rate Mechanism crisis of 1992–93; and the slump in industrial country stock markets in October 1998. Among the developing countries the 1990s' episodes include the Mexican peso debacle of 1994–95 and knock-on banking crises in Argentina and Brazil in 1994; the (non-Japan) Asian crisis beginning in mid-1997 and continuing; the Russian debt default of August 1998; the steep falls in many developing country stock markets in October 1998; the near-currency-crisis in South Africa, Africa's largest economy; the Brazilian devaluation of January 1999; and a wider severe Latin American downturn in 1999. Meanwhile old investment banks like BCCI (1991) and Barings (1995) collapsed, followed by new hedge funds like Long Term Capital Management (September 1998). The latter's collapse was considered to pose such a serious risk to the US financial system that the Federal Reserve organized a bail-out rather than let it go bankrupt.
3. Cases where the financial data are less than fully satisfactory (notably those of the former Soviet Union) would raise the figure to at least 89 countries. Gerard Caprio and Daniela Klingebiel (1998), 'Bank insolvencies: cross-country experience,' Policy Research Working Paper 1620, Washington, DC: World Bank.
4. See J. Frankel and Andrew K. Rose (1996), 'Currency Crashes in Emerging Markets: An Empirical Treatment,' *Journal of International Economics* (41): 351–68.
5. The US case does not make it into the top 50 when the sample includes countries for which the data are not fully satisfactory.
6. Jason Furman and Joseph Stiglitz (1998), 'Economic crises: evidence and insights from East Asia,' *Brookings Papers on Economic Activity*, 2: 1–114. Emphasis added.
7. Linda Weiss (1999), 'State power and the Asian crisis,' *New Political Economy* 4: 317–42, at 319.
8. I omit the 1970s because the fourfold rise in oil prices set off a turbulence that swamped the effects of the mechanism described here, whose effects can be seen more clearly after the 1970s inflation ended.
9. IMF (1996), *International Financial Statistics Yearbook*, pp. 458–61.
10. I am indebted to Richard Duncan, 'The origin of economic bubbles,' unpublished mimeo, May 1998.
11. I draw on Giovanni Arrighi and Beverly Silver (1999), 'Hegemonic transitions: past and present,' *Political Power and Social Theory* 13: 239–75, at 254.
12. Quoted from 1985 in Nicolas Kristof with David Sanger, 'How U.S. wooed Asia to let cash flow in,' *New York Times*, 16 February 1999: A10, emphasis added.
13. Jeffrey Garten, a former senior Commerce Department official, quoted in Kristof with Sanger.
14. 'The case for mild repression,' *The Economist*, 18 September 1997: 81.
15. Kristof with Sanger, op. cit.
16. 'Sick patients, warring doctors,' *The Economist* 18 September 1999, p. 81.
17. Stephen Fidler, 'Pruning the IMF,' *Financial Times*, 10 December 1999: 14.
18. Kendall Stiles (1991), *Negotiating Debt: The IMF Lending Process*, Boulder, CO: Westview.
19. Tony Killick (1995), *IMF Programs in Developing Countries: Design and Impact*, London: Routledge.
20. The US has systematically manipulated the UN for its own agenda, 'as if its own brand of internationalism should not be polluted by this multilateral Tower of Babel' (Dominique Mosi, 'World needs a referee with a rule book,' *Financial Times*, 20 December 1999). As the chair of the Senate Foreign Relations Committee, Senator Jesse Helms, explained, 'Americans ... see [the UN] as just one aspect of America's diplomatic arsenal ... If the United Nations ... serves [the American people] as an effective instrument, it will earn and deserve their support. But a United Nations that seeks to impose its presumed authority on the American people ... begs for ... eventual U.S. withdrawal.' (Jesse Helmes, speech to the United Nations Security Council, excerpted in 'In the words of Helms: "Lack of gratitude,"' *New York Times*, 21 January 2000: A8.)

21. Strom Thacker (1999), 'The high politics of IMF lending,' *World Politics*, 52: 38–75, p. 64.
22. Ibid., p. 65.
23. On the beliefs of American economists compared to those of several continental European countries, see Bruno Frey et al. (1984), 'Consensus and dissensus among economists,' *American Economic Review*, May. For example, asked to 'agree,' 'agree with qualifications,' 'disagree' to the question, 'Tariffs and import controls lower economic welfare,' almost 80 per cent of the American economists said 'agree,' compared to 27 per cent of French economists, with the other national samples in between.
24. R. Wade (1996), 'Japan, the World Bank, and the art of the paradigm maintenance: *The East Asian Miracle* in political perspective,' *New Left Review* 217: 3–36.
25. I am indebted to Devesh Kapur for discussion of the US influence over the Bank; and to Catherine Gwin (1997), 'U.S. relations with the World Bank, 1945–1992,' in Devesh Kapur, John Lewis, and Richard Webb (eds), *The World Bank: Its First Half Century*, vol. 2, chapter 6, pp. 195–274.
26. For example, Hardev Kaur (1997), 'The world negotiates with US chief execs,' *Business Times* (Malaysia), 15 December; Aviva Freudmann (1997), 'WTO financial services agreement in sight, despite snags,' *Journal of Commerce*, 11 December 1997.
27. IMF (1995), *Capital Account Convertibility: Review of Experience and Implications for IMF Policies*, Washington DC; Stanley Fischer (1997), 'Capital account liberalization and the role of the IMF,' mimeo, IMF, September.
28. Nicholas Kristof with David Sanger, 'How the US wooed Asia.'
29. Ibid.
30. John Whitehead, temporary alternative governor, Asian Development Bank, statement to Board of Governors, 32nd Annual Meeting, 30 April-2 May 1999, Manila.
31. The Treasury's wish to be rid of Stiglitz was an element in his move, but he had then been in the council for four years, longer than the normal tenure, and a move was due. As Chief Economist at the World Bank, Stiglitz continued to voice his criticisms, sometimes in public, of some elements of Treasury/Fund policy, for example, the Treasury/Fund bail-outs in Asia and the privatization program in Russia. President Wolfensohn, seeing Treasury indignation as an obstacle to vital Treasury support for his reappointment to a second term, and worried about rumours of Stiglitz' unprofessional conduct in promoting a staff member, asked him to step down as Chief Economist before his normal tenure was up.
32. Quoted in Wolfgang Reinicke (1998), *Global Public Policy: Governing Without Government?*, Washington, DC: Brookings, p. 106, emphasis added.
33. Louis Uchitelle, 'A crash course in economics: rethinking what's driving the emerging-markets crisis,' *New York Times*, 29 January 1999.
34. I am grateful to indefatigable Brown undergraduate Jordan Wolff for help in tracking down the material on which this argument is based.
35. Jung-en Woo (1991), *Race to the Swift: State and Finance in Korean Industrialization*, New York: Columbia University Press, p. 193, passim. Woo cites returns on capital of over 300 per cent in 1980.
36. James Fall (1995), 'The US–Korea financial dialogue,' in Kim Young-suk and Oh Kap-soo (eds), *US–Korea Economic Partnership*, Brookfield: Avebury Press.
37. Soogil Young (1996), 'Korea–US economic relationship in 1990s: conflict or cooperation?,' in *Korea–United States Cooperation in the New World Order*, Institute for International Economics, Washington DC and Institute for Global Economics, Seoul, February.
38. Doug Bereuter, 'US congressional agenda,' in *Korea–United States Cooperation in the New World Order*, pp. 115–19, emphasis added.
39. Stephen Krasner (1978), *Defending the National Interest: Raw Materials Investments and U.S. Foreign Policy*, Princeton, NJ: Princeton University Press, p. 348.
40. Gerard Baker, 'Greenspan hails US economic system,' *Financial Times*, 9 September 1999: 7.
41. Benjamin Cohen, 'Capital controls: why do governments hesitate?,' paper presented at the 1999 Annual Meeting of American Political Science Association, 2–5 September 1999.
42. Jane D'Arista, 'Credit to the creditors,' *Flow of Funds*, 1st quarter 1999, Financial Markets Center.

43. In the rest of this section I draw on Ronald Dore (2000), *Stock Market Capitalism: Welfare Capitalism*, Oxford: Oxford University Press.
44. I take the term Wall Street–Treasury complex from Jagdish Bhagwati (1998), 'The capital myth: the difference between trade in widgets and dollars,' *Foreign Affairs*, 77: 7–12. In earlier papers I extended his usage to 'the Wall Street–Treasury–IMF' complex. But adding the IMF muddies the analytical waters, because the complex operates through several other organizations as well as the IMF.
45. 'European M&A activity doubles to hit $1,213bn,' *Financial Times*, 23 December 1999.
46. US Department of Commerce (2000), *Survey of Current Business*, March, table G.2.
47. Jane D'Arista and Stephany Griffith-Jones (1998), 'The boom of portfolio flows to "emerging markets" and its regulatory implications,' Table 5, in Manuel Montes (ed.), *Short-term Capital Movements and Balance of Payments Crises*, Helsinki: World Institute for Development Economics Research, Table 5.
48. There is another story to be told about the US's instrumental role, to do with US exchange rate diplomacy on Japan and Asian currencies. For example, the US Treasury pressured the Bank of Japan in the mid and late 1980s not to tighten credit, in order not to appreciate the yen and weaken the dollar. The failure to tighten monetary policy earlier made the bubble worse.
49. Arrighi and Silver, 'Hegemonic transitions,' p. 255.
50. 'Fallout from a global crisis,' *Financial Times*, 8 December 1999.

8. Contagion: From higher risk to risk aversion and the danger of protectionism

Mario I. Blejer and Graciana del Castillo

1. INTRODUCTION

August 1998 was a turning point in the world financial saga. Contagion from Russia changed the character of the crisis; default on domestic debt, a large part of which was in the hands of foreign investors, led to a reassessment of lending and investment strategies and a re-evaluation of the type of financial instruments demanded. In the earlier phase of the Asian crisis, sovereign borrowers had to confront higher interest rates caused by the perception of higher risks, but access to international capital markets was largely preserved, even if at less attractive terms. In the period immediately following the Russian debacle, financial flows to emerging economies evaporated and spreads shot up. These changes, which were also reflected in a selective deterioration of ratings by credit agencies, were caused by a sharp increase in risk aversion and a clear shift in preferences towards more liquid instruments from mature markets.

The financial environment that settled in world markets in the fourth quarter of 1998 was particularly harsh on countries that were highly dependent on foreign savings to finance large budget imbalances and external current account deficits. In Brazil, especially, government dependence on foreign finance at a time when it had dried up brought to the fore existing policy inconsistencies. Despite a large assistance program from the IMF, Brazil had to discontinue using the exchange rate as an anchor, which had been the key feature of the 'Plan Real,' which succeeded in bringing inflation down to about 3 per cent, from hyperinflationary levels five years earlier.

The impact of the Brazil devaluation on the financial markets was not as severe as was initially expected and financial flows were not largely affected. However, the crisis seems to have unfolded from a financial crisis to a crisis of the real sector of the economy as recession, unemployment, and lower levels of economic activity continue to prevail, particularly in the Latin American region. In these circumstances, the danger of protectionism has become more real. Protectionist pressures are gaining new momentum not only in emerging countries but also in industrial countries.

The purpose of this chapter is as follows: first, to cursorily review the factors that triggered the Asian crisis in July 1997 and led to contagion within and outside the region. Second, to discuss the channels through which the Asian crisis had an impact on other emerging markets, particularly in Latin America and Russia and to describe the policy response in these countries as well as the factors that increased their resilience to contagion up to the summer of 1998. Third, to analyse in more detail the deepening in the emerging market financial crisis resulting from default in Russia which changed the nature of the crisis. Fourth, to show how policy inconsistencies and the high dependence on foreign savings to finance large budget and external deficits made Brazil particularly vulnerable at a time foreign financing had dried up. We shall conclude that investors have become more discriminating and risk averse, as a result of which reinsertion into the international capital markets has been increasingly dependent on countries following appropriate and consistent policies. We shall also caution on the danger for governments – both in emerging and mature countries – to yield to protectionists pressures from the private sector arising from competitive devaluation of the currencies of major trading partners.

2. ERUPTION OF THE CRISIS IN ASIA

The eruption of the Asian crisis took many observers by surprise.[1] Critical indicators of previous crises showed low risk. Many of the southeast Asian economies had experienced an excellent macroeconomic performance for at least a decade and had been heralded to the rest of the developing world as a role model of successful development. To a larger or lesser extent these economies had achieved high rates of growth with low inflation, strong fiscal positions, high domestic savings and investment rates, dynamic export performance, and a high level of foreign exchange reserves. At the same time, no world commodity or interest rate shock was about to trigger a crisis, as had often been the case in previous times.

But success helped to hide some of the weaknesses that were widespread in these economies. The inflow of private capital through the international capital markets in the form of fixed income securities (largely bonds), loans, and equities to the Asian emerging markets before the crisis was large indeed. These markets received private capital inflows, excluding foreign direct investment, amounting to $120 billion in 1996 and $130 billion in 1997 ($70 billion in the first half of 1997).[2] The countries most affected by the crisis (Asian-4: Indonesia, Korea, Malaysia and Thailand) received 53 per cent of all flows to Asia and 29 per cent of all flows to emerging markets in 1996.[3] Although large inflows of capital had been central to the development of the region, they presented inherent risks for host countries: a rapid expansion of money and credit put upward pressure on prices, created bubbles in stock and real estate markets, appreciated the real exchange rate and deteriorated the current account, and made the banking system more unstable and vulnerable. The vulnerability of the banking system was dramatically increased by the large short-term (unhedged) exposure of the banking and corporate sectors. This was particularly true in Korea and Thailand which encouraged short-term flows at the expense of long-term ones, including foreign direct investment.[4]

Intermediation of such large capital inflows was done by weak financial sectors. The number of banks had expanded very rapidly. In Indonesia, for example, the number of banks grew from 75 in 1988 to 205 in 1996 and there was an excessive dependence on banks as financial intermediaries; bank loans represented 62 per cent of total private market financing, as compared to 42 per cent on average in the Asian-4 and in emerging markets as a whole. A growing banking sector was not accompanied by increased supervision and prudential regulation. On the contrary, inadequate supervision and regulation as well as poor governance allowed for directed credits and for the accumulation of non-performing loans to go unchecked.

Domestic credit creation as a percentage of GDP increased rapidly in 1995–97: in the Asian-4 the compounded annual rate of growth averaged about 20 per cent. In Korea, Malaysia and Thailand, domestic credit creation was about 130–150 per cent of GDP in 1996. A large over-expansion of credit resulted in over-investment, creating excess capacity in many industries and spilling over to non-productive assets, thus fostering the bubbles discussed above. Credit over-expansion also led to dangerous levels of leverage (high debt to equity ratios) in the private sector. Although difficult to measure, there are some indications that leverage of private sector firms in the Asian-4 had been increasing rapidly in the pre-crisis period. At the time the crisis erupted, the average debt of the top 30 Korean conglomerates (chaebol) was over four times equity,[5] with much of the corporate debt supplied directly by, or guaranteed by, Korean financial institutions. Increase in debt had in turn increased the debt burden; in Thailand, for example, interest payments represented 14 per cent of GDP.

In search for high returns in emerging markets foreign investors underestimated risk. At the same time, lack of transparency and governance problems resulted in an inefficient allocation of resources in the private sector. In the public sector, international reserves of the monetary authorities, impressive in gross terms, were largely committed in future market transactions. An important factor that diffused the perception of the looming crisis was the inadequacy of data. Overheated economies with appreciating real exchange rates had large current account deficits. The erosion in external competitiveness, which had started in 1994 with the devaluation of the yuan in China, accelerated as the dollar appreciated and many of the southeast Asian currencies were pegged to it. Thailand's current account deficit in 1996 remained at 8 per cent, while Korea and Malaysia showed deficits of 5 per cent of GDP. Their dependence on foreign savings was thus significant.

In July 1997, the crisis in Asia was precipitated by a rapid withdrawal of foreign funds, as investors herded together in reaction to the increasing weaknesses of these economies. During the first half of 1997, concern about the sustainability of the currency peg in Thailand resulting from the large current account deficit and poor export prospects, contributed to a collapse of the real estate price bubble and put pressure on a fragile and over-exposed financial system. The financial system in Thailand, just as in other countries of the region, was characterized by poor quality of loan portfolios, high short-term debt to international reserve ratios (roll-over risk), and a large unhedged currency exposure (currency-mismatch risk).

The inceptive policy response to the crisis in Thailand was through a combination of spot and forward exchange market intervention and the imposition of capital and exchange controls in May, without an effort to address the underlying structural weaknesses. As could have been predicted, exchange controls increased uncertainty and further undermined confidence, thus accelerating capital outflows. The authorities abandoned the policy of pegging the baht to the dollar and its value rapidly deteriorated. The devaluation of the baht put pressure on the value of the currency of trade competitors and neighbors and in this way the first contagion effects were set in motion. During the summer of 1997, Thailand, Indonesia, and Malaysia abandoned their policies of pegging to the dollar and increased interest rates to various degrees to avoid sharp devaluations. Currency depreciation and hikes in interest rates had a devastating effect on highly leveraged corporate and financial sectors, with high short-term and unhedged exposure in foreign currency.

By the end of 1997, spillover effects had become more far-reaching. Contagion to Korea (the 11th largest economy) in October, the perceived lack of commitment for financial sector restructuring, political uncertainty, and mixed policy signals in Thailand, Malaysia, and Indonesia intensified exchange market pressure even in countries with solid fundamentals (such as Hong Kong and Taiwan), and extended contagion to Latin America.

3. EARLY CONTAGION TO OTHER EMERGING COUNTRIES: POLICY RESPONSE IN LATIN AMERICA

Despite having better governance and lacking the weak financial systems that triggered the crisis in Asia, Latin America has been the region most prone to contagion. The first sign of contagion appeared in October 1997. The policy response in Latin America was swift: countries responded with very orthodox monetary and fiscal measures. Brazil doubled interest rates to 40 per cent and weathered the attack on the real. Argentina and Mexico also raised interest rates, although they did not need to increase them as much. All countries took measures to tighten the fiscal stance.[6]

Despite the success in fending off contagion at the time, the early impact of the Asian crisis on Latin America was nevertheless important and left the region more vulnerable to future attacks. The impact took place through three basic channels: trade, investment, and policy design. At the inception of the crisis, several countries exported a significant share of their products to Asia.[7] More importantly, Latin American countries had to compete in third markets with exports from southeast Asian countries in unfavorable conditions, given Asia's gain in short-term competitiveness due to currency devaluation. Furthermore, some critical commodity prices plummeted as a result of the crisis, resulting in the deterioration of the terms of trade of copper producers (Chile, Peru) and oil producers (Mexico, Venezuela, Ecuador, Colombia), and in higher price volatility of many commodities. Lower growth in the large countries (particularly Brazil and Argentina), dragged by higher interest rates adopted in response to the crisis, have also had a negative effect on their smaller trade partners in the region. Concurrently, the cost of financing in international capital markets which had been falling, started to increase. Although in part covered by a continued flow of foreign direct investment, the region had to finance a current account deficit of some $70 billion in 1998. Some countries, notably Brazil, were also negatively affected by the higher cost of financing sizable fiscal and external deficits.

The quick and credible policy response to early contagion in Latin America through the adoption of orthodox macroeconomic adjustment was able to contain the effects of the shock, particularly in avoiding the speculative attacks on their currencies. The crisis itself facilitated the adoption of certain fiscal and structural policies that had been difficult to adopt in the past. More importantly, investors were reassured that the liberalization policies of the past were not to be reversed. The resilience of the Latin American countries to contagion at this early stage was not only the result of the policy response to the crisis itself, but also of major policy changes of the past: countries had abandoned statist and populist policies, had adopted efficiency-enhancing structural reforms that had increased investment opportunities and had attracted foreign direct investment, and had not relied as heavily as the southeast Asian countries on speculative short-term financing. After the Mexican crisis of 1994, Latin American countries had also been better positioned to deal with external shocks as a result of widespread financial reform, which had improved supervision and prudential regulation of the banking sector, closed or merged weak banks, increased foreign ownership and therefore competition in the domestic market, avoided excessive credit (lending booms), and hedged bank currency and maturity exposures.

4. DEEPENING IN EMERGING MARKETS FINANCIAL CRISIS: TURNING POINT IN RUSSIA

In August 1998 the Asian saga took a new twist when the crisis hit Russia. The speculative attack on the ruble in October/November 1997 was successfully curbed by a sharp rise in interest rates, increasing reserve requirements on foreign exchange deposits, and intervening in the foreign exchange and treasury bill markets. Interest rates had peaked at 50 per cent in late January but had declined to about 25 per cent by mid-year. While monetary policy had been successful in fending off contagion, little progress was made on the fiscal front or to correct other critical structural deficiencies, including the perverse relationship existing between government, banks and the corporate sector, which was totally lacking in transparency as in many of the Asian countries.

As a result of lack of progress on fiscal and structural reform, Russia remained vulnerable to swings in investors' confidence and succumbed to a new speculative attack on the ruble in mid-August 1998. A large fiscal deficit, in part due to chronically weak government revenues and the dependence on short-term government borrowing led the government to devalue the ruble, to default on its domestic debt (a large part of which was in the hands of foreign investors), and to declare a moratorium on payments by Russian commercial banks to foreign creditors. This resulted in a serious reversal of progress achieved toward macroeconomic stability in Russia, particularly the decrease in inflation, the maintenance of a stable exchange rate, and a resumption, albeit small, of economic growth.

Russia's policy response to the speculative attack in August 1998 changed the character of the world financial crisis and led to a swift and rash reassessment by investors of their lending and investment strategies and a re-evaluation of their financial instruments. At the same time, the deterioration of credit ratings of many emerging markets limited the continued participation of institutional investors who are restricted to holding primarily investment-grade securities. The deteriorating health condition in the Japanese banking and financial sectors as well as the collapse of major hedge funds in the United States aggravated the overall situation. Hedge funds suffered large losses on their holdings of Russian securities and as their losses became apparent, they began to face much higher margin calls from their creditor banks. The imposition of capital controls by Malaysia soon after the Russian default raised further concerns about investing in emerging markets securities. The increase in the risk aversion of investors made them switch to liquid assets in mature markets, despite their low return.

The factors that triggered the crisis in Russia and the policy response of the authorities were somewhat different from those that precipitated the original crisis in Asia or those that existed at the time of contagion to Latin America. The trade effect of the Asian crisis in Russia took place basically as a result of the sharp fall in the price of oil. On the investment side, despite an external current account near balanced, the impact was felt through the increased cost associated with borrowing in the international capital markets to finance the fiscal deficit.

The nature of contagion at this time was also different from that of the early phase;[8] by this time, contagion was due to both psychological and technical factors: the former resulting from the herding instincts of investors when confidence breaks down; the latter resulting from the need for investors to sell equity in profitable companies and markets when large and highly leveraged hedge funds stopped having access to further financing and had large short-term liabilities to cover.

5. SYSTEMIC CONSEQUENCES FOR EMERGING MARKETS: FROM INCREASED RISK TO RISK AVERSION

The deepening of the financial crisis in the third quarter of 1998 had systemic consequences for emerging markets. Private sector financing for emerging markets dried up, spreads shot up, the price of securities in the secondary markets fell, and domestic interest rates rose.

Despite the Asian crisis, private market financing to emerging markets grew by over 30 per cent in 1997 (see Table 8.1). Fixed income securities (mostly bonds), which accounted for 51 per cent of total financing, grew by 24 per cent, and loans, representing 42 per cent of total financing, grew by 36 per cent. Equities, which represented less than 8 per cent of total financing in 1996, grew by over 50 per cent. If we look by region, financing to Asia grew by close to 8 per cent but financing to the countries most affected by the crisis (Asian-4) contracted by over 20 per cent. In Latin America, financing continued at a rapid pace (43 per cent).[9] The three largest countries (Argentina, Brazil, and Mexico or LatAm-3), which attracted about 80 per cent of all private market financing to the region, experienced lower growth (34 per cent). Flows to Brazil, however, experienced very fast growth (87 per cent), with both loans and equity growing rapidly. Flows to Argentina grew by 40 per cent but those to Mexico remained stagnant. In Russia, financing grew by nearly four times in 1997, from \$4.4 billion in 1996 to \$16.6 billion in 1997.

Table 8.1 Private market financing for emerging markets (quarterly data)

	1996	1997	1998	1999	1998				1999			
					1Q	2Q	3Q	4Q	1Q	2Q	3Q	4Q
					In billions of US dollars							
ISSUANCE	**218.4**	**286.1**	**149.7**	**173.2**	**40.5**	**50.9**	**30.5**	**27.8**	**32.6**	**53.0**	**34.7**	**52.9**
Bonds[a]	111.3	138.2	80.2	87.0	26.7	28.6	14.0	10.8	21.8	27.5	15.9	21.8
Loans	90.7	123.2	60.0	63.0	11.0	18.7	16.2	14.2	8.4	18.9	12.6	23.1
Equities	16.4	24.8	9.4	23.2	2.8	3.6	0.3	2.8	2.4	6.6	6.1	8.0
ISSUANCE	**218.4**	**286.1**	**149.7**	**173.2**	**40.5**	**50.9**	**30.5**	**27.8**	**32.6**	**53.0**	**34.7**	**52.9**
Asia	118.5	127.5	34.5	62.9	7.6	13.9	5.6	7.7	11.9	17.1	17.4	16.5
Latin America	63.1	90.3	66.1	64.3	22.5	22.5	10.2	10.9	13.2	22.0	9.8	19.3
Europe, Middle East, Africa	36.8	68.3	49.1	46.0	10.4	14.7	14.7	9.2	7.6	13.9	7.5	17.1
MARKET INDICES												
Bonds[b]												
J.P. Morgan Emerg. Mkt. Spread	537	510	1151	824	462	641	1330	1151	1171	1070	1098	824
US 30yr. Treasury Yield	6.3	6.0	5.1	6.4	6.0	5.7	5.2	5.1	5.6	6.0	6.1	6.4
Merrill Lynch High Yield	9.4	12.8	3.7	1.6	2.8	1.7	–3.6	2.9	1.1	0.7	–1.2	1.1

Equities[c]												
IFC Investable Composite	9.4	–14.8	–21.9	67.1	7.0	–21.2	–21.7	18.1	10.9	23.8	–3.2	25.7
Asia	10.5	–56.6	0.7	72.6	19.4	–35.7	–7.6	41.5	6.5	43.2	8.0	23.1
Latin America	17.2	29.2	–35.5	61.8	–1.1	–18.1	–26.6	8.2	13.4	15.4	–7.9	34.2
S&P 500	22.9	33.4	28.6	21.0	13.9	3.3	–9.9	21.3	5.0	7.0	–6.2	14.9

Notes:
[a] Including other fixed income (certificate of deposits and others).
[b] Spreads (in basis points) and yields (in per cent) are shown at end-period.
[c] Total returns are based on the entire period.

Sources: Bloomberg; BEL, DCBEL, International Finance Corporation, and Emerging Markets Data Base.

The market spread in secondary bond markets, as indicated by the J.P. Morgan Emerging Market Spread, continued to fall in 1997 by over 6 per cent. In equity markets, total returns, as indicated by the IFC Investable Composite Index, showed a 15 per cent fall, with returns in the Asian markets falling by close to 57 per cent and those in Latin America experiencing an improvement of close to 30 per cent.

While in 1996 the Asian-4 had received private market financing flows amounting to over $60 billion, comparable to those of Latin America as a whole, the situation changed significantly in 1997. While flows to the Asian-4 fell to less than $50 billion in 1997, those of Latin America increased to $90 billion. Also, the first and second semesters were comparable in terms of the amount of flows to Latin America but they differed in those to Asia and Russia, where the first semester flows were about 55–60 per cent of the annual flows.

The situation changed quite dramatically in 1998. Activity in the private market financing for emerging markets plummeted from $286 billion to less than $150 billion (a 48 per cent fall). The fall in Asia was as high as 70 per cent. In Latin America the fall was below 30 per cent. Investors had become quite discriminating and, because of this, the fall in Brazil was 43 per cent while in Argentina there was hardly any fall. In Russia, the fall was slightly over 20 per cent. The situation was particularly bad in the second semester of 1998.

The negative market sentiment and the increase in risk aversion in the advent of the Russian crisis more than doubled spreads on the emerging market bond index from 644 basis points at end-June to 1 481 basis points at end-August 1998. Equity markets collapsed, with the IFCI plummeting 22 per cent over this period (a 27 per cent fall in Latin America as compared to an 8 per cent fall in Asia where the collapse of the stock markets had taken place earlier). International fund raising by emerging markets fell from $51 billion in the second quarter to $31 billion in the third (a 40 per cent fall). The fall was 60 per cent in Asia and 55 per cent in Latin America. Activity in the equities markets came to a virtual standstill.

The *composition* of the private market flows to emerging markets (Figure 8.1) did not change significantly as the crisis evolved but this was not the case with the *geographical distribution* of the flows (Figure 8.2). While at the end of 1996, bonds accounted for 51.0 per cent of the flows, loans for 41.5 per cent and equity for 7.5 per cent, by 1998 bonds accounted for 52.6 per cent of the flows, loans 40.7 per cent and equity 6.7 per cent.

At the same time, the geographical distribution changed with the relative situation of Asia deteriorating notably *vis-à-vis* Latin America. While in 1996 Asia accounted for 54 per cent of private market financing to emerging markets, in 1998 its share had fallen to 23 per cent. The respective share for Latin America, on the other hand, had increased from 29 per cent to 44 per cent.

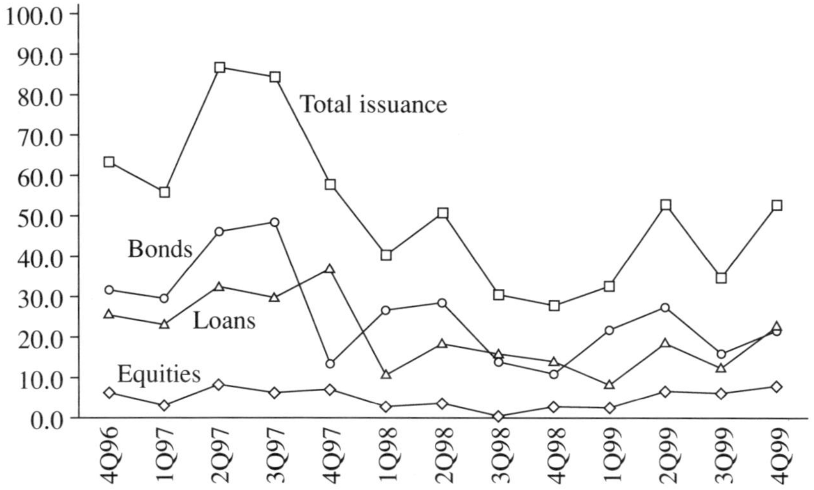

Sources: Bloomberg; BEL, DCBEL, International Finance Corporation, and Emerging Markets Data Base.

Figure 8.1 Private market financing for emerging markets in billions of US dollars

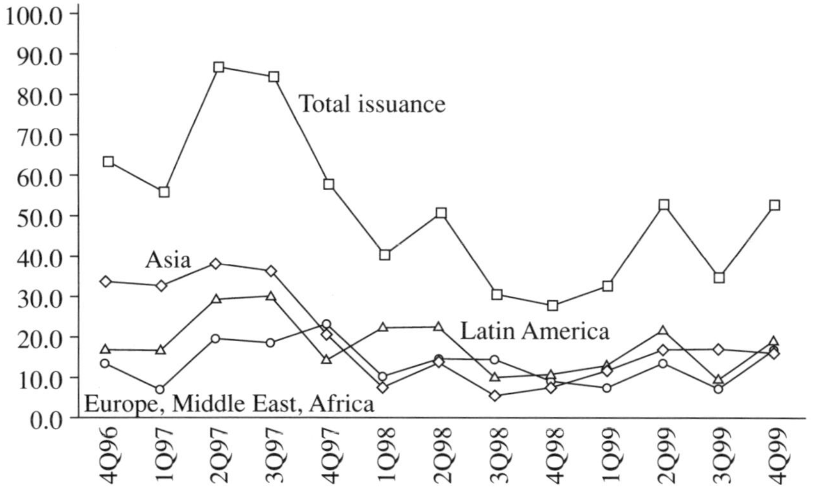

Sources: Bloomberg; BEL, DCBEL, International Finance Corporation, and Emerging Markets Data Base.

Figure 8.2 Private market financing for emerging markets by region in billions of US dollars

If we compare the crises countries (Asian-4 to the LatAm-3), we observe that flows to the Asian-4 fell from \$61 billion in 1996 to \$14 billion in 1998. Flows to the LatAm-3, which amounted to \$50 billion in 1996, increased to \$66 billion in 1997 and remained at close to \$50 billion in 1998. Flows to Brazil fell from \$23 billion in 1997 to \$13 billion in 1998 and those to Mexico from \$21 billion to \$13 billion. Interestingly enough, flows to Argentina remained the same at about \$22 billion in 1997–98.

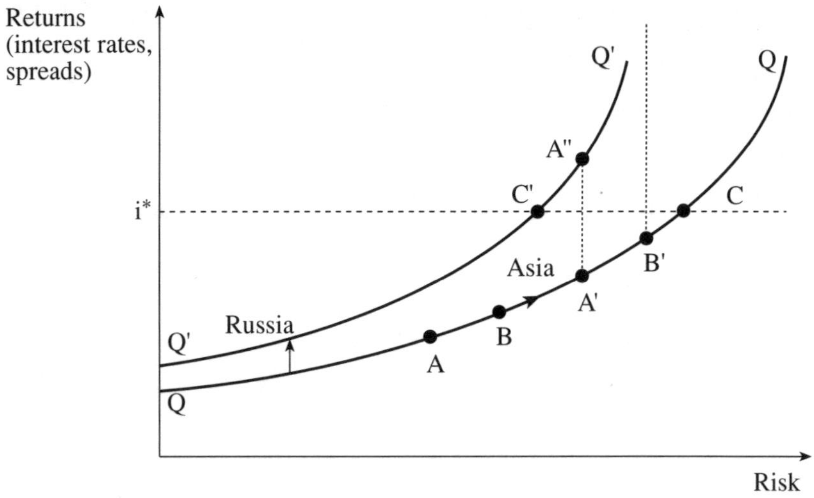

Figure 8.3 Increase in risk vs. risk aversion

An analysis of Figure 8.3 allows us to track the change from increased risk to higher risk aversion as the Asian crises evolved into the Russian crisis. The upward sloping QQ curve in Figure 8.3 shows that at higher risk investors expect a higher return. A country such as Argentina, with lower risk than other emerging markets in mid-1997, was on a point such as A on QQ. As a result of the Asian crisis, the perceived risk of emerging markets rose and therefore countries had to pay higher spreads (a movement up the curve QQ). Thus, Argentina would have moved from A to A' where borrowing conditions had deteriorated but there was still ample access to international private market financing. The situation changed qualitatively after the Russian crisis; rather than a movement along the curve, there was a shift upward in the curve to Q'Q': with the same risk countries now facing a higher spread. To put it in a different way, at a certain interest rate such as i*, investors accepted risk at C before the Russian crisis, and after the crisis they only accepted risk at C'. The shift in the curve represents an increase in risk aversion and a change in preferences. A flight to quality benefited bond markets in the United States and Europe and caused new highs in their stock markets. Most emerging markets, on the other hand, were left without access to financing.

A good credit rating country at the time, such as Argentina, which had moved from A to A' as a result of the Asian crisis, moved to point A" after the Russian crisis. At A" the country had to pay a higher spread but it still enjoyed access to private market financing. On the other hand, a country such as Brazil (and most other emerging markets), which showed a much higher risk to start with, and was at a point such as B in QQ, moved to B' as a result of the Asian crisis. When the curve indicating the tradeoff between risk and return shifted upwards to Q'Q' after the Russian crisis, Brazil and many other emerging countries lost access to international private market financing.

6. CHANGE IN POLICY RESPONSE: DEVALUATION IN BRAZIL

The disappearance in practice of private market financing to emerging markets after the Russian debacle was particularly painful for countries that were highly dependent on foreign savings to finance large budget imbalances and external current account deficits. In Brazil, the difficulties in financing the twin deficits at a time when foreign financing had dried up brought to the fore policy inconsistencies. These had existed for a long time but, in the presence of massive capital inflows, the urgency to solve them had been lacking. Despite a large financial program accorded with the IMF in November 1998, Brazil was forced to discontinue its policy of using the exchange rate as an anchor that had been the key feature of the Plan Real. This plan succeeded in bringing inflation down to less than 3 per cent, from hyperinflationary levels five years earlier, in combination with significant growth in real GDP per capita and notable improvements in the poverty situation.

Brazil had reacted to a speculative attack on its currency in October 1997 with prompt and credible orthodox macroeconomic policies. The crisis itself facilitated the adoption of tough monetary and fiscal policies, some of which had been difficult to adopt in the past. As the external pressure ebbed, however, the initial fiscal tightening was eased and the ability of the government to deal with existing inconsistencies was very much reduced. The persistence of the twin deficits made Brazil once again prone to contagion from the Russian crisis in August 1998. Although the government once again reacted with a new hike in interest rates and the announcement of expenditure cuts for the last quarter of the year, which was subsequently converted into a comprehensive three-year fiscal adjustment program, credibility of the government was low as a result of the previous fiscal adjustment failure and the impending national elections. Nevertheless, the government hoped that the three-year $41.5 billion international assistance package agreed to with the IMF on 13 November would supplement central bank reserves and suffice to create confidence in the currency and maintain the exchange rate anchor.

But political opposition to the adjustment program was underestimated. Opposition in Congress and at the state and local levels to many of the measures proposed by the federal government delayed indispensable fiscal adjustment. Uncertainty about the ability of states to service their debts further aggravated matters. This in turn undermined confidence and contributed to a shift in investors' sentiment, making higher interest rates unavoidable. Higher real rates of interest increased the cost of servicing domestic debt and made fiscal adjustment more burdensome. For the first time, starting in August 1998 and until the end of the year, Brazil had to rely on domestic savings to finance the fiscal deficit.

At the same time, powerful private sector groups opposed high interest rates and put pressure on the government to change its policies. Thus, the higher interest rates necessary to stop capital flight, which continued at a worrisome pace, were avoided by loosening the monetary stance. A new speculative attack on the real took place. In early 1999, Brazil abandoned its policy of supporting the currency, and after a failed attempt to widen the intervention band, let the real float on 15 January.[10] The real quickly depreciated by about 40 per cent and interest rates had to be raised to avoid a sharp overshooting. International reserves fell to $36 billion in early March 1999 (including IMF funds already released).

On 8 March, Brazil and the IMF reached agreement on a revised program, the key elements of which were a strengthened fiscal adjustment and the adoption of a new nominal anchor for monetary policy, given the floating exchange rate system. The adjustment program has exhibited early signs of success and its sustainability will depend on the strengthening of confidence and the ability to reduce interest rates and to keep inflation under control.

The Brazilian crisis did not have much of an impact on financial markets. The impact on private sector financing to emerging markets was quite different from that of the Russian crisis. As a result of the latter, total flows fell by 48 per cent and spreads increased by 120 per cent in 1998. On the other hand, if we compare the first semester of 1999 with 1998, flows to the emerging markets grew by 12 per cent (on an annualized basis) and spreads fell by the same percentage. Most of this growth, however, is explained by growth in Asia (70 per cent), since flows to Latin America only grew by 2.2 per cent (those to the LatAm-3 fell by 2.6 per cent) and those to Europe fell by close to 40 per cent.

The *composition* of the flows (Figure 8.1), however, changed after the Brazilian crisis. While bonds accounted for 52 per cent before the crisis, their share grew to 58 per cent in the first two quarters of 1999. Equity flows also grew from 7 per cent to 11 per cent during this period. On the other hand, loans fell from 41 per cent to 31 per cent. The geographical distribution (Figure 8.2) also changed after the Brazilian crisis, with flows to Asia increasing from $34 billion in 1998 to $58 billion (on an annualized basis) in the first semester of 1999, and those to Europe falling from $36 billion to $22 billion. Surprisingly, flows to Latin America increased marginally from $65 billion to $66 billion.

In Latin America, however, the impact of the Brazilian devaluation of the real was large, not because of its impact on the financial markets, but as a result of the trade impact on economies highly integrated through Mercosur and other trade arrangements.

The future of Latin America is inextricably linked to that of Brazil. The crisis in Brazil has increased the vulnerability of neighboring countries, even those with strong fundamentals and micro-foundations and has undoubtedly set the stage for a new phase of instability, protectionist pressures, social distress, and political changes in Latin America. The difficulty of many of these countries to finance large current accounts and debt repayment will put pressure on domestic interest rates, slow down their economies, and aggravate the unemployment problem.

7. THE DANGER OF PROTECTIONISM

Crises do tend to generate a rethinking of economic relations and, as the current crisis unfolded from a financial crisis to a crisis of the real sector, the danger of protectionism has become a reality. Obstacles to trade negotiations are shifting from tariffs to invisible barriers which might hamper trade between nations in the future. Some of these barriers are environmental laws, labor standards, rules for competition, and corruption.

Protectionist pressures are gaining new momentum. In November 1999, the World Trade Organization (WTO) met in Seattle at the ministerial level to launch a new round of trade liberalization. These efforts were marred by tens of thousands of protesters ranging from labor unions to consumer groups, participating in anti-WTO rallies.

Liberalization efforts are not only being resisted at the multilateral level but at the national level as well. In November 1998, President Clinton's plans to cut tariffs on $1.5 trillion in global trade fell through. As a start toward APEC's ultimate goal of a free trade area in the Pacific by 2020, tariffs were to be cut in nine areas effectively by 2002. Plans for liberalization fell through as Japan refused to cut tariffs on two sensitive areas – forestry products and fish – at a time its economy was in recession. At the same time, anti-dumping cases are being prosecuted in the United States, the country with the harshest anti-dumping statutes, at an alarming pace. With currencies in some Asian countries, Russia, and Brazil 30 per cent to 50 per cent below their pre-crisis levels, these countries are trying to increase their exports to the United States and other dynamic markets. Several industries in the United States have been affected. The most notorious is the steel industry which has brought anti-dumping cases against producers from Brazil, Korea, Russia, and Japan.

Another example of the danger of protectionism is the escalation of the banana conflict between the United States and the European Union and the meat conflict between France and the United Kingdom at the turn of the twentieth century. In general, demand for protection has not been as outspoken in Europe as in the United States, in part because import volumes have been growing less rapidly (7.5 per cent in 1998 as compared to 10.5 per cent in the United States and Canada) and better export prospects as a result of the depreciation of the euro. Although there is no evidence of increased protectionist pressures in Japan, imports continue to fall. Since over 30 per cent of Japan's imports come from South East Asian countries, Korea, and China, this is making recovery of these countries more difficult.

In Latin America, the common external tariff of the Mercosur was raised in 1998 on a supposedly temporary basis until 31 December 1999. Also, the list of exemptions has been a source of friction between the Mercosur countries, as there were indications that Brazil intended to change it unilaterally.

The devaluation of the real in early 1999 has put strong pressure on Brazil's trading partners, particularly within Mercosur, but also on other countries of the region. In Argentina, the automobile industry has been very much affected since a large part of its production is directed toward the Brazilian market. Agricultural sectors in both Argentina and Uruguay have been affected not only by the drop in demand in Brazil but also by lower commodity prices. At the same time, Brazilian products have become very competitive in their markets. Dairy products, fruits, rice, garlic, sugar, olives, paper, and many other sectors have been severely affected by the change in comparative advantage within Mercosur countries. This and other factors have led to the awakening of always latent demands for protectionism and the adoption of unilateral measures outside the Mercosur framework. Argentina introduced a system of minimum import prices on steel from selected sources. Brazil unilaterally decided to lower the import tariffs of hospital equipment. Both Argentina and Brazil have cut down bilateral credits which have negatively affected their exports and those of other trading countries, particularly Uruguay and Paraguay. In the Andean countries, Bolivia adopted health and safety measures supposedly designed to protect domestic production against Brazil's imports. Also, the Andean Group adopted selective tariff safeguards.

8. CONCLUDING REMARKS

The Asian crisis brought to light some of the very different conditions in what has been collectively referred to as *emerging markets*. These conditions triggered the financial crisis and led to contagion. In Asia, large capital inflows in the 1990s were inefficiently intermediated by weak financial institutions with poor regulatory and supervision systems, lack of foreign competition, and governance problems relating to the close links between the government, the banks, and the corporate sector. As the competitiveness of these overheated economies fell, in part due to the policy of pegging to the dollar at a time the dollar was appreciating *vis-à-vis* their main trading partners, market sentiment shifted and sudden capital outflows triggered the crisis in July 1997. In Russia, in addition to poor governance and a weak and under-developed financial sector, there were basic macro-imbalances, particularly in the fiscal area, that eventually made this country succumb to a speculative attack. In Brazil, with better governance and a well-developed and supervised financial sector, macroeconomic policy inconsistencies were the main factors that made the country prone to speculative attacks. A fixed exchange rate policy is not sustainable unless financial policies support it. In the case of Brazil, the government failed to tackle the chronic fiscal deficit in a serious and sustainable manner. The fiscal imbalance also resulted in the deterioration of the current account. As financing dried up in the international capital markets, Brazil's twin deficits made it vulnerable to the currency and reserve attacks to which it was subjected.

In the aftermath of the Asian crisis, world growth decelerated from over 4 per cent in 1996–97 to an estimated 2 per cent in 1998–99. Some countries in Asia experienced deep recessions resulting in sharp deterioration of living standards together with rising unemployment and social dislocation. All emerging countries have seen to varying degrees a fall in their living conditions and in their prospects for coming years. Some have been cut off from private market financing altogether. Despite lack of financing, other emerging countries did not follow Russia in unilaterally restructuring their debt obligations.

To reinsert themselves back into the international capital markets, emerging markets will need to regain the confidence of investors by putting macroeconomic policies and microeconomic foundations on a solid footing, including good corporate governance and transparent policymaking.

The danger of protectionism (even if in a disguised form), and certainly the possibility of delays in further liberalization, has become real once again. Emerging and mature markets are unlikely to revert to extensive tariff liberalization. The danger, however, is in the imposition of ad hoc non-tariff barriers to discourage trade: these barriers could take the form of administrative or technical barriers, health, sanitary or environmental restrictions and, also, could appear as a consequence of lack of credit financing from large countries to smaller ones.

Rather than letting the crisis undermine their process of trade liberalization and integration, countries should pursue this goal even more determinedly. Mercosur has been a success to its large members in particular and it should be preserved. However, in the wake of a large devaluation in Brazil and amid evidence of a deep slowdown in economic activity in the region, Mercosur countries should abandon their customs union characteristics to behave more as a trading bloc to penetrate outside markets, particularly in the USA and Europe. These economies have been buoyed by earlier terms of trade gains from lower prices of oil and other raw materials, lower yields in capital markets, and downward pressure on inflation from competition from Asian products. Mexico exported its way out of the 1994 financial crisis. Countries in Asia have not managed to do so since exports to the United States and Europe rose but those to Japan have fallen. Countries in Latin America should deepen their trade integration to the world, rather than restrict themselves to the regional market.

NOTES

1. For a detailed analysis of the Asian crisis see Corsetti et al. 1998a, 1998b, Goldstein 1998, and Rivera-Batiz, Chapter 2, this volume. For a review and evaluation of Fund-supported programs see Aghevli 1998, Lane et al. 1999, and IMF 1998a, 1998b. See also World Bank 1998.
2. In addition to financing through the capital markets, the region received close to $80 billion in foreign direct investment in 1996; half of this went to China and 90 per cent to East and South East Asian countries. Data on foreign direct investment are from UNCTAD's databank. Other data are from IMF sources.
3. Their respective shares fell rapidly in the first half of 1997 to 41 per cent of Asian flows and 20 per cent of flows to emerging markets
4. Total foreign direct investment (FDI) to the Asian-4 amounted to $15.5 billion in 1996 and fell slightly in 1997. Flows to Thailand and Korea in 1996 were practically the same ($2.3 billion), but while those to Korea remained unchanged in 1997, FDI to Thailand increased to $3.6 billion, in part as a result of mergers and acquisitions.
5. Corsetti et al. (1998a) show that the debt-equity ratio of the 30 top chaebols was 333 per cent and that the comparable figure for the USA was close to 100 per cent.
6. By end-1998, all large countries in the region increased taxation, which is likely to have a negative impact on investment and growth. While Brazil increased corporate income tax from 33 to 37 per cent, raised its tax on gross revenues from 2 to 3 per cent, and increased a tax on checks from 0.2 per cent to 0.38 per cent, Argentina and Mexico, which had much better fiscal situations, also tightened their fiscal policy. Argentina broadened the VAT base, imposed a 1 per cent tax on assets, increased income tax from 33 to 35 per cent and increased the withholding tax on interest. Mexico increased corporate income tax from 34 to 35 per cent and imposed a withholding tax on dividends of 5 per cent.
7. Chile: 33 per cent; Peru: 26 per cent; Brazil: 18 per cent; Argentina: 13 per cent.
8. For an analysis of contagion effects by regions of the world see IMF (1998a).
9. Data on foreign direct investment to the region collected by UNCTAD shows that FDI grew rapidly as well (28 per cent) to reach $56 billion. Brazil, which had attracted only $1.3 billion in 1993, received $16.3 billion in 1997, outperforming Mexico for the second year as the largest single recipient.

10. As pointed out by Blejer and del Castillo (1998), an exchange rate rule, with full capital mobility, can only succeed if compatible financial policies are strictly adhered to even when severe negative shocks take place *and* if reliance on persistent capital inflows is not essential.

REFERENCES

Aghevli, Bijan B. (1998), 'Asian Crisis: Causes and Remedies,' paper presented at the Conference Asia: An Analysis of the Financial Crisis, sponsored by the Federal Reserve Bank of Chicago and the IMF, 8–10 October.

Blejer, Mario I. and Graciana del Castillo (1998), 'Déjà vu all over again?: The Mexican and the Stabilization of Uruguay in the 1970s', *World Development*, 26 (March): 449–64.

Corsetti, Giancarlo, Paolo Pesenti and Nouriel Roubini (1998a), 'What Caused the Asian Currency and Financial Crisis? Part I: A Macroeconomic Overview,' paper presented at the CEPR/World Bank Conference on Financial Crises: Contagion and Market Volatility, May 8–9, London.

Corsetti, Giancarlo, Paolo Pesenti and Nouriel Roubini (1998b), 'What Caused the Asian Currency and Financial Crisis? Part II: Interpreting and Modelling the Crisis,' paper presented at the CEPR/World Bank Conference on Financial Crises: Contagion and Market Volatility, May 8–9, London.

Goldstein, Morris (1998), *The Asian Financial Crisis: Causes, Cures and Systemic Implications*, Washington, DC: Institute for International Economics.

International Monetary Fund (1998a), 'The IMF's Response to the Asian Crisis,' (http://www.imf.org).

International Monetary Fund (1998b), 'How Has the Asian Crisis Affected Other Regions,' *Finance & Development* 35(3).

Lane, T., A Ghosln, J. Hamann, S. Phillips, M. Schulze-Ghattas and T. Tsikata (1999), 'IMF-supported Programs in Indonesia, Korea, and Thailand – A Preliminary Assessment,' IMF Occasional Paper No. 178, Washington: International Monetary Fund.

Radelet, Steven and Jeffrey Sachs (1998), 'The East Asian Financial Crisis: Diagnosis, Remedies, and Prospects,' *Brookings Papers on Economic Activity*, **1**: 1–90.

Rivera-Batiz, Francisco L. (2001), 'The East Asian Crisis and the Anatomy of Emerging Market Disease,' in A. Lukauskas and F.L. Rivera-Batiz (eds), *The Political Economy of the East Asian Crisis and its Aftermath: Tigers in Distress*, Cheltenham, UK: Edward Elgar.

World Bank (1998), *East Asia: The Road to Recovery*, Washington, DC: World Bank.

PART IV

Roundtable Discussion

9. Roundtable on the causes and consequences of the East Asian financial crisis

Graciana del Castillo, Albert Fishlow, Miles Kahler and Paolo Pesenti

1. INTRODUCTORY PRESENTATION BY PAOLO PESENTI

I want, first of all, to make the traditional but important remark that these are my own views and need not reflect those of the Federal Reserve Bank of New York.

Let me talk broadly about what is currently emerging in the policy literature as a consensus view of the East Asian crisis and its implications. Of course, like any kind of consensus view, chances are that nobody in this audience will agree with it, but let me still try to present it!

A few months ago, when my first contribution to this debate came out on the Internet, in a joint work with Giancarlo Corsetti and Nouriel Roubini, the gap between the various views of the East Asian crisis was somewhat wider than it is today. The 'Asian Crisis' was seen in the context of a longstanding debate between two competing interpretations of currency and financial collapses. One saw crises as caused primarily by fundamental weaknesses and policy distortions and the other one saw them as self-fulfilling prophecies and financial panics. We have gone through these arguments before, both at this conference and in the existing literature, so there is little need for me to enter into the details of these different interpretations. However, one thing that is important to notice about the East Asian case is that it has never fitted neatly into either of these two approaches. For instance, given the magnitude of the financial distress in 1998, even the most fervent believers in the fundamentalist approach to crises generally recognize that, in practice, some form of panic did occur and caused the market to overreact to economic news. And by the same token, faced with the extensive evidence of the fragility of the banking and financial sectors in East Asia well before the Thai crisis in 1997, the most balanced supporters of the panic view have also highlighted the role played by fundamental and institutional distortions in the unfolding of the crisis.

In other words, I find that the points of consensus and agreement are far more substantial than the points of controversy between the two camps. Here is a list of what fundamentalists and non-fundamentalists agree upon. First, policy inconsistencies enhance the vulnerability of the economy to speculative runs. Second, size does not matter in the generation of a crisis, that is, large capital inflows need not be destabilizing. Third, what really matters in precipitating a crisis is a mismatch in the maturity structure of the assets and liabilities of domestic financial institutions; it is the short maturity of capital inflows that contributes to bank failures in the presence of shocks to long-term lending, and there is also a role for the mismatch between the currency composition of assets and liabilities. So, it is not the size, but the composition of the capital inflows that matters. Fourth, financial liberalization, in the absence of monitoring and supervision, can produce a set of circumstances under which greater instability is possible. I will elaborate on that later on. Fifth, attempts at deregulating the banking sector and increasing domestic competitiveness can make the system more fragile to a destabilizing shock. Sixth, the availability of foreign exchange reserves is a precondition for financial stability, independently of the issue of determining the optimal amount of foreign reserves. Seventh, flexible exchange rates can help to reduce financial rigidity to a larger extent than fixed exchange rates. Eighth, infusions of capital by international lenders of last resort may be indispensable to contain the impact of the crisis but may also worsen the conditions for the crisis by enhancing the moral hazard distortions. And finally, and the key issue in all of this: it is always the combination of elements that matter, not the single elements, taken in isolation.

With the benefit of hindsight, we are now quite ready for a balanced, consensus view that attributes the crisis to premature financial liberalization, that is, liberalization of financial markets prior to the adoption of adequate mechanisms of supervision and regulation of financial intermediaries. The emerging consensus view argues that two decades of rapid and sustained growth with high savings and investment rates and high rates of human capital accumulation occurred despite – and perhaps because of – the significant distortions of the market mechanism in the financial sector. To a large extent, the performances of the Asian economies were the result of growth-oriented strategies based on various forms of centralized coordination of production activities, resource allocation, protection of domestic industry, and implicit or explicit government guarantees on private investment projects. Such projects allowed firms to undertake very risky projects by relying heavily on bank credit. The prevailing practice of relationship banking gave incentives to develop strong informal ties between creditors and debtors. This provided the economy with the resources required to finance high-growth objectives, but it also downplayed the role of prices in project selection.

In the presence of limits to foreign borrowing, these distortions did not translate into high domestic vulnerability to external shocks, which is why the crisis occurred in the 1990s and not before. This key feature changed with the process of domestic financial liberalization. In the 1990s, international capital markets became more accessible, and domestic markets were deregulated. With supervision of the financial system inadequate, there was a strong corporate bias in favor of debt financing. The World Bank points out that leverage rose sharply prior to 1997 in the crisis countries. For instance, between 1991 and 1996, it doubled in Thailand and Malaysia.

Notwithstanding the specific factors that varied across countries, there is still a common phenomenon that characterizes all the relevant countries in East Asia prior to the crisis: rising financial vulnerability. Short-term borrowing to finance long-term projects became increasingly important, especially in Korea, Malaysia and Thailand, generating a mismatch in the maturity of assets and liabilities. Second, domestic banks were lending to domestic firms mainly in local currency, while borrowing short term in foreign currency. This created of course a second mismatch, a currency denomination mismatch in the balance sheet of domestic intermediaries.

When we analyse the East Asian crisis as being related to financial liberalization, we should not forget that this is by no means an exclusive feature of the East Asian economies. As a matter of fact, if you want a model, that is, an intellectual framework, to analyse emerging market crises, the most appropriate model that I can think of falls back to the work of the late Carlos Diaz-Alejandro, who wrote about the financial crisis experienced in Chile during its own process of deregulation and liberalization in the early 1980s. He suggested that, whether or not there are explicit or implicit government guarantees, if the economic situation gets bad enough, the public expects governments to intervene to save them from losing bank deposits. Now, expectations of a future bailout need not be based on an explicit promise by the government or any existing institution. It does not even matter if the government warns that there will be no intervention. As Diaz-Alejandro puts it: 'agents expect to be bailed out regardless of the "laissez faire" commitments which a misguided minister of finance or central bank president may occasionally utter in a moment of dogmatic exaltation.' Simply, investors understand that in the event of a crisis no government will cross its arms and let the system go belly up. It should be stressed that this argument applies to the banking sector as well as other financial firms whose collapse may generate significant externalities.

In the light of these considerations, to argue that the East Asian crisis is different from anything else seen before, simply because the East Asian countries did not display the usual symptoms – chronic inflation, huge budget deficits, and high unemployment – needs to be qualified. The difficulties in the financial sector constitute a contingent public liability that is real even if it is not reflected in the official data on public deficits until the crisis occurs. And, in this respect, once again, previous episodes are illuminating. Diaz-Alejandro examined the budget deficit of the Chilean government before the crisis in that country in 1982. He found that, if you look at the official public sector budget deficit in the very early 1980s, it was non-existent. Economists at the time thus approved Chilean policies, failing to foresee the coming crisis. What they were missing in their analysis, though, was that the public sector was accumulating an explosive amount of contingent liability to both foreign and domestic agents. You take this situation, and it perfectly describes the East Asian situation of the late 1990s. Historically, the East Asian crisis does not really represent a new case. The policy lessons that one should draw from the East Asian crisis are really similar in spirit to the ones that have been learned from other episodes of currency and financial collapses.

Should countries take a few steps back from integrating their economies in world markets in the aftermath of what happened? Should policymakers maintain financial markets relatively closed to the rest of the world? There are at least two skeptical views of the benefits from world market integration. One stresses that national economies can benefit greatly from the gains from free trade in goods and services without opening up their asset markets. The second view argues that the efficiency gains from opening up the economy are more than offset by increased uncertainty. Each view has its strengths and its weaknesses. Nevertheless, I would say that most experts agree that the benefits from capital account liberalization are sizable, but that they can be obtained only if countries have their house in order. Indeed, the consensus view of the East Asian crisis is that local weaknesses, and not globalization, have to be blamed as the culprit of trouble. A process of capital market liberalization, unaccompanied by effective supervision or regulation of financial intermediaries, increases the vulnerability of the system to external shocks, it magnifies the existing distortions, and weakens the financial sector.

As a matter of fact, most of the East Asian countries involved had officially adopted rules consistent with international financial standards well before the crisis started. What was lacking was compliance and enforcement of these rules. In this respect, and I think this is a key message of my intervention, the essential issue is enforcement, not the formal adoption of new rules.

What is a cautious approach to capital account liberalization? If there is a basic lesson from the Asian crisis it is that a high priority should be given to measures preventing the mismatches that I talked about before, that is, preventing the growth of large stocks of foreign-currency-denominated debt, and preventing and controlling the magnitude of the maturity mismatches of assets and liabilities of corporate and financial firms. There are many practical proposals to discourage short-term borrowing, such as high reserve requirements, limits on inter-bank loans in foreign currencies, foreign currency deposit limits on domestic banks, the use of high-risk weighting in setting capital standards for foreign currency loans, and many others. All these measures concern capital inflows. According to the consensus view of the sequencing of liberalization measures, existing controls on capital outflows should be quickly phased out and replaced with regulations that simply limit capital inflows. Underlying these policy recommendations, however, is the assumption that the enforcement and compliance problems involved in regulatory reforms have found convincing solutions.

Do we need to include the regulation of lending banks in policy recommendations? The answer is yes, for several reasons. First is realism. The regulator of a borrowing bank will not necessarily operate at the same standard as the regulator in the country of the lender bank, so it is up to the latter to compensate to the extent possible for the deficiencies in the borrowing country. The second reason is moral hazard, which reduces the incentive of the lending banks to engage in proper risk assessment. How do we deal with this? One possible approach is to increase the risk-based weight of capital standards for short-run and cross-border inter-bank loans. This is one possibility. An alternative, and possibly more radical approach, is to move to a system emphasizing less externally-imposed standards and rely more on internal bank models in the assessment of risk, such as voluntary risk models. The third approach would be to rely more on market discipline for bank regulation. So, there is a broad debate on the optimal tactic or way to achieve this task, but the point remains that we should go in that direction.

I want to talk about three more issues. One is the role of transparency. There is a broad consensus that the lack of transparency played a huge role in the East Asian crisis. There is agreement on the need to have greater openness on the part of both the debtor countries and on the part of official institutions such as the International Monetary Fund. Of course, we are also aware that while transparencies are important – and were certainly lacking before the crisis – they are not enough to prevent another major debacle from occurring. Information on specific statistics, such as the countries' net foreign reserves and the official liabilities with financial and corporate systems, would have been useful and there is no question that their unavailability may have exacerbated the uncertainty facing investors. But it is hard to argue that the most important information was all hidden. The current account imbalances, the level of short-term and foreign currency liabilities, and a myriad of other data were quite well known and regularly published. There is no doubt that more transparency, with an effective implementation of disclosure rules and international accounting standards, will be very useful, but benefits may show up only in the long run.

A second set of remarks regards the role of the foreign banks and the lessons of the East Asian crisis. One issue that has importance for the analysis of the East Asian crisis is whether the substantial ownership by foreign banks of a domestic financial system could have beneficial effects for a country and could contribute to prevent financial crises. Apart from generating greater domestic competition, stimulating efficiency, introducing new managerial skills, and transferring innovative banking know-how, the idea is that international banks can provide other benefits to a domestic financial system in a period of crisis. If a foreign bank just simply lends to a domestic bank in an emerging market, it does not have any stake in the loans that the domestic bank makes to local firms using those funds. In fact, in a situation of potential crisis, the international bank may have an incentive to call-in the loans, and that might actually trigger a crisis by running down foreign reserves and forcing the local bank to call in its own loans. Instead, if a foreign bank operates locally, say by lending through a local branch, it has much more at stake on the stability of the domestic banking system and it is much less likely to call-in loans and repatriate its liabilities. Second, since one cannot always ensure that governments in emerging markets are fulfilling their responsibility to properly supervise and regulate the domestic banking system, the presence of foreign banks could mitigate this problem. Foreign banks may adopt more rational lending practices than domestic banks, relying less on the basis of relationship banking and using more arm's length banking. They may also be subject to less pressure and arm-twisting on the part of local political and economic elites seeking support for particular projects. Strong regulations on multinational banks by home country governments – such as US government regulations of the activities of US banks – indirectly provide regulation of the foreign-based branches of those banks.

What are the counter-arguments here? Should a large fraction of the banking system in an emerging market be controlled by foreign banks to ensure competition, efficiency and stability? Well, the obvious counter-argument is political sensitivity. Banks in emerging markets are often used for political purposes, directing lending to particular projects desired by the leaders in those countries. This is why the governments are wary of letting the domestic banking system be dominated by foreign countries. Now, this argument can be used to explain positively, in political economy terms, why governments do not want foreign ownership of domestic banks. But in fact they provide a stronger, normative argument in favor of opening up the financial sector to foreign ownership.

Let me make a final set of remarks. By the end of 1998, the amounts required for public bailouts of financial institutions in the East Asian countries was estimated to be in the order of 20 to 30 per cent of Gross Domestic Product (GDP). By the standard of solvency, this means that the fiscal cost of the bailout, consisting of the budget surpluses required to finance the interest bill of the additional public liabilities, is equal to two to four percentage points of GDP per year. Basically, the longer Asian countries are required to cut spending and increase tax revenues toward this target, the longer the dampening effect on national welfare. This actually appears to be the position that was adopted by the IMF when it approached the crisis countries. The IMF sought to improve public sector primary balances as a way of contributing to the financing of the cost of the bailouts. However, these conditions were met by widespread criticism. As a result, the Fund decided to relax substantially its public sector budgetary targets. It is worth reconsidering this issue in some detail.

There are two possible criticisms to the implementation of strict quantitative targets on the public budget in the aftermath of a crisis. The so-called 'panic view' argues that, if international investors are fleeing in a panic, any constraint on the ability of the monetary and fiscal authorities of a country to provide liquidity and resources to the domestic public sector can only exacerbate the crisis. Obviously, it is argued, domestic policymakers need these resources and any strict limit on what they can do is going to make the crisis much worse than it is. There is a different type of criticism that is a little more balanced and maybe more fair to the rationale behind IMF targets. It argues that the need for an improvement in the fiscal position of a government, if required to absorb the fiscal costs of bailouts, is a long-run argument that should not guide policy design in the short-run. By contrast, in the short-run you should allow for the possibility that the crisis leads to a cyclical downturn that dries up domestic credit and cripples growth. If you try to impose strict, short-run fiscal targets, exactly at the time when the economy is entering a recession, this will worsen the situation. Furthermore, the fall in domestic demand will worsen the fiscal deficit, which is really endogenous. The bottom line is that, in the short-run, unrealistic fiscal targets on the budget deficit will force the government to adopt unnecessarily restrictive policies. What is required is a long-run adjustment, a structural adjustment in the order of 2 per cent to 4 per cent of GDP to cover the fiscal costs. When should these adjustments start? Definitely not during a recession. And I think I will stop here.

2. INTRODUCTORY PRESENTATION BY ALBERT FISHLOW

It is important to start by noting the fact that the world economy is entering a period of time in which financial flows have again gone back to what they had been before 1914. Despite all the recent attention dedicated to capital flows, and the extent to which they are upsetting the world markets and alike, one must appreciate that financial flows as a percentage of income were substantially larger before the First World War than what they were afterwards, until recently. Much of the period after the Second World War was in fact a rejection of the high capital mobility strategy of earlier years. It was a period in which most of the foreign transfers were direct investments, not portfolio investments, and in which most of the capital was made available through the World Bank and other official agencies. So that is a first observation, which should lead us not to exaggerate the significance of the magnitude of the capital flows today, relative to what they have been in the past. Still, one must recognize that there is an important technological difference in the flows today. You can tell immediately how much money is flowing from here to there, at a moment's notice. This is quite new. Ten years ago one would have had some difficulty. You would have had to wait quite a bit until the figures were collected and made available, and then you would have had to check them. The immediacy of information makes the increased globalization much more real in its impact.

A second observation to make is that one can view the 1990s as the moment in which East Asia became capitalist, in the same way that Latin America became capitalist in the 1980s. It is interesting that Paolo quoted from Carlos Diaz-Alejandro, in terms of describing the Chilean situation in the early 1980s. One of the things that we clearly see in Latin America after the 1980s is that all of the countries managed to convert to capitalism. They managed to rid themselves of inflation. They managed to rid themselves of very substantial fiscal deficits. They managed to open up their trade accounts. They managed to enter this New World. To some extent, the nature of the present crisis in East Asia mirrors what happened in Latin America in the 1980s. We are really seeing the extent to which the countries of East Asia, which earlier had adopted a different model, are now being required to conform to a general capitalist scheme and model.

A third observation that I would make is that the process of liberalization has made it much clearer that the exchange rate is central to the domestic economy. The notion that the exchange rate deals with the external sector and domestic policy deals with the internal economy is fundamentally wrong. This is very obvious in the case of Thailand, which was a classic case of currency overvaluation, anticipated by the IMF two years before the crisis occurred. The stock market in this country peaked much earlier than the 1997 crisis would indicate, responding to sluggish exports and a growing current account balance deficit linked to the overvalued currency.

What is rather clear now is that there are only two real possibilities for an effective exchange rate regime. One is to have a currency board, such as Argentina has. The other alternative is a floating rate. The notion that there is an intermediate possibility, an attempt to combine the two in a variable-weight kind of strategy, is increasingly becoming an unlikely phenomenon. The fundamental point to recognize on this is that no country nowadays has sufficient reserves to defend its exchange rate against massive capital flight. The volume of reserves that individual countries are able to hold are no longer adequate. In the case of Brazil in 1998, for example, Guillermo Calvo estimated that its central bank needed somewhere in the order of $300 billion dollars in reserves in order to make its exchange rate credible.

Audience Question to Mr. Fishlow: Assuming no capital controls?

Fishlow: Yes, but capital controls do not make a difference. They do not make a difference for one fundamental reason: they have been shown to be effective only in very short-term circumstances and only to deal with very short-term disequilibria. Capital controls cannot effectively deal with long-term disequilibria.

To come back to the issue of the exchange rate regime, I would suggest that one of the characteristics of the East Asian crisis, which is really shared by the more recent Russian and Brazilian crises as well, is that they are all fundamentally different from earlier crises. We are now talking about IMF packages of an order of magnitude of $45 billion, which are much greater than what had been historically the case before the Mexican case in 1994. And as I have mentioned, even these huge bailouts provide inadequate foreign exchange reserves in the new world of capital flows that exists today.

The final observation that I want to make comes down to the question of allocation of the losses. What is different about the present situation, in comparison with the Latin American debt crisis in the 1980s, is the fact that lending banks moved relatively quickly to take some of their losses. In the 1980s, they took something on the order of five years, while in the East Asian crisis, one year later the banks were actively engaged in writing off the bad loans. One is seeing a much greater ability of banks to take those losses, in part precisely for the reason that Paolo gave earlier: banks are now becoming international. They are becoming international not only within the developing countries, but also among the developed countries. This phenomenon is changing the character of financial markets and is an important trend at the beginning of the new century.

3. INTRODUCTORY PRESENTATION BY MILES KAHLER

I will make my presentation by raising three sets of questions. One is under the heading of fundamentals; the second includes some questions about financial markets; and the third regards some political economy questions.

On the question of the fundamentals behind the crisis, I would argue that there is much more consensus about what countries should do in this new environment than one might expect, given the theoretical debates that have occurred. One can see that in Paolo's presentation, and in the papers presented at this conference. My concern is that the new fundamentals, as I will call them, are going to be overplayed, like the policy prescriptions that have been given to countries in the past. These policy changes, or policy steps, really have to be portrayed as a modest insurance policy that may help deal with future financial crises. They are not, however, a guarantee that such crises will not occur, even if the policy measures are fully implemented. I worry that the way these reforms are being portrayed in the new financial architecture rhetoric is that financial markets will reward countries that implement these reforms. Is this necessarily the case?

Financial market issues raise additional questions. My first, most basic, question is: what is an emerging market? How do we get this classification? We know historically how this came to be. It was an International Finance Corporation marketing device. They did not want to call developing countries any more by that name so they called them emerging markets, to encourage investment in them. Most of the attention about this category in the 1990s was how you get into the emerging market category from the bottom up. In other words, how do we make Zambia into an emerging market? But the interesting question seems to me: how do you graduate out of an emerging market? What is it that makes some countries more stable, less prone to crisis, more acceptable to international investors?

There are a number of possibilities. It is important to look back and realize that 20 years ago, two of the industrialized countries were in some sense emerging markets, according to our criteria. Britain and Italy were in quite severe balance-of-payments crises in the 1970s. In the British case, they risked being cut off from the financial markets altogether. Since the late 1970s, none of the G-7 or the G-10 countries has been involved in financial crises of that kind (they have been involved in banking crises, very severe ones in some cases, but not financial crises). What is it that has made some countries fall into the emerging market category and what does this do to perceptions in the financial markets? I would argue, for example, that Greece is an emerging market by most criteria, but it happens to belong to particular clubs, and I think club membership is rather important in allowing countries to stay out of the category. That gets to the issue of regional groupings and how they could assist countries into moving out of the negative connotations of emerging markets and into some other category that might be more beneficial. OECD membership in the early 1990s unfortunately had a perverse and negative effect in that regard, but it seems to me that European Union (EU) membership has had a very positive effect on some countries, which might otherwise be regarded as emerging markets.

Two other brief points on financial markets. First, I am still puzzled on how much of a constraint technology imposes on governments who wish to control or regulate capital inflows and outflows. Ralph Bryant tried to estimate more than ten years ago the relative importance of technology in encouraging financial market integration. I am not sure if anyone has done a careful analysis of how technological change has made this issue more relevant today than it was then. Any talk about capital controls of any kind is subject to the presence of technological constraints. Second, there is the question of differential behavior of financial institutions. There is a recent study on hedge funds that Barry Eichengreen contributed to the IMF. It gets at some of the regulatory issues, particularly from the side of the G-7, that are definitely going to be on the future policy agenda. We really need to know more about the differential behavior of various financial institutions and how they interact with regulatory structures. I get the sense that we are really walking blind in that area.

There is, finally, a set of political economy questions that I want to comment on. Hearing the discussion so far today, it seems to me that the political economy issues discussed have been a tale of two regions, Latin America and East Asia, which go up and down against one another. The 1980s was the decade of East Asia and not the decade of Latin America and the 1990s was until recently the decade of Latin America and turned out not to be the decade of East Asia. And this raises three different questions to me. One regards the theory of optimal collusion, as I will call it. The lessons drawn from Latin America that always impress me are the political disadvantages of polarization and its wide swings in economic policy. The classic case was of course Argentina, but there are other Latin American examples as well. By contrast, East Asia became the case of collaborative or cooperative economic policy. Good government institutions and what I would call optimal collusion were the hallmark of the Asian miracle. Now, of course, we are swinging the other way, emphasizing the values of competition, transparency and so on. It is not clear to me that these two run completely counter to one another, but we do not really have a very good political economy sense of what degree of collusion is desirable among the elites in a country. In the relations between government and business, collusion in one setting becomes cooperation in another. Therefore, the advice that is going to be given to governments now is not going to be terribly helpful if it emphasizes just one set of values and under-emphasizes the other, leading to wide swings in policy regimes, as in Latin America.

The second political economy point concerns implementation. The new fundamentals that Paolo Pesenti presented earlier are very different from the old fundamentals and implementing them over time seems to be extremely difficult. There are going to be strong incentives to defect from these new arrangements constantly. The political incentives to encroach upon financial regulation and supervision, for example, are likely to be irresistible. These are not issues that have gone away in G-7 or OECD economies, which are constantly being undermined by the political process. So, it is not as if these countries are going to adopt these standards and then everyone can go home breathing a sigh of relief. There are major policy shifts that need to be dealt with and it is not clear to me that international institutions are set up to deal with them effectively.

My third political economy issue relates to Al Fishlow's remarks presented earlier about the pre-1914 world. I would suggest that the big difference with that world is that governments today are much more accountable for economic policies than they were before 1914. There are, in addition, many more governments. And the financial markets are evolving constantly and more rapidly than they were before 1914, which indicates a very different environment.

To conclude, let me just say that how the opposition to neoliberalism or market reforms is going to stack up during the first decade of the new century is a major question. There are three potential sources of opposition – economic nationalism, populism, and redistribution – but it is not clear that any of them necessarily are going to turn to full-fledged opposition to economic openness or financial liberalization. In terms of economic nationalism, we see from the case of Malaysia that it is very hard to turn back to autarky policies. The elites that would like to use that ploy, like Mahathir, are in some sense committed to a policy of export orientation and involvement with the international economy that they find extremely difficult to reverse to any significant extent. In the case of redistributive coalitions, that appears to be the way the situation in Latin American is moving, as may be suggested by the election of Chavez in Venezuela. But even there, you may see substantial opposition, except perhaps on the issue of debt repayment and renegotiation. For example, putting in place real taxation systems necessarily runs counter to redistributive programs of various kinds. Democratic oppositions, particularly in Asia, might find neoliberalism and market reforms more useful for their purposes. If you look at the Chinese dissidents, for example, they see market reform as a way of undermining collusive bargains and as actually contributing to democratization rather than running counter to it. But this may be an optimistic view. Let me end on that note.

4. QUESTIONS AND DISCUSSION

Audience question to Mr. Pesenti: What policies do you feel are needed to avoid future crises?

Mr. Pesenti: Drawing on the issues that have been discussed so far, let me go on record on the type of reforms that I think are the logical outcome of the East Asian crisis. These go in two directions: first, more prudential regulation and more supervision, and, secondly, real liberalization and real globalization, meaning more openness of the domestic financial sector to foreign ownership. I see the implementation of these policies as representing medium-term to long-term implications.

Audience question to Mr. Pesenti: Who is going to gain from them? Is Wall Street going to be happy about it?

Mr. Pesenti: These are very good questions. They are also very tough ones and I do not have an answer. If you think about it, there are both pros and cons for US banks. On the one hand, they gain opportunities and access to the East Asian market. On the negative side, more regulation and supervision means that the lending US banks will be more controlled in the host countries. Also for the new financial architecture, or whatever you want to call it, to be successful, it will be absolutely crucial to make sure that the safety net involved in the public guarantees of bank deposit insurance is not going to cover at all foreign cross-border liabilities of the banking system. This has to be absolutely clear, not just in terms of regulation but in terms of compliance. From this point of view, I do not think that the lending banks, whether located in the USA or in Germany or Japan, are going to be terribly happy about it. So, in the end, it is not quite clear whether Wall Street is going to be happy or not. But I think the really important question is: are these changes necessary? And the answer to that is a clear yes. If we want to avoid the huge social costs associated with crises, this is something that we should go for. I am not arguing that it is a sufficient condition, but it is a necessary condition for the social cost of these crises to be avoided.

Audience question to Mr. Pesenti: In your presentation, you addressed an issue that I want to pursue a little bit further. You seemed to argue that macroeconomic stability and domestic banking reforms are needed before you liberalize the capital account. Given the fact that the capital account in East Asian countries has already been liberalized, and that it would be extremely difficult now to close the economies, how do you reform their banking systems?

Mr. Pesenti: My answer is to pay more attention to lender banking. I would argue that the key element is to promote a different mentality and culture and the best way to achieve this is to push hard for an effective opening up of frontiers to foreign ownership of financial institutions in these countries.

Mrs. del Castillo: I would add that there are really two different policy-oriented issues that deserve to be considered on the topic of policy sequencing. During the 1970s, the debate in Latin America was whether you should liberalize first the current account or the capital account. The consensus there was that you should liberalize the current account first. The East Asian countries moved in that direction. But in the 1990s, the sequencing debate has turned on the issue of how to liberalize the capital account, and in this arena the East Asian countries did not follow the appropriate sequencing of policies, which required regulatory reforms of the financial sector first. In the case of South Korea, the situation was even worse because they initially liberalized short-term capital flows and only later long-term flows. And in this I think that they are now making substantial progress. They have implemented a whole set of new regulations with respect to foreign direct investment (FDI), which will attract FDI and redress the short-term versus long-term imbalance.

Audience question to Mr. Kahler: You have mentioned the definition of emerging markets and you have been talking about policy responses. But I am wondering to what extent one can look outside emerging markets for solutions. Specifically, do you think that the rule of law associated with participation in organizations such at the European Union, is important?

Mr. Kahler: Well, just as a point of agreement, I think it is. There are many aspects to being part of the European Union (EU) club. Regulatory harmonization is part of it. Having financial support from the EU is part of it. You also have to be a democracy to be part of the EU club. They have been absolutely adamant about this since the early 1960s and it kept Spain out of the EU for some time. So, in the EU case, the club is so comprehensive that it is hard to specify what is important about being a member, from the perception of outside investors; furthermore, most EU members are members of other clubs, like the OECD or the G-7, so that there are many overlapping memberships for this particular group of countries. What is striking to me is that both Latin America and South East Asia have not constructed such clubs and I think that one of the untold aspects of the crisis is that regional solutions were not seriously examined. We have seen that contagion is not limited to regions but it certainly tends to be regional, and that to me provides a very large incentive to think carefully about regional solutions of various kinds. I do not think that either region has been particularly good in exploring this policy avenue.

Mrs. del Castillo: But trade arrangements embodied in regional blocs have made countries more prone to contagion.

Mr. Kahler: Well, it is Barry Eichengreen's argument about Europe and other regional arrangements that one cannot have a trade arrangement that is stable without dealing with exchange rate and other financial issues. It is politically hard not to also, and Mercosur is facing this. Certainly the Argentines would agree with you. What do you think, Al?

Mr. Fishlow: This is what we have seen recently, and not only in Mercosur. I think that within the next five years you are going to see the dollar as the currency of Mexico, and the reality of the matter is that given the trade relationship in the first instance and the interplay with immigration and the proximity, the next step is really in the movement toward a common currency.

Audience question to Mr. Kahler. Following up on the last question, what has been the role of ASEAN in setting a rule of law?

Mr. Kahler: One can begin to detect a greater willingness on the part of some of the governments in ASEAN to critically examine some of the other governments in the club, but it is a very small step. There is a real need to engage in some sort of mutual surveillance at least in some narrow areas, like in the areas that Paolo was talking about earlier. This is justifiable in that what you do wrong in your country could have a very severely negative effect on me in my country, something that has been made clear in this crisis. This would be a big step for most of the East Asian countries to take and it will probably take a while to get there.

Mr. Fishlow: I would just add that the rule of law is now really being pushed quite extensively in East Asia when you begin to talk about provisions for bankruptcy, conditions that had not been present before. And this can have immense impact. Rules that initially seem to be exclusively financial can manage to cross over and begin to affect other sectors.

Audience question to Mr. Fishlow: What has been the impact of the East Asian crisis on the United States?

Mr. Fishlow: I think in the case of the United States, one of the things that we should recognize is that, with the exception of the downturn in the early 1990s, we have had a continuing rate of expansion for more than 15 years, and this is really now moving into new economic territory. Part of what has happened is that wages, real wages, have not shown the tendency to rise as they have during every other cyclical process. That is one of the big differences between the recent US expansion and the historical record. Historically, when the economy was faced with relative shortages of labor, wages would rise, and inflation would start. Then came the Federal Reserve with an interest rate hike and the economy would slow down. We have not seen that occur and that is one of the novelties of the present situation in the United States.

Obviously, the United States economy cannot grow at 6 per cent a quarter forever, but the expansion has shown a remarkable resilience. Many of the banks had previously projected the first half of 1999 as a major downturn and it did not happen. All of the indications are that it is not happening for one very important reason: Americans are not saving. They are continuing to spend, and with consumption spending rising at very high rates, the performance of the economy is necessarily high. This depends obviously on the ability of the rest of the world to finance the deficit in the US balance of payments. This deficit now comes close to 3 per cent of GDP. We are in the position of being exactly in the same situation as the Latin American economies that we have always criticized: high consumption spending financed by foreign money coming in. The one great virtue that we have is that the dollar is a very solid currency, and this provides an incredible degree of flexibility in policy.

Mrs. del Castillo: I believe that the East Asian crisis benefited the United States in many ways. There was a clear flight to safety in financial markets and this favored the USA. Furthermore, in the manufacturing sector there were high profit margins and US firms managed to keep their market shares by lowering those margins. They thus managed to compete effectively with firms in East Asian economies, despite the enhanced competitiveness these had as a result of devaluations. There are two other factors that have had a positive effect on

US consumers. One is the fall in the price of oil and raw materials. The other one is the drop in the relative prices of goods from East Asian countries. The real danger for the US economy is the very large trade deficit and the protectionist policies that have resulted from this.

Question to Mr. Fishlow: You mentioned how in the 1980s, the crisis in Latin America led to major structural improvements in the economy. Is this happening in East Asia now?

Mr. Fishlow: I do see major changes in bankruptcy law, in foreign direct investment laws, and in a number of other areas. More importantly, one of the key impacts that this is likely to generate is that there will be more pressure on China to introduce reforms.

Question to Mr. Fishlow: Can you say something more about the prospects for some sort of dollarization in either the Western hemisphere or in the East Asia region?

Mr. Fishlow: There will be many Americans who will object when the first Mexican is appointed on the Federal Reserve Board! Well, Alan Greenspan basically voiced this concern recently, suggesting that there would be no foreign voice on dollar monetary policy. As you all know, Argentina has raised the dollarization issue very aggressively in the last year, and one of the reasons is that they are hopeful of relieving any pressure on the peso as a consequence of what has happened to the real in Brazil. But it is very difficult to avoid dollarization in a situation like that of Mexico, where you have relative free exchange of goods and services with the USA, major population movements between the two countries, and two economies that are so integrated that Mexico is currently receiving 80 per cent of imports from the USA and exporting 80 per cent of its products to the north. It is very difficult to conceive of the situation as not being one that comes very close to the conditions for an optimal currency union. I think that the reluctance of the USA is based on the fact that the country does not want to accept responsibility for being the banker of last resort for what happens south of the border. And I think that is the key question that will have to be resolved for dollarization to happen in Mexico.

Anyway, any country can accept the dollar. Panama has done so historically. You also have it circulating widely in Argentina, Bolivia and other countries. Ecuador is also considering dollarization. So this is something that is happening anyway.

Index